The Speaker's Compact Handbook

Second Edition

prague

University

Douglas Stuart

WADSWORTH
CENGAGE Learning

Australia · Brazil · Japan · Korea · Mexico · Singapore · Spain
United Kingdom · United States

Publisher: Lyn Uhl
Executive Editor: Monica Eckman
Senior Development Editor: Greer Lleuad
Assistant Editor: Kimberly Gengler
Editorial Assistant: Kimberly Apfelbaum
Technology Project Manager: Jessica Badiner
Marketing Manager: Erin Mitchell
Marketing Assistant: Mary Anne Payumo
Marketing Communications Manager: Shemika Britt
Content Project Manager: Sarah Sherman
Creative Director: Rob Hugel
Art Director: Linda Helcher
Print Buyer: Sue Carroll
Production Service: Matrix Productions
Cover Designer: Brittany Singletary
Compositor: Newgen

For more information and technology assistance, contact us at
Cengage Learning Academic Resource Center
1-800-423-0563
For permission to use material from this text or product, submit all requests online at **http://www.cengage.com/permissions.**
Further permissions questions can be e-mailed to
permissionrequest@cengage.com.

Library of Congress Control Number: 2007935006

ISBN-13: 978-0-495-57079-0
ISBN-10: 0-495-57079-6
Wadsworth, Cengage Learning
25 Thomas Place
Boston, MA 02210
USA

Cengage Learning products are represented in Canada by Nelson Education, Ltd.

For your course and learning solutions, visit:
academic.cengage.com
Purchase any of our products at your local college store or at our preferred online store **www.ichapters.com.**

Printed in Canada
3 4 5 6 7 12 11 10 09

Using This Book

The Speaker's Compact Handbook provides a concise and portable resource for speakers. It's not coincidental that it shares these characteristics with its sister text, *The Speaker's Handbook,* the first handbook of its kind and now in its eighth edition. Even more concise and portable than that full handbook, *The Speaker's Compact Handbook* is appropriate for certain kinds of academic public speaking classes, the student who has to give an individual or group presentation in a class from any department, the beginning speaker who needs individual guidance in preparing for a particular kind of speaking situation, and the professional who wants a quick refresher on the basics or quick pointers on topics such as the effective use of presentation software.

Why a *Handbook*

A handbook differs from a textbook in a few important ways.

- First, handbooks are brief: They present a distilled version of the most useful advice gleaned from centuries of academic research and decades of practical experience.

- Second, handbooks are reference books. They are not intended to be read from cover to cover, but are designed to help you locate what you need when you need it.

- Third, handbooks are *handy.* Quite literally, this compact edition fits in your hand. It's easy to keep on your desk or in your briefcase, coat pocket, or purse without adding weight or bulk.

Starting Out in This Book

To make the most efficient use of the *Speaker's Compact Handbook,* we recommend that you take a few minutes now to look it over. You will see that the inside front cover and first page give an overview of part and chapter titles and that the last page and inside back cover of the book give a more in-depth picture of the content of each chapter. Explore these chapters in any order that works for you (see the section How to Put Together a Speech, below, for the quickest approach to getting started on a speech); but here are two basic suggestions to help you begin using this book as effectively as possible.

1. *Take time to establish a foundation.* In the first four chapters (Part 1—Approaching Public Speaking), we pulled together those topics that give you ways of thinking about and beginning the task of preparing a speech. We suggest that you read these chapters before delving deeper into the book.

2. *Consider the context in which you will be speaking.* Before you go about selecting sections of the book to guide you, it is essential that you understand the expectations of your particular situation, be it the classroom, the workplace, or the public arena. We suggest that you look at chapters 5 through 9 (Part 2—Speech Contexts), where you'll find sections that discuss which elements of speaking are most relevant in each of four general contexts.

How to Put Together a Speech

Three important charts in this book provide an easy reference to the basics of speech planning, creation, and organization.

■ **The Five Steps of Public Speaking**, Figure 1-1, page 7. This figure lays out the elements that go into just about every speech and provides cross references to the chapters that deal with each element.

■ **Speech Planning and Practice**, Figure 10-1, page 53. This timetable graphically demonstrates the relationships of the elements described in Figure 1-1 and shows where tasks overlap and ways for progressing through them.

■ **Speech Structure Chart**, Figure 32-1, page 172. This chart shows the relationship of a speech's main points, subpoints, supporting materials, transitions, introductions and conclusions and how they flow together in a standard speech.

Other Features to Help You

Emphasis and Review Tools

■ **Key points**. Throughout the text you will find Key Point boxes. These brief discussions highlight related ideas or information to consider or present helpful hints about, or a review of, the subject under discussion.

■ **Checklists**. The Checklists, which also appear in boxes throughout the text, provide a summary of steps that must be taken in a process, or a list of questions that must be asked to help define a situation or find a solution to a problem.

Appendixes

At the end of the book you'll find three supplemental sections for further reference:

■ Appendix A, **Sample Speeches and Outlines**. This appendix contains an example of a persuasive speech and the outline created during its development, an example of an informative speech, and an example of an outline used to develop a second informative speech.

- Appendix B, **Citation Guidelines**. Using the wrong word, mispronouncing it, or using bad grammar can distract your audience from your message. This appendix lists some common errors to watch out for.

- Appendix C, **Common Pronunciation and Usage Errors**. This appendix contains a sampling of citations for 13 types of print and nonprint sources. The samples model how you cite sources using APA and MLA style in a list of references or works cited, or in a bibliography.

Remember, a handbook is a reference text, a resource that tells you how to do what you need to do when you're getting ready to do it, or are in the middle of doing it. This handbook, like all other handbooks, is therefore intended to be a lifelong tool. We hope that you use it whenever you need or want to speak in public and that it contributes to the success of your presentations.

Acknowledgments

For their helpful suggestions that influenced several important decisions during this book's development, we owe thanks to these dedicated public-speaking teachers:

Daryle Nagano, *El Camino College*

Diane Reuszer, *Northeastern Junior College*

Beth Von Till, *San Jose State University*

Kathleen Zaworski-Burke, *San Diego City College*

Preface

Online Technology Resources

While using this text, you have the option of using a rich array of resources to enhance and extend your learning. If your instructor did not request that these digital resources be packaged with this text, they are available to you for individual sale. Available resources include the ThomsonNOW online study system, interactive speech videos within Thomson's unique video interface, the Speech Builder Express program for customized coaching throughout the speech-making and outlining processes, and the InfoTrac College Edition periodicals database. For more information and to access this book's online resources, visit **http://www.thomsonedu.com.**

Brief Contents

Contents

Contents

1 Approaching Public Speaking

CHAPTER 1. Understanding Public Speaking

Public speaking is the act of creating meaning with your listeners. As a speaker, you consciously combine communicative resources you already have at hand.

CHAPTER 2. Listening

Listening skills enhance your own speaking and help you meet your obligations as an audience member.

CHAPTER 3. Speaking Ethically

Ethical principles can guide you as a public speaker.

CHAPTER 4. Overcoming Fear of Speaking

Combining thorough preparation with relaxation and visualization techniques will increase your confidence.

CHAPTER 1

Understanding Public Speaking

Giving a speech is never a simple act. There are dozens—or perhaps hundreds—of decisions to make. This daunting task becomes more manageable, though, if you approach it with a few basic principles and theoretical frameworks to guide you.

As with any other skill (such as dancing, programming, or tree surgery), with public speaking there are principles to be mastered, there is a need for concentration and practice, and there are benefits to working with a skilled teacher and supportive colearners. That's why so many colleges and universities require or strongly recommend courses in public speaking, why thousands of people join groups like Toastmasters International, and why corporations and public agencies spend millions of dollars on presentation training.

1a. What it means to be a speaker

You are a public speaker when you stand behind the lectern at an awards banquet, or when you approach the floor microphone at a planning commission meeting, or when you sit at a table with three other members of your work group and present your proposal for tackling some problem. You are a speaker in class, at work, and among friends and family. And in any one of these settings, you are a different speaker from the speaker you'd be in another. Though listeners contribute to the creation of meaning, as speaker you are an originator and inventor, and you bring something uniquely "you" to shape the transaction.

However, not all oral communication in a group setting is public speaking. Perhaps the distinguishing characteristic of **public speaking** is that it is an event when a contract is reached among a group of people such that one person, the speaker, is given consent to direct the event.

1b. Public speaking as meaning-centered communication

Viewing communication as the transmission of information from a sender to a receiver makes "giving a speech" simply a matter of selecting ideas, packaging them, shipping them efficiently, and verifying their receipt. For most purposes, speakers are better served by embracing a more collaborative and complex model of communication.

Think about a group of filmmakers at work, or a software design team. At any given time, one individual may be putting forth ideas while the others listen and react. The result is a composite that did not exist in any one person's mind at the outset. The difference between *messages* (speaker controlled) and *meanings* (jointly created) has important implications.

1   Meaning is social

No individual, either sender or receiver, can control the "true meaning" of a statement. For example, a speaker who has violated a social norm cannot get off the hook by saying, "I did not intend that remark to be offensive, so it wasn't."

2   Meaning is contextual

Words take their meanings not just from a dictionary but from all that surrounds them—their context—as they are uttered. A message can be repeated verbatim, but its meaning will not be identical if the context has changed: when and where a statement was made, who was present, what happened previously, and what tone of voice and expression accompanied the utterance.

3   Meaning is contingent

No sentence or act frozen in time has acquired its "true meaning." The meaning has to be interpreted within a chain of events. A speech may begin with an anecdote that initially seems to reflect the speaker's view but is later revealed as exemplifying what the speaker opposes. Meaning becomes clear as it unfolds in the interplay between speaker and listeners. Often, we do not know what something meant until we reflect on an entire encounter.

4   Meaning is negotiated by discourse communities

Sometimes the "true meaning" of a message has to be worked out over time by larger groups in society, whose members already agree on some things. An example is the definition of sexual harassment in the workplace.

1c.   Familiar communicative resources

When you enter into the contract that designates you as a speaker, your challenge is to adapt three communication skills that you already have in your repertoire: conversation, writing, and performance.

1   Conversation skills

In everyday conversations, you are probably relaxed and spontaneous, responsive to the situation, and naturally expressive of your changing feelings. You do not worry about your exact words because meaning is clarified in the give-and-take.

One of the highest compliments a speaker can receive is to be called "conversational." The skills drawn from conversation that are useful to a public speaker include speaking in a comfortable and confident manner, listening to and considering the perspective of others, and adapting constantly to feedback. A lot of apprehension about public speaking can be dissipated if you incorporate this conversational model into the speaking event.

2   Writing skills

The written word enables you to distance yourself from your ideas, which allows you to craft and tinker. Writing can create the distance you need to view your ideas objectively, test them for logical coherence, and see how well they fit together. In writing, you can weave in multiple voices of authorities along with your own.

In writing, you pay close attention to word choices and organization to produce a carefully crafted message. You have the time to enjoy wordplay, to explore nuance, and to find elegant phrasing that makes the message memorable.

From writing, then, a speaker draws on the attention to language, the order of ideas, and the internal unity of the speech. Good writing requires time to rework and polish your words to achieve the most economical and forceful way to convey your message.

3   Performance skills

We are all performers—whenever we *do* something rather than merely think about it. In this handbook, when we talk about your performance skills, we mean the ways you have learned to use certain physical qualities—tone of voice, gestures, movement—to create a focal point for a group.

The performative aspects of public speech are what makes a speech more than conversation, more than an outline or a transcript. *Performance* refers not to display or phoniness but to the enactment of an event between speaker and listeners that transcends the message or exchange of information. This transcendence is what makes people say, "You had to be there."

Performance skills useful to the speaker include the ability to pay attention to the entire effect, the knowledge of how to use setting and timing, and the capacity to turn a collection of individuals into a cohesive group. Performers know how to make use of all the senses. They tie together visual effects, lighting, sound, music, humor, and drama. They have a superb sense of timing and understand how to direct emotional buildup toward the right moment for climax. Speakers can make use of these skills by learning to visualize the desired impact and carefully planning details that contribute to that overall effect.

CHECKLIST

A Balance of Skills

Conversation skills

❏ Underreliance leads to stiffness, excessive formality, distance, lack of spontaneity.

❏ Overreliance leads to uneconomical use of time and language, blunders, disorganization, the tendency to go off on tangents and lose focus.

Writing skills

❏ Underreliance leads to imprecise word choice, repetition, scattered organization.

❏ Overreliance leads to unnatural use of language and a "canned" sound, inability to adapt to an audience, an almost inevitable tendency to read or memorize the text.

Performance skills

❏ Underreliance leads to monotony, low emotional impact, reduced energy level.

❏ Overreliance leads to distraction from the message, unnatural or melodramatic persona, audience passivity, questions of sincerity.

1d. The skill-learning process

We learn complex skills differently from the way we learn simple facts. A complex skill like public speaking involves the combination of a number of intellectual and physical operations. Most of these operations are already in your repertoire. What you may not know is how to combine these skills to make an effective public speech.

KEY POINT **The Four Stages of Skill Learning** There are four stages in learning any skill:

1. unconscious incompetence (ui)
2. conscious incompetence (ci)
3. conscious competence (cc)
4. unconscious competence (uc)

As we move through the stages, we progress from not being aware that we are making errors in some area or that we need to learn a particular skill (ui), to realizing that there's room for improvement (ci), to working toward improvement and being vigilant when we use the skill (cc), to, finally, integrating the learned skills to the extent that competence comes naturally, and we no longer need to devote conscious attention to them (uc).

A great deal of your communication behavior is unconscious. You do not think about how you move your lips to make sounds or why you speak one way with your friends and another with your boss. These may be areas of unconscious competence (uc). At the same time, you may not be aware that you mispronounce "escape" or twirl your hair when you are nervous. These are examples of unconscious incompetence (ui). When do your communication behaviors receive your conscious attention? Usually when you are learning a new skill or when you run into difficulties in communicating. As soon as a skill is mastered or a communication problem is solved, your behavior becomes unconscious again.

1e. Common misconceptions

There are many approaches to teaching public speaking and much folk wisdom about how people become effective speakers. Four misconceptions can get in the way of becoming an effective public speaker.

- *Misconception 1: Good speakers are born, not made.* No one is born an effective speaker any more than one is born a good tennis player or an accomplished violinist. Inborn predispositions and early learning help some people learn faster and go further. However, virtually anyone can learn to give a clear, effective public speech.

- *Misconception 2: Good speaking should be easy right away.* Many speakers think, "I know how to talk, so I must know how to give a speech." When they recognize this fallacy after a speech that fails badly, they become discouraged. In addition, the discouragement may be compounded by Misconception 3.

- *Misconception 3: Speaking will always be difficult.* Although learning a skill requires effort and attention, performing the skill becomes much simpler, and almost automatic, once you reach a certain level of mastery. When you get discouraged with a speech outline that just won't come together or with phrasing that just won't flow, remember: It *will* get easier.

- *Misconception 4: There are simple formulas.* Communicating with an audience is a complex and sophisticated act. Every public speaking event is unique. There is no all-purpose recipe for preparing or delivering a speech. The quickest way to do something is not always the best way. In the area of public speaking, certain basic principles date back over two thousand years to Aristotle's *Rhetoric* and continue to be refined through social science research. We have confidence in these principles. The advice in this handbook is what has proved to be the soundest. With these sound public-speaking techniques, you will be more flexible and effective than if you had only some all-purpose recipe.

> **KEY POINT** **More Than Prescriptions** Although the chapters of this handbook are written as prescriptions, you will not find simple dos and don'ts to apply automatically to every situation. The fundamentals of speaking are stated simply, but the application and combination of these principles depend on your good judgment in each speaking situation.

1f. Five steps for speech preparation

Preparing a speech is complex and can be daunting. We offer this streamlined list (see Figure 1-1) of the bare essentials that go into preparing any speech, even the most basic one. These ideas and references will guide you as you get started. Later chapters describe variations to these steps, different speech formats or types of speeches, and sophisticated strategies.

THINK Initial decisions and analysis	Prepare plan 10 Select and narrow topic 11 Consider occasion 11 Clarify purpose 11 Determine mode of delivery 28 Frame thesis statement 11 Analyze topic 11 Analyze audience 12 Counter anxiety 4
INVESTIGATE Research for resources and materials	Locate resources 13 Investigate articles, books, and websites 14 Conduct interviews 15 Keep research notes 16
COMPOSE Development of speech materials	Develop rough working outline 17 Develop full-sentence outline 20 Add supporting materials 16 Add attention factors 30 Prepare introduction, conclusion, and transitions 31 Prepare presentation aids 27 Prepare speech notes 33
PRACTICE Preparation for oral performance	Give the speech aloud 33 Practice with presentation aids 36 Work on vocal delivery 34 Work on physical delivery 35 Get feedback 33
PRESENT The culmination of all your work	Relax, enjoy, connect with your audience, and debrief to learn something for next time.

FIGURE 1-1 The Five Steps of Public Speaking (with chapter references)

For simplicity the five steps are laid out in a linear fashion, but in fact they are recursive. This means that a speaker is always revisiting earlier steps in the *Think–Investigate–Compose–Practice–Present* cycle to ensure analytical and developmental completeness, and to facilitate polishing of the message. For a major speech you might return to refine your analysis after some research. Or when putting the speech together, you may discover the need for further research. In any speech, even a simple one, we certainly hope you don't stop thinking *after* Step 1 (Think)!

The first four steps are developed in more elaborate form in Figure 10-1, which shows how they overlap in time and how important *oral* activity is at every step of the process.

CHAPTER 2

Listening

Listening is a crucial communication skill; it is an essential component for most careers and a key factor in why relationships fail or succeed. Listening is not something experienced passively; it is a complex set of actions that requires explicit attention and practice.

Effective speaking and listening go hand in hand. Listening in a close and thoughtful way to public speakers gives you rich information about what works and what doesn't. You will be more appreciative of good speaking when you hear it. You will also be more critical of speaking that fails to measure up to the standards you set for yourself. Improving your habits and attitudes as a listener will directly enhance your effectiveness throughout the steps of preparing and delivering a speech.

2a. Prepare to listen

It is not necessarily instinctual to take time to prepare before a situation that requires skilled listening.

■ *Banish distractions, get physically set*. In our multitasking society, we are used to doing many things at once. When listening is a priority, we need to break that pattern by sitting up straight, looking at the speaker, and clearing away all materials except those needed for note taking.

Recognize that speaking in public takes courage and effort. Give the gift of your full attention, and adhere to the courtesies of a public situation.

■ *Stop talking*. Beyond the obvious, this principle applies to keeping up a running internal commentary as you focus on composing rebuttals. (See **2b**.) Also, when interviewing someone, don't do most of the talking.

■ *Decide on your purpose*. There are many possible objectives to listening, including to learn, to understand a new point of view, to evaluate an argument, or to enjoy a narrative. Marshal the resources you will need—your empathy, your curiosity, your critical analysis, your concentration—to meet your goal as a listener.

2b. Be curious and think critically

Effective listeners balance a charitable and open receptiveness with a critical assessment based on their real-life experiences and common sense.

> **KEY POINT** **Listening to Nonnative English Speakers** We encourage native speakers of American English to make a special commitment to understanding the speech of those for whom English is a second or third language. Learn to listen past any unusual pronunciations or inflections that may be by-products of the speaker's original language. Remember that, to communicate with you, the speaker has learned American English vocabulary, grammar, and syntax, and then has risked speaking publicly in that new language. In return, the only contribution required of you is to accustom your ear to a somewhat different pattern of sounds.

■ *Be open to the speaker's point of view.* Although people cannot help evaluating everything they hear as they hear it, you can make a conscious effort to substitute an attitude of curiosity. What, exactly, is this person saying? What led to that position? How did the person come to these conclusions, with what assumptions?

■ *Follow the structure of the speech.* Try to identify the thesis, main points, supporting materials, and crucial links, whether these are explicitly stated or not. Looking for structure aids your retention of content and your evaluation of its validity.

■ *Assess the speaker's claims.* In the same way you would listen to any speaker who makes a controversial claim, engage your critical thinking skills to test the validity of the argument.

■ *At the designated time, ask questions.* Frame questions that deepen your understanding of what the speaker is trying to get across.

Evaluating Claims Critically

❏ Do the main points taken together justify the thesis? (See **18a**.)

❏ Is each claim stated clearly? (See **21a**.)

❏ Is this claim a proposition of fact, value, or policy? (See **11d**.)

❏ Is the support offered for each claim relevant to the point? (See **16**.)

❏ Does each piece of evidence meet the appropriate tests for examples, testimony, or statistics? (See **16**.)

❏ Are the links between the points logically drawn? (See **24d**.)

❏ What premises are taken for granted without being stated? Are these assumptions valid? (See **21c**.)

❏ Are any fallacies present? (See **21f**.)

❏ Does the speaker misuse emotional appeals or substitute them for intellectual argument? (See **25d**.)

2c. Listening to learn

Effective listening will enable you to reach a deeper understanding of your topic and to use your time more efficiently when you seek information from other people as you research your speech. (See **15**.)

■ *Paraphrase.* Check your understanding of the points being made by paraphrasing and clarifying. This involves restating what you think you heard so the speaker can confirm or correct your interpretations.

■ *Ask follow-up questions for clarification.* As the expert answers your open-ended questions, careful listening will enable you to follow up with more-specific questions in response to those answers: "You said a minute ago that the issue of class size may be more important in the long run than teacher development. Why do you say that?"

■ *Take notes.* Be sure to take notes as you gather information from another person. Because the object is to optimize learning, it can make sense to employ this tool, which forces you to think about what is being said so that you can write notes that make sense as well.

2d. Constructive feedback

In a class or a workplace, you may be asked to provide feedback on the decisions the speaker has made and the effectiveness of the presentation. The role of critic/consultant requires a special blend of honesty and tact. The supportive critic bears in mind the fragility of partially formed ideas and the close connection between the person's speaking personality and the person's self-image. The following guidelines are for listeners who have been asked to give feedback.

- *Start with the positive.* Acknowledge what the speaker has tried to do and how it has succeeded. Try to communicate some sense of priority. There is no profit in refining the phrasing of a sentence if the whole point is going to be cut from the speech. Think first about whether the message makes sense and whether the overall strategy is effective. When those issues are settled, move on to the refinements.

- *Be specific.* It is more helpful to say, "You were discussing causes of the problem in Point 1 and then again in Point 3" than "This speech was disorganized." The same is true for positive comments.

- *Give suggestions, not orders.* Your comments should acknowledge the fact that your response is the reaction of just one listener and that others may differ. For example: "I have never cared for a big dramatic introduction, though I know it works for some people. Have you thought about . . . ?"

- *Be realistic about the amount and kind of feedback a speaker can receive.* Always consider the speaker's feelings when deciding what to say and how to phrase it. Be aware of the time constraints a speaker faces. Early in the development of the speech you can make some major suggestions for revision, but if the speech is in final rehearsal, it's too late to suggest going back to the drawing board.

- *Use the 90/10 principle.* This principle, developed by one of the authors in teaching interpersonal communication, states that people's weaknesses are rarely the *opposite* of their strengths. More often, they are the *excesses.* This awareness suggests a way of phrasing feedback: "The first 90 percent of quality A is a positive addition to your speech, but the last 10 percent of quality A begins to work in the opposite way." You are not suggesting that speakers eliminate a characteristic behavior, but that they

---

CHECKLIST

Constructive Feedback
- ❏ Start with the positive
- ❏ Be specific
- ❏ Give suggestions, not orders
- ❏ Be realistic
- ❏ Use the 90/10 principle

hold it in check. Actual feedback phrased this way might sound like this: "Your informal conversational style works wonderfully for most of the speech, except that at one or two points it becomes so colloquial and casual that your credibility suffers a bit."

2e. Common listening pitfalls

1   Daydreaming, doodling, and disengaging

It's easy for your mind to wander, in part because it takes a speaker longer to state an idea than for a listener to think the same thing. Listening experts recommend using that time differential constructively. Fill in your own examples. Think of questions to ask later. Stay mentally active in ways that connect to the speech topic. (See **2a**.)

2   Being distracted by appearances

You may notice that a speaker sways back and forth, or has a vocal inflection that makes every statement sound like a question. Or you may notice that the speaker looks wonderful in that shade of blue. In either case, letting yourself be distracted by these traits hinders your listening to the message of the speech.

3   Uncritically accepting a message

Don't automatically assume that if a speaker makes a statement it must be true. If something sounds wrong, it may be because it *is* wrong. Listeners share ethical responsibility for the meanings that come out of speeches. Give ideas the scrutiny that respect for them requires. (See **2b**.)

4   Prematurely rejecting a message

Hear the speaker out. Listen attentively, and you may hear a new argument or find an intriguing point you hadn't considered. (See **2b**.)

5   Planning your rebuttal

You can certainly be critical and analytical, but unless you are in a debate that requires on-the-spot refutation, don't divert your attention to the extent of composing your own responses. (See **2a**.)

6   Looking inattentive

As a matter of courtesy and respect, assume a supportive and responsive listening demeanor. The International Listening Association website **http://www.listen.org** provides some short articles on the value of listening as well as a list of 10 irritating listening habits.

CHAPTER 3

Speaking Ethically

Sometimes, a speaker succeeds in getting a point across or in persuading an audience but does so in a manner that is manipulative, exploitative, dishonest, or otherwise offensive. These cases raise questions about the ethical obligations of all speakers. Ethical questions do not ask, What works? but rather ask, What is right?

In one sense, ethical beliefs are a matter of each person's own conscience. Yet our beliefs about right and wrong are highly influenced by other people. Codes of ethical conduct come to us through family, religion, and culture. The National Communication Association has also established a code of ethics to guide communicators; it can be reviewed at http://www.natcom.org/policies/External/EthicalComm.htm.

3a. The ethical implications of your choices

No decision a speaker makes is morally neutral. We speak because we believe that what we say will make a difference. And it does. The results of a speech can be as serious as persuading others to follow a dangerous course of action or as apparently harmless as wasting their time with an unprepared and unfocused message. Every time you speak, you exercise power and assume responsibility for the consequences of what you do or do not say.

1 Ethical decisions are complex

Often, the answer to questions about what works in public speaking is, It depends. Questions about what is the right or ethical course of action are just as complex. Our ethics grow from our values, and values sometimes conflict. Rarely are there black-and-white choices. The best we can do most of the time is to select the lighter shade of gray. As communicators, we are obligated to think hard about each case and to develop our judgment through experience and reflection.

2 Ethical decisions vary with context

In a speech tournament, a debater might argue for legalized prostitution at 9:00 and argue against it at 10:30. In this context, it is understood that the rules of the game are to defend the assigned side of a topic as vigorously and skillfully as possible. This is considered no more unethical than a football team's defense of the north goal in the first and third quarters and of the south goal in the second and fourth. However, we judge as very unethical a candidate who takes one position when addressing voters in Oregon and the opposite position in Kansas. This is because, as critical listeners in the political arena, we view such public speeches not as part of a game but as sincere statements of the speaker's true beliefs.

What you can pass off as your own words varies as well. Political leaders are assumed to employ speechwriters who draft many of their speeches for them. This is considered ethical because the demands on public servants make it impossible for them to personally prepare each speech they give. However, in an academic speech class, it is well understood that students are expected to create and deliver their own speeches because the learning experience depends on acquiring a variety of skills and being assessed in them. To use your friend as a ghostwriter is clearly plagiarism in this context. (See **3b**.)

> **KEY POINT**   **Be True to Yourself and Your Listeners**   As a public speaker, you are not simply a transmitter of messages; you also put yourself (your individual self) in contact with an audience. Though you may adapt and adjust and accommodate to meet your goals, you have an ethical obligation to be true to yourself. When you've finished a speech, regardless of how anyone else responds, you should always feel good about what you said and how you said it.
>
> Public speakers have a special kind of power. When audience members entrust you with their time and attention, you take on an obligation to treat them with fairness and concern. You have every right to pursue your own reasons for speaking, but not at the expense of your listeners' welfare.

3b.   The integrity of ideas

A commitment to integrity requires that you take a larger view of how each individual speech act either reinforces or abrades the fabric of society. To live and work together, people have to trust that, on the whole, communication proceeds honestly and reliably.

1   Don't plagiarize

Besides yourself and your audience, there are others, not present, to whom you have some ethical obligations. These are the people whose ideas and words you draw into the speech situation. Some individuals who would never dream of stealing another person's property seem to think it is somehow acceptable to steal a scholar's solution to a problem or to borrow a friend's outline for a speech. The ethics of public speaking generally proscribe using another's major ideas or exact words—or even paraphrasing them—without giving credit to the source. Plagiarism is a serious offense in academic institutions and in the world of publishing. Careers have been ruined when public leaders have been exposed as plagiarists.

To avoid even the appearance of unethical appropriation of speech content, form the habit of taking careful notes of the sources of all your ideas, statistics, and evidence. And when you hear a wonderful anecdote, story, or turn of phrase you might like to quote someday, make a note right then so you will remember to give credit to the source. (See **16d, f**.)

There are several resources to guide you in avoiding even the appearance of plagiarism. Refer to **http://northwestern .edu/uacc/plagiar.html** or **http://www.uwtc.washington .edu/courses/231/documents/plagiarism.pdf** or **http://owl .english.purdue.edu/owl/resource/589/01/**

2   Don't lie

Rarely do we live up to the standard of "the truth, the whole truth, and nothing but the truth" in everyday interactions. The phrase *it depends* always crops up in conversations about what counts as a lie, a white lie, a fib, a prevarication, or tactful phrasing. In public speaking, however, the following categories of behavior cross the line between honest and dishonest speech.

■ *Making statements that are counterfactual.* This is pretty obvious. Saying, "I have no financial interest in this fitness center. I just care about your health" when you receive a commission for every new member you enroll is dishonest.

■ *Playing word games to create a false impression.* Sometimes, a speaker can use words with precise definition, being technically correct but totally misleading: "In response to allegations of illegal drug use, let me say that I have never broken the laws of this country" [when the drug use was in another country].

■ *Leaving out some part of "the whole truth" that, if known, would reverse the impact of the statement.* Saying "We have totally dominated the Smurge Company in our market" is misleading if you neglect to mention that the domination happened in only one quarter out of four.

3   Don't oversimplify

Another dimension of the integrity of ideas has to do with faithfulness to the facts and realities of your subject matter. Although we can hardly say that there is one "real truth" on any complex issue, we can say that some accounts are so shallow or oversimplified as to provide a basically false picture. Before you speak in public, thus contributing to and shaping the public discourse on a topic, you have an ethical obligation to look beneath the surface.

Another form of oversimplification is exemplified by the classic list of propaganda devices identified by a group of journalists some decades ago that sets forth the techniques unethical speakers can use to short-circuit an audience's rational processes.[1]

---

[1]Adapted from Alfred McClung Lee and Elizabeth Briant Lee, *The Art of Propaganda* (New York: Harcourt and Institute for Propaganda Analysis, 1939), 23–24.

CHECKLIST

Finding a Balance in Ethical Decisions

❏ Balance the value of using language in a lively and forceful manner against the risk of causing pain and offense.

❏ Balance the importance of appealing to your audience at an emotional level against the risk of abusing emotional appeals.

❏ Balance the right to use compelling persuasive appeals against the obligation to avoid simplistic persuasive techniques.

■ *Name-calling*. By attaching a negative label to an idea or a person, a speaker can provoke fear or hatred in an audience. The speaker hopes this tide of emotion will gloss over the lack of substance in his or her position.

■ *Glittering generalities*. At the other extreme is the use of words or phrases that represent some abstract virtue like patriotism or motherhood to generate a positive response rather than dealing with the merits of a position.

■ *Testimonials*. Another way to generate positive emotions is to link a popular figure with some cause or product. Here, the speaker replaces sound argument with a possibly inappropriate extension of the person's credibility from another area.

■ *"Just plain folks."* It is fine to build identification with an audience so that members are receptive to the ideas presented. This process goes too far, though, when the speaker implies, "You should believe me, not because of the inherent validity of what I say, but because I'm just like you."

■ *Card stacking*. In this method, a speaker carefully uses only facts or examples that bolster a particular position, and the highly biased selection is passed off as representative.

■ *The bandwagon*. This technique is useful to a speaker who wishes to discourage independent thinking. The "everyone is doing it" approach appeals to the need for security and plays on fears of being different or left out. A proposition should be sold on its merits, not on its popularity.

This list is far from comprehensive. Effective persuaders also use such techniques as snob appeal (the opposite of "just plain folks") and stand-out-from-the-crowd (the opposite of the bandwagon). Such persuasive appeals are questionable whenever they serve to distract listeners from important issues, cloud important distinctions, introduce irrelevant factors in the decision-making process, or use emotional appeals inappropriately or excessively. (For more about fallacies in logic, see **21F**. For fallacies in statistics, see **16b**.)

CHAPTER 4

Overcoming Fear of Speaking

Stage fright, communication apprehension, speech anxiety, reticence, shyness—these are among the most researched and analyzed variables in the literature on communication, precisely because the problem of feeling fearful about a public presentation is so widespread. Experts offer ways of thinking about this problem that can help you become more comfortable and confident when you speak in public. There are techniques you can use to work toward this goal as well.

4a. Put your fear into perspective

Many speakers try to be calm in every speech situation. This is unrealistic.

1 Some fear is normal

All speakers feel some fear, and for most of us the feeling can be managed and sometimes even turned to positive effect. The more speeches you give, the more confident you will become. You will recognize that fear is usually worst just prior to the speech and during the introduction. Once your speech is under way and the audience responds to you, negative emotions are often replaced by exhilaration.

2 Analyze your fear

"I'm scared to death" is a common statement that describes the emotional intensity of stage fright, but in reality, few people expect the experience to be fatal. An amorphous, ill-defined fear cannot be dealt with, though. Dealing logically with this fear requires examining its components so you can isolate a number of specific problems to be solved.

It is helpful to list your fears on paper. Be as specific as possible. If you write statements like "I'm afraid I'll make a fool of myself," ask yourself these follow-up questions: "How will I do that?" ("I'll forget my speech"); and "What will happen next?" ("The audience will think I'm dumb"). Use this format for your list:

I am afraid that [specific event] will occur and then that [specific result] will follow.

When you have generated your list, you can classify your fears. For items like "I'm afraid my visual aids won't be clear," the solution is simple. Check out the clarity of your visual aids with a few people, and if there is any problem, redesign them. As **4b** points out, many fears have roots in inadequate preparation. The mere act of writing the fears down often points immediately to a solution.

Other fears on your list may relate to physical responses: "I'm afraid my hands will shake and my voice will crack." If many of your concerns fall into this category, pay special attention to the suggestions in **4c**.

A number of items on your list may relate to failure to meet your own high standards. Recognize this concern as a positive motivation to do the best you can. But also realize that the power of suggestion is great and that dwelling on failure can cause it to happen. Use some of the visualization and verbalization techniques recommended in **4d** to create positive self-expectations.

> **KEY POINT** **An Offering, Not a Performance** One technique in particular has helped people cope with stage fright: seeing their listeners as "recipients" rather than "critics." A speaker must break out of the self-absorption of speech fright: "How do I look? Will they like me? Is my speech good enough?" Remind yourself that you are there not to perform but to share. How will the ideas and information you offer enrich their lives?
>
> Some recent research findings suggest that the best way to reduce communication apprehension is to change how you view the public-speaking event. It is not easy, but if you can think of yourself more as "talking with" the listeners and less as "performing for" them, you will feel much more comfortable.

4b. Prepare and practice

Although good speakers can make delivery seem effortless, their skill is based on extensive preparation over a period of time. The confidence they exude is also a result of preparation, not genes or fate or dumb luck.

If you feel uneasy about starting your speech, perhaps your introduction needs more work. If you are fearful of losing the continuity of the speech, you may need to practice it aloud several more times to internalize the flow of ideas. If you find yourself becoming generally anxious, use this as a stimulus to review your preparation. Whatever else you do, remember that time spent fretting about the outcome could better be used taking positive action to ensure a positive outcome.

As you prepare, follow the suggestions on practice sessions in chapter **33**. Avoid making last-minute changes in the speech.

4c. Relaxation techniques

When too much adrenaline makes you jumpy, physical activity usually helps you cope with the physical effects of fear. Avoid heavy exercise, but a brisk walk around the block or a little pacing in the hall—or a few arm swings and neck rolls—can be enough to bring your body back to normal. Once the speech begins, take advantage of the extra energy that the adrenaline provides to make your delivery more vigorous. Appropriate, dynamic gestures will help you discharge the nervous residue.

You can also handle symptoms of nervousness by learning and practicing relaxation techniques. Explore such methods as tightening and then relaxing certain muscle groups, breathing deeply, visualizing serene settings, or imagining sensations such as warmth or heaviness in parts of your body.

Chemical aids to relaxation—alcohol, drugs, tranquilizers—are highly inadvisable.

4d. Positive self-suggestion

When you experience fear, you are visualizing the most negative outcome for your speech. It is possible, however, to turn these fearful visions around. For example, tennis players, field goal kickers, and concert pianists, among others, have found it helpful to visualize what they are striving for.

1 Visualize success

When you prepare a speech, do not let yourself think about failure. When you detect such thoughts in your mind, replace them with a positive scenario: "I will approach the lectern calmly, smile at the audience, and begin. My voice will sound strong and confident." Do not, however, set unrealistic standards of perfection. Build some contingencies into your fantasy: "If I forget a point, I'll look down at my notecard and concentrate on the main idea I am conveying." Run through these positive visualizations a few times a day before you speak. As you practice, picture the audience responding favorably to the speech. And just before you get up to speak, remind yourself of the general tone and image you wish to project: "When I get up there, I am going to communicate my sincerity and concern in a warm, natural, confident manner."

2 Replace negative internal statements

One approach to reducing fears is to use "cognitive restructuring" to probe our mental commentaries, identify the unrealistic or irrational statements that cause fear, and replace them with more positive, logical, and realistic beliefs. We all have constant narrations running through our minds, so familiar that we are barely conscious of them. With some introspection, you can bring them to the mental fore and examine the effect they have on your behavior. It is helpful to remember that these are not statements of fact but statements that you yourself have created and that you can choose to replace if they interfere with your efficient functioning. Once you become fully aware of the commentaries that govern your response to public speaking, you can work on replacing the unproductive beliefs with more positive ones. Table 4-1 gives some examples.

TABLE 4-1   **Replacement Statements**

False Belief	Positive Replacement
A good speaker never says "uh" or "er."	A few nonfluencies aren't even noticed unless attention is called to them.
I'm going to go blank.	I've practiced several times, and I know the basic structure of this speech.
I can't handle this tension!	Even though I feel uncomfortable, I'm able to cope with tense situations.
No one will be able to understand me because of my accent.	My listeners will want to hear what I have to say, not how I say it.

Your unproductive responses are habitual and will not change easily. At first, you will have to repeat the replacement sentences mechanically, over and over. Because the replacement sentences are so reasonable and logical, a large part of your mind will want to accept them. The reassuring nature of the words often helps you to become physically calmer, and this more comfortable sensation acts to reinforce the new beliefs.

4e. Further assistance

Some fear of speaking is too deeply rooted to be remedied by the methods suggested here. If your fear of speaking is almost paralyzing, if none of the preceding suggestions work, you may need help in coping with it. Research shows that even severe fear of speaking can usually be reduced to a manageable level when treated by a qualified professional.

2 Speech Contexts

CHAPTER 5

Analyzing Speech Contexts

The skills and recommendations discussed throughout this handbook are necessarily general. They become useful to you when you are able to tailor them to the demands and expectations of a particular context. A person with excellent generic speaking skills may still be at a loss if a situation requires knowledge of a particular format. For example, it does a concerned citizen no good to prepare a compelling persuasive argument if the person cannot penetrate the rules of parliamentary procedure to gain recognition to speak. Ultimately, what is important to a speaker is not what is said but what meaning is created through the saying. Any given message or **text** takes on meaning from the circumstances that surround it—from the **context**. (See **1b**.) Both speakers and listeners rely on the context to make sense of messages. So knowing the rules and customs of a given speaking occasion will reduce the uncertainty you feel and thus minimize your fear.

5a. The basics

You will save time and work more efficiently if, before you even begin to plan a speech, you think carefully about the overall context of the speech. You can do this by starting with some fundamental questions: Who, where, what, when, why, and how?

- *Whom* will you be speaking to? And *where* will you be speaking? It's virtually impossible to begin to design a speech without having some picture of the situation that you will be entering. The people gathered in a particular place, or linked electronically, constitute the audience that will help define the meaning of your speech. As soon as you identify them, you can use chapter **12** to guide your more detailed audience analysis.

- *What* will you speak about? Topic selection is rarely completely under your control or completely out of your control. In every case an early determination must be made to map out the general content area you will be working with. Then, and only then, can you begin to gather materials and organize, develop, and craft them into an effective speech.

- *When* will you be speaking? Both the calendar and the clock have much to do with your overall approach to the speech. Be realistic about how soon you need to have the speech ready and how long you will be talking. This information is necessary to manage your preparation time (chapter **10**) and to practice your speech (chapter **33**).

- *Why* are you giving the speech? You always have some *reason* for speaking. Maybe you were invited to speak at some event, assigned to speak in a class, or have sought an opportunity to address a particular audience. Additionally, you have some *purpose* for speaking. In this handbook we classify general speaking purposes as to persuade, to inform, and to evoke, but we hasten to add that most situations involve a blend of these goals. Chapter **11** goes into more depth about how to identify these purposes and how to refine them into specific objectives and thesis statements.

■ *How will you be presenting the speech?* From the outset, make the decision as to whether your speech will be extemporaneous (carefully planned and outlined but not planned word for word), delivered from a written manuscript, memorized, or impromptu (off the cuff). The decision will influence how you prepare, following the guidelines for each mode of delivery as presented in chapter **28**.

5b. The format and models

Just as there are genres of literature—fiction, nonfiction, poetry—each with multiple subgenres such as the thriller, romance, and space opera, there are familiar categories of speaking. When one conducts a training workshop, delivers a sermon, or participates in a debate, there are some well-known, albeit general, expectations about the shape that speech will take. In other cases, there are more specific formats speakers typically follow. Examples of some workplace, civic, and ceremonial formats are found in chapters **7**, **8**, and **9**. If you've purchased the online Technology Resources that come with this book, you can access them to find other examples of some detailed speech formats used in classroom speaking assignments in various disciplines and in particular professional settings. (See page vii to learn about these resources.) Whenever such standard formats exist, it is your responsibility to learn about them and to adhere to them.

If you are not given a particular format to follow, your first research task should be to seek out models to study. How do social workers present case reports at staff meetings? What is included in a progress report on an engineering project? What kind of speeches have been presented as keynote addresses to this particular organization? There may be a set of written guidelines to follow. If not, ask for manuscripts, outlines, and videos of previous presentations. Interview members of the organization about what is expected. Whenever possible, sit in as an observer on presentations of the type you will be making. Make note of the steps that are followed, the kinds of arguments and evidence that are used, the style and tone that are common; from these observations generate a template for your presentation.

5c. The specific situation

Besides finding out the essential information about a speech situation and researching existing formats, speakers benefit by thinking about the many factors that define every context for speaking. These dimensions might be arrayed along several continua. Locate where your speaking situation falls within each category.

←——————————————————————————→
Public sphere   **Private sphere**

A context is established in part by the venue or domain in which speaking occurs. One set of expectations accompanies a meeting in a legislative hall, a large city square, or a cathedral. Even if the same topics are being talked about, quite different expectations will come into play if the speech takes place in a private office or a living room.

←——————————————————————————→
Formal demeanor   **Informal demeanor**

Some contexts are highly formal and require dressy attire, use of titles and respectful forms of address, dignified word choice, and a setting that is orderly and perhaps ceremonial. The informality of other contexts is signaled by casual dress, use of first names, colloquial speech forms, and everyday physical arrangements.

←——————————————————————————→
Monologic   **Dialogic**

Contexts are also defined by the role of the participants. In monologic situations, it is assumed that a featured primary speaker will dominate the event, taking primary responsibility for what is talked about. In dialogic situations, other participants can direct both the topic and the form of the interaction. As with all the other continua, there are many contexts that fall between the extremes or that blend the norms. At a public lecture, for example, the expectation is that the main speaker will be listened to without interruption or heckling until the question-and-answer period begins. Then the norms of dialogic speech take precedence and it is considered inappropriate for the speaker to give another speech.

←——————————————————————————→
Highly prescribed   **More open**
rules of speaking   **rules of speaking**

All public speaking is rule-bound to some extent, but there is tremendous variation in how explicit or specific those rules are. Some contexts have very rigid rules about who may speak, for how long, and on what topic. In a formal parliamentary meeting, a speaker must receive recognition and then link the discourse to a particular motion before the house. In a legal proceeding, advocates can ask questions only in certain ways and at certain times, and they can present arguments only during opening and closing statements. Contrast this to a meeting of a small task force, in which participants might seize the floor at any time and change subjects at will. The rules in the latter case either are implicit—group members may subtly sanction those who talk too much or too long—or evolve on the spot—as when someone suggests that each person take a few minutes to state a position on the topic.

← →

Power resides with speaker   **Power resides with listeners**

Power differences between speakers and listeners inevitably influence context. Sometimes, the power resides with the listeners: Bosses control paychecks, teachers assign grades, judges make rulings, and homeowners' association boards approve projects. Whether motivated by common sense, self-preservation, or genuine respect, speakers usually show a degree of restraint in addressing those in higher-power positions. At other times, power resides with the speaker. Here, the expectations differ: The speaker doesn't deny the power but often chooses to downplay it to avoid being intimidating or threatening to listeners.

← →

Existing community   **One-time assembly**

The context of a speech differs based on the relationship among the participants. When an already established group comes together, speeches typically include in-group jokes, use of abbreviations and shorthand expressions, and references to shared history. There is no need to spend time building a sense of community as there would be in a situation in which individuals have gathered for the first time, primarily because they are interested in a common topic or in the speaker.

← →

Immediate audience   **Extended audience**

Most often, a speech is intended for those who are present. But there are occasions when everyone understands that the real context of the speech involves a much wider audience that will read it or hear it broadcast.

These dimensions illustrate the uniqueness and complexity of speech contexts. A speaker could be right on target in analyzing most of the relevant factors in a situation but, by misreading just one of these—say, the expected level of formality—could jeopardize effectiveness. Do not be afraid to ask questions about any new situation that you enter. If you are in charge of an event, be sure that invitations and announcements communicate shared expectations.

An additional and important determinant in each speaking context is culture. Mastering the marketing presentation in a U.S. business context will not prepare you to give a similar presentation in Japan. Knowing about different cultural norms and expectations also helps listeners to be respectful of international guests.

Each of the four chapters that follow offers preliminary suggestions for a particular kind of context: the educational, the business and professional, the civic and political, or the social and ceremonial. We offer these suggestions with caution, because even these generalizations need to be adapted and combined for each specific event. For example, a training workshop within a company would combine the expectations of workplace communication and the education setting. Or, an inaugural address would draw in elements of both political and ceremonial speaking.

CHAPTER 6

Educational Context

Though it is common to contrast academic life with the "real world," the classroom speaking context is a real one in all important respects. Classroom presentations involve real people who are involved in the mutual creation of meaning with significant consequences. Speakers are challenged to analyze the expectations and requirements of each educational context. To adapt the recommendations from other sections of this book, begin by determining why the oral assignment is being used.

6a. Oral assignments to develop speaking skills

Academic speech classes, presentation skills training programs, speech contests, and Toastmasters' groups represent the few types of contexts in which the presentation of a public speech is the primary activity rather than a means to some other end. In these situations, the assignment is typically designed around the skills students need to practice. You may be required to give a speech to inform or to persuade, to include a variety of types of supporting material, or to use different kinds of reasoning. Admittedly, such speech experiences are artificial in some ways; you may be asked to cover a great deal within a restricted time limit and to provide detailed outlines with speech components labeled. But there is no need to chafe against the constraints of classroom speaking. Try to select topics that excite you and engage your listeners. Take advantage of this special opportunity to receive detailed feedback on both the overall impact of your message and the technical aspects of your presentation. To succeed in these assignments, it's important to learn exactly what each one entails and to touch every base.

6b. Oral assignments to provide practice for professional contexts

In advanced academic classes and in organizational training programs, you will have opportunities to learn how the generic speaking skills of analysis, research, organization, and delivery are modified in various contexts. To present a literary critique, a social science research report, an engineering design review, a health care plan for a patient, or a training program for employees, you must master a new set of conventions. Oral assignments are designed to simulate situations you will face in career settings. Audience members may be asked to role-play colleagues, customers, or clients. Outside experts are sometimes invited to presentations to give you feedback. It is particularly important in these projects to get detailed information about the purpose of your presentation and the expectations of your listeners.

Though we always encourage you to "be yourself," assignments of this sort invite you to project yourself into a new persona to some extent. If you aspire to be a chemist or a journalist or a physical therapist, the classroom setting provides a safe environment to explore how you will communicate in those roles. Step up to class assignments and try on the conventions, speaking style, and even the clothing that will be expected in the new role.

6c. Oral assignments to help you master subject matter

The most common use of oral assignments in educational contexts is as a means to a broader end. Oral reports, debates, and group presentations are powerful ways to explore and master subject matter. When student presenters know they have to talk about ideas in public, they are forced to engage material deeply to synthesize points and make them clear to others. Members of classroom audiences often find that peer presentations help reinforce course content, possibly because their classmates explain things in more accessible ways than professors sometimes do. And instructors find oral presentations to be one important way to assess student learning, sometimes superior to papers or exams in showing how fully students understand course material and how creatively they can apply it.

For these assignments, success depends on taking the extra time, after studying the topic and doing research, to follow the principles of effective speaking. An oral presentation doesn't consist of just reading an academic paper. Clarify the expectations and time limits and then plan and rehearse a lively, well-organized presentation that will engage the audience and boost your credibility.

CHAPTER 7
Workplace Context

Generally, in business and professional settings formats have been created and norms have evolved, and the emphasis is on efficiency and clarity. Speech in workplace settings is expected to be stream-lined and unadorned. A routine report to a work group typically does not begin with an attention getter, but rather features a detailed logical orientation to locate the topic within the organization's multiple tasks. Visual aids (including handouts) are central to professional presentations, in part so that technical details can be available for examination and reference. Within organizations, because goals are assumed to be shared, listeners may ask each other tough questions and play devil's advocate. In a team environment, internal communication is a way to test ideas so that they can be improved before costly mistakes are made.

Typical presentations in a business and professional context include the employment interview, the marketing presentation, the technical presentation, and project proposals and status reports. We also discuss chairing a meeting.

KEY POINT **Professional Benefits** A quick glance at job descriptions on the web reveals regular and frequent use of phrases like "excellent oral and written skills," "strong ability to motivate others," and "excellent interpersonal and communication skills." The skills you develop as a public speaker will help you get a job: The candidate who gives answers that are concise, who can express ideas and desires in memorable ways, and who remains calm in a stressful situation will make the better impression. Once you get the job, you can use these communication skills to shape your career environment so that you gain personal satisfaction while being an effective and valued professional resource.

7a. Job interviews

Traditionally, the job interview consists of an applicant and a personnel director, with a desk as a prop. However, more interviews are now being done in a group, with a number of people from different departments and levels talking with the applicant. Other events that resemble interviews are the performance review and the sales presentation to a committee. In any of these situations, you may not be successful if you come prepared only to answer questions. When you speak to a group, even a small one, you should apply several public-speaking concepts, of which the following are the most important.

1   Audience analysis

Learn all you can about the people who will be interviewing you. (If the organization has a website, mine it for information.) If possible, get a list with their names, so you can learn to pronounce them, and their positions, so you can think about the various perspectives they represent. When you are introduced, you can quickly associate faces with the names and roles you have studied. Throughout the interview, you can adapt your answers to their perspectives: "That brings up the whole question of the cost effectiveness of surveys. I'm sure you confront that issue all the time, Mr. Keenan, being director of marketing research."

2   Opening statement

The first question of a job interview likely will be, "Tell us a little bit about your background—how you got to where you are now, and how you describe your orientation to our field." Seize this opportunity to set the tone. Make a brief statement that serves the purposes of a speech introduction: gets the audience's attention, creates rapport, and establishes a framework for the main content to follow. Do not assume that on the day of the interview your résumé or sales brochure is fresh in the interviewers' minds. Besides reiterating what you sent earlier, you can also update it if further developments would be of interest to the group.

You can use your opening statement to describe a general philosophy or position. You may highlight aspects of your experience to show trends or directions that led you to the present interview. Whether you are selling yourself, a service, a product, or an idea, use this opportunity to establish credibility.

It seldom hurts to compliment their organization. Be as specific as possible to show your knowledge of its workings.

3   Answers to questions

Review the guidelines for answering questions in chapter **37**. Try to tie questions together in a group interview: "This question spotlights another side of the training issue Ms. Herman raised a few minutes ago." You can also demonstrate your powers of synthesis by relating certain common threads to your opening position.

4   Problem–solution–result (PSR) statements

A PSR is a brief, memorable personal success story. In it, you succinctly state a *problem,* describe your *solution* to that problem, and then list the components of the beneficial *result* of your solution—and all in 90 seconds or less. By preparing a collection of PSRs, you can ensure that in an interview you are primed to respond positively to a variety of questions concerning your skills and achievements. Ninety seconds is not much time at all, but for PSRs, brevity is important.

Describing the problem should take about 50 percent of your time. You set the stage, laying out what was at stake, what the consequences would have been if the problem had not been solved, and what constraints you may have operated under. The solution should take no more than 25 percent—what actions you took and what skills and abilities you brought into play. Summarize the key steps, and avoid the temptation to go into the kind of detail that comprehensively demonstrates your understanding of your field (save this for follow-up questions). The result should show quantifiable results if possible, but it should be a concise and powerful description of the immediate and long-term benefit of your actions, along with any awards or recognition that came with them.

Here is a sample of a PSR:

Problem

When I was the publications manager for a small software company, there was one time when my leadership, management, and organizational skills were really put to the test. We had a telecommunications management package under development and in trial at a large potential customer. At a status meeting it was let drop that Sales had promised a complete documentation set for a week from Friday, eight days away, instead of the eight weeks agreed upon in the original development plan. Well, this was a problem, because the documentation consisted of 10 manuals, many of which were not started yet. But if we failed to produce the manuals, no matter how ridiculous the deadline, the image of the company would suffer, as would the chances for landing the customer.

Solution

I immediately pulled my staff off all other projects and divided the workload according to their various talents. I made the rounds of the other departments in the company, negotiating new delivery dates for their existing projects while gaining assurance of easy access to subject matter experts for my staff. As the days passed, I adjusted workloads to respond to evolving needs, did subprojects where necessary, and continued to work on interdepartmental cooperation.

Result

On the appointed Friday, three sets of a 10-manual, 800-page documentation suite went into the arms of DHL for delivery. As a result, my team was stronger, with the confidence that comes from meeting an impossible goal; the other departments knew they could count on us in a pinch; the potential customer was very pleased with the documentation and became a customer-in-fact not long after—which landed the company a $12 million receivable.

By keeping your PSRs brief, you make them memorable, and you also allow your interviewers to set the level of detail. If the interviewers want to know more, they can ask more questions, and, of course, you will have prepared more PSRs to cover the more in-depth questions. In the preceding example, an interviewer could ask to find out more about how the speaker negotiated the new internal delivery dates or what the most difficult project assignment was.

PSRs are not only for job interviews. They are also very handy in performance reviews and salary adjustment meetings, in which having such a store of examples demonstrating the benefits that accrue to the organization because of your presence can only work to your own benefit. Although by no means exhaustive, Table 7-1 lists a representative set of topics for PSRs.

Prepare the PSR when events are still fresh in your mind. Don't wait until the annual performance review, or until you start job hunting, or until you've finished school.

5   Effective delivery

You are "on stage" the entire time, even though you are seated and in an informal setting. (Delivery skills are discussed in **34** and **35**.) When you answer a question from one group member, be sure to include the entire group in your eye contact.

T A B L E 7 - 1   Topics for Problem–Solution–Result Statements

Specific personal attribute	Decisiveness
	Creativity
	Spoken/written
	     communication
	Fast learning curve
	Adaptability
		Versatility
		Leadership
		Confidence
		Analytical problem
		     solving
		Organization

Specific work skill	Report writing Supervision Manual dexterity Crisis management Negotiating experience	Accounts receivable Medical knowledge Government relations Facility with computers Budget preparation

Accomplishment	Designed and
	     implemented X
	Lowered costs
	Staffed X
	Set record for X
	Recruited and
	     trained X
		Improved productivity
		Organized and directed
		Enhanced customer
		     relations
		Met goals and
		     objectives
		Devised new strategies

7b. Team presentations

Often, interdepartmental teams form within an organization to present information on products, processes, or decisions to internal and external audiences. This means that, in addition to good speaking skills, success depends upon planning, coordination, and teamwork.

1   Preparation plan

In the workplace, everyone is already overtasked, so it is crucial at the beginning of a project to ensure that people's time will be used efficiently. This responsibility falls to the project manager, who should initiate the first planning session well before the date of the presentation.

CHECKLIST

Key Tasks for Group Planning

1. Clarify the purpose, including identifying who the stakeholders are, what their expectations are, and what constitutes success. (See **11c** and **22a**.)
2. Agree on the core message, the equivalent of the thesis statement, which will serve as a touchstone against which all content will be evaluated. (See **11d**.)
3. Divide the labor among team members.
4. Establish the timeline, making sure to cover intermediate milestones and practice sessions.

---

2   Content outline with speakers' responsibilities

For the steps in organizing a presentation, see **10, 17, 18, 19**. We recommend that a team presentation be thought of as one "macrospeech" rather than as a series of individual presentations. We have all heard group presentations in which the speakers contradicted each other, overlapped in content, left out key points, jumped ahead and stole the thunder of upcoming presenters, and even squabbled publicly about the order and coverage of points. To provide coherent content and project a professional image, it is crucial that each team member have a picture of the whole presentation and how each piece relates to that whole.

Before an outline can be decided upon, the group will have engaged in initial brainstorming and preliminary decision making. When the topic is narrowed and focused, someone needs to create a detailed outline of the speech, complete with an introduction and a conclusion, transitions, time limits for each segment, and a list of visual support and equipment needed.

In this process of decision making and outline crafting, the group should come to agreement on several issues:

■ *The introduction*. This may be done by the team leader or the first speaker. In any case, the introduction should cover the basics: making the audience want to listen, telling them what will be discussed, and introducing the team members. (See **31**.)

■ *The main points*. Each segment needs to serve a clear purpose in developing the core idea. If the group merely decides that Andrea will talk about her part of the project, and then Clint will talk about his, and so on, there is no guarantee that the components will be relevant and will fit together. As with a speech, it is prudent to have only a few key ideas and, generally, a few speakers. However, in an extended presentation, each group leader can present the main idea, and additional speakers can present segments that function as subpoints under the topic. However simple or complex the organization, there needs to be prior agreement on the goal of each part of the presentation and on the time allotted for it.

■ *Transitions*. Listeners need to be reminded of the overall road map for the presentation. The transition from segment to segment can be handled by a group leader, or each speaker can be charged with building a bridge to the next. For the principles of transitions, see **31**. It is important to go beyond "Here's Johnny" to offer a statement like "Once the basic design has been completed, it needs to be tested. Here is where John Carlton and his able group come in. John is now going to tell you about the steps they go through to make sure our clever designs actually work."

■ *The conclusion*. Again, a group leader or the final presenter can review and integrate the material presented. The important point is that there be a planned wrap-up that ties things together and ends on a positive note. (See **31**.)

■ *Question-and-answer period*. The plan needs to build in a question-and-answer period after each segment of a long or technical presentation or to allow for questions at the end. Decide who will field questions and direct them to the appropriate person. Sometimes, individuals are present who do not participate in the main presentation but are available as resources during the question-and-answer period. (See **37**.)

3   Unifying elements

Projecting the impression of unity, mutual respect, and teamwork should be one of the goals of each presentation. Having a clearly organized presentation is the most important way to make this point; however, there are a few additional steps a team can take to show they are "on the same page."

- *Make the segments parallel.* This may involve common phrasing of the main idea of each piece: "With our technological innovations, we will own this marketspace next year. . . . With our dedicated and knowledgeable sales force, we will own this marketspace next year. . . . With our uncompromising support, we will own this marketspace next year." Or it may be appropriate to use the same suborganization in each part of the presentation. In a cross-departmental status report, each department might follow this pattern: (1) review the goal, (2) report on progress to date, (3) report on problems encountered, (4) identify solutions, and (5) provide a current timetable.

- *Use common themes and phrases.* Develop a glossary of technical terms, abbreviations, and acronyms, and get agreement within the group to adhere to the "approved list." Once the substance of the presentation is in place, look for ways to emphasize the unique approach of your organization or the special features you are offering. Just as the main ideas can have common phrasing, other integral concepts and themes can be consciously woven throughout the presentation.

- *Find opportunities for cross references.* Speak of your copresenters with respect and admiration. Use terms like *colleague.* Briefly forecast or refer back to their points, and direct questions to them, acknowledging their expertise.

- *Present a consistent visual message.* Slides, presentation software, and diagrams should have a common look. Agree on a template at the beginning of a process, and have a designated specialist to polish and unify the material coming in from all the presenters.

4 Practice

Busy professionals who know their topic well often are reluctant to have formal practice sessions. Practice is important for an individual talk, but it is *essential* for pulling together a team of speakers.

- *Schedule at least one early run-through even if some pieces are still under construction.* The goal is to get a sense of how the presentation fits together and to find opportunities to improve it.

- *Schedule at least one final run-through.* This will serve to polish the transitions and to familiarize the speakers with the equipment and visual aids used.

- *Arrange for feedback on the presentations during the practice stage.* Participants may comment on one another's content and clarity. It is also common for managers or other organizational members to sit in on practice sessions to make suggestions. For very important presentations, simulations may be staged with persons role-playing audience members, and communication consultants may be brought in to videotape the rehearsal and even coach individuals on presentation skills.

■ *Pay attention to the timing of the overall presentation, whatever the level of rehearsal.* It is not inappropriate to have someone give time signals during the actual presentation to keep the team on track.

5   Debriefing

Shortly after a presentation, the team should meet to talk candidly about what worked and what can be improved in the future.

7c.   Project proposals

To pursue a plan, you often have to convince others that your ideas are worth their time, money and energy—with a **project proposal**. The project might be a research idea, services for a possible client, a course of action to reach an institutional goal, or an innovation you would like your organization to adopt. In each case, you are addressing the decision makers who will endorse or reject your plan.

1   The evaluation criteria

If you are proposing a research idea for your senior thesis, look at the standards set by the faculty. If you are applying for funds from an agency or bidding on a contract, carefully review the Request for Proposals (RFP) and be sure you address every point. If you are making a pitch to a client or customer, find out what is important for their decision among competing proposals. As with any form of audience analysis, listening is key. Talk to the decision maker directly or get information from documents and experts. If possible, study models of successful proposals.

2   The introduction

After a greeting and introducing yourself and any colleagues, concisely state the problem the proposal addresses. You will probably include a brief description of the background, showing your awareness of its significance. You might mention alternative approaches that have been tried or are available. In any case, within the first couple of minutes, state your proposal. (This is similar to a thesis statement, described in **11d.**) Include the positive results of the proposed action, as in these examples:

■ My partner and I would like to contract to handle all your public relations and advertising placement needs, *freeing you to concentrate on your business operations.*

■ Our agency is requesting funding from your foundation to provide a pilot program that will *empower senior citizens* by teaching them how to access health information online.

■ I would like to have 10 percent of my time released from my other assignments for the next six months to conduct research on a data security application that would *enhance several of our existing products*.

3 The body of the presentation

Explain the overall strategy and the rationale for it. Move to an explanation of the steps you propose. Probably you will also discuss timelines, costs, personnel, and so on. If there are deliverables, such as product designs, prototypes, and documents, be specific in your commitments. It can sometimes be helpful to define what certain deliverables are *not*. For example, "We will deliver 6,000 widgets in bulk, but it will be up to you to provide the packaging." If there are limitations or risks, mention them briefly, but don't dwell on them. Be ready, however, to discuss them if there are follow-up questions.

Presentation aids are especially helpful in making your vision clear. (See **27**.) Handouts can show that you have thought about specifics, while allowing your oral presentation to focus on the major concepts of the proposal.

4 The conclusion

After a short recap of your key points, make a direct appeal for the acceptance of your proposal. (See **31b.2**.) Once again, emphasize the benefits of your plan by linking to the needs and values of the decision makers.

> *Not:* Our consulting firm has an excellent reputation and we take pride in doing exceptional work.
>
> *But:* Adopting our plan will help you to refashion your website to better serve your current customers and to attract new ones.

7d. Project status reports

A **project status report** can be delivered to an advertising campaign's project team, a church's search committee looking for a new minister, or the funding agency for a multimillion-dollar government contract.

1 The introduction

Start your report with a very brief summary of what is being undertaken and where you are in the process. Assume that listeners are familiar with the overall project.

2 The body of the report

Depending on the project, this detailed account of the progress can be organized into categories, such as task, objective, or department. For large projects, several speakers might report on different areas, such as the development, testing, documentation, and marketing of a software application. (See **7b** for suggestions on group presentations.)

When addressing problems, such as delays in the schedule, be open and direct, but maintain a tone of confidence and optimism. Choose words carefully. Don't whine, apologize, or point fingers. Tell what you have done to rectify the situation and what adjustments you have made to minimize impact on the total project, as in these examples:

- While we are waiting for delivery of replacement parts, we have shifted three production engineers to work on packaging.
- Recent server problems at the university library have curtailed access for students, so I have not been able to see the appropriate research. However, I have applied for an account with the county library system so that I can log on to the necessary databases there.

3   The conclusion

End with a realistic assessment of the status of the project. If changes in budget or timelines are inevitable, state them directly. If you have proposals to overcome problems or to make improvements, declare them here. If things are going well, don't be bashful about saying so!

Allow plenty of time to answer questions. Welcome them and respond directly and nondefensively. (See **37**.)

CHECKLIST

Sample Agenda for a Project Status Meeting
1. Welcome, introductions, overview
2. Goal review
3. Progress to date
4. Problems encountered
5. Identified solutions
6. Impact on timetable and budget
7. Summary, Q&A

7e. Training sessions

Examples of **training presentations** include workshops for new employees about the corporate style guide for documents, training sessions for an organizational customer about a new software package, and health-education classes for people who have recently been diagnosed with a disease or condition.

Making information clear and usable is the centerpiece of training. (For more on informative strategies, see **22**.) However, one key difference between training and informative speaking is that training is typically expected to produce some verifiable skills in the participants. To get people to change their behavior, you need not only a strong informative message but also persuasive skills of motivation.

1   The objectives

It's essential for trainers to discover what trainees already know and what they need to learn. A *needs analysis* is similar to an audience analysis (see **12**). However, the frequent challenge for trainers is to satisfy both the organizational decision makers who requested the training and the training participants. For example, management might envision a training presentation on conflict resolution as a workshop to teach skills for responding to customer complaints, but the employees might expect to learn how to deal with difficult coworkers or supervisors. Trainings should use a variety of sources of information such as *interviews, observations,* and *questionnaires* to identify the various perceived needs of organization members and to clarify expectations about what the training will cover.

In planning the training, you should use the needs analysis to identify the training objective or the behavioral outcomes you are aiming for. (See **11c.3**.) What, exactly, will participants be able to do that they can't do now?

2   The mix of activities

A good workshop or training program always includes discussions and opportunities for practice. It is usually a mix of activities such as group exercises, analysis of case studies, role-playing, brainstorming, and sharing. Selecting and facilitating such activities builds on your speaking skill but usually requires additional preparation in training techniques. Besides enrolling in train-the-trainer programs, you will find it useful to observe effective trainers in action and to work with a more experienced co-trainer at first.

Another expectation of a training program is the extensive use of clear, useful, and professional visual and presentation aids. Pay particular attention to the suggestions in **27** and **36**.

3   The agenda

The training should follow principles of organizing any presentation (see **19**), with a logical progression of content, coherent groupings, and effective transitions between points (see **32b**).

However, because you are involving the participants, you will not have complete control of the timing. You may have planned for 10 minutes of questions after your first "mini-lecture" but find that there is only one brief question. Later, an activity you had thought would require about a half hour ignites the group and they spend twice that long discussing it. Experienced trainers work from a careful plan, but they have contingency plans at hand. Sometimes you may need to redesign on the spot, dropping some planned components and making smooth transitions between the rearranged pieces. (You can see how experience in impromptu speaking is good preparation for such occurrences! See **28b**.) At other times you will need to wrap up a discussion skillfully and move on.

To maintain your credibility as a trainer, avoid seeming rushed or disconcerted by the inevitable adjustments to your goals.

> *Not:*   I had two more really great activities planned, but now I guess we don't have time for them.

> *But:*   You've brought up most of the key points I wanted us to consider in this discussion. For a little more depth on [subject *x*] and [subject *y*], look over these pages in the printed materials you received.

> *Not:*   Well, this framework has seven components, but I only have time to cover three of them.

> *But:*   You see from this slide that this is a robust theory with several components. For our purposes in this workshop, we will be discussing three of them.

4   The introduction

Begin by explaining the importance of the material to be covered and then be quite specific about the objectives: "When this workshop is over, the participants will be able to [do these particular things]." Typically, the participants are invited to introduce themselves and to state their goal for the training. In dealing with busy adults, it's always a good idea to give a detailed agenda of what is to come and to be specific about timelines and breaks. You will also need to establish your credibility on the topic and to establish rapport. People learn better when they like and trust the instructor.

5   The two-part conclusion

The wrap-up of a training program differs from a simple conclusion in a speech. During the training you provided opportunities for questions and comments throughout the session, but also allow for additional time for discussion during the wrap-up. In addition to a summary of what has been covered, which provides closure, it is a good idea to have participants state what has been most meaningful and useful for them, because training often includes explicit plans for the application of the concepts covered. Participants might be asked to draw up an action plan for using the material on the job, or they might be invited to a follow-up session to discuss how the training has influenced their work. Finally, always save time at the end of training for feedback and a written evaluation of some sort.

7f. Chairing a meeting

Although individual speakers need to fit into an existing format, people who find themselves in leadership roles can often shape the context for speaking. Participants usually look to the leader to define the ground rules and facilitate the interactions. Here are suggestions for some common leadership roles.

1 Planning and preparing

Clarify the format, coordinate the participants, and anticipate contingencies.

- *Agenda planning.* Determine what will occur and in what order. Typically, the items of an **agenda** follow a hierarchical order. Routine reports, announcements, and introductions come first, and they lead-up to the major speaker, presentation, or discussion. (For many organizations and governmental bodies, the general format is already set by bylaws and custom. See the *Checklist: Sample Agenda Based on Parliamentary Procedure* in this section.)

    Try to have all potential agenda items submitted to you well in advance. Many meetings have been thrown off schedule by the surprise request for a "brief announcement," which turned into a 15-minute speech. It is your responsibility to manage communication so that the group's goals are met efficiently. Be firm in sticking to the agenda and moving the proceedings along.

- *Coordinating participants.* Give a *written* copy of the agenda to all participants in a formal business meeting. Confirm how and when they will participate: "I'll call on you for the treasurer's report right away. Save your idea for fund-raising, though, and introduce it under new business." For a decision-making session, let every participant know what to expect so that each can come prepared with the right information and some prior thoughts. For an informal program such as a banquet, you might not write out the agenda, but you should still apprise each person of your plan: "Right after the ventriloquist performs, I'll introduce you for the presentation of the Scholarship Award."

- *Manage the logistics.* As chair of any event or session, you are a coordinator, facilitator, and host. You are not the "star"; you are there to serve the group by helping members meet *their* goals efficiently and pleasantly. To this end, prepare by visualizing the event. Anticipate issues that may arise.

    Will the group need information for its discussion? Perhaps you should bring minutes, policies, reports, and data for reference. Prepare handouts, slides, or charts to put key information before the group.

Consider the comfort and convenience of the participants. At a business meeting, will there be writing materials, name tags, refreshments, and scheduled breaks? At a banquet or public program, oversee or delegate even such small details as seating arrangements, water at the speakers' table, and audiovisual equipment.

CHECKLIST

Sample Meeting Agenda Based on Parliamentary Procedure

1. Call to order includes: checking credentials; calling roll; introducing observers, parliamentarian; honoring any ceremonial functions
2. Approval of agenda
3. Reading (or distribution) and approval of minutes of previous meeting
4. Treasurer's report
5. Reports of other officers
6. Reports of standing committees
7. Reports of special committees, task forces
8. Old business
9. New business
10. Announcements
11. Adjournment

---

2 During the meeting

Beyond the logistical concerns of agenda setting and troubleshooting, an effective leader can shape a context that helps a group meet its goals for communicating.

■ *Introduction, transitions, and conclusion.* Carefully plan your opening and closing statements. Try to develop coherent, even graceful, transitions to bridge the parts of the program so that you do not fall back on "We're moving right along" or "Last, but not least, . . ."

   As the person who speaks first and from a position of leadership, you can model appropriate communication for the meeting by the way you present yourself, the tone you take, and the level of formality you assume.

■ *Communication ground rules.* Sometimes it is necessary to be more explicit about the way communication will proceed. In these cases, a leader should *metacommunicate*, or talk about talk. For example, you might say:

   ▫ At our meetings, we agree to seek the floor by raising a hand and letting the speaker call on people.

- Because of the sensitive nature of our topic, we request that you not use names or identifying information when you share examples from your organization.

- So that more people have time to participate, we request that you keep questions and comments brief.

- This morning, we will only be discussing the problems that have brought us together and the causes we can identify. After lunch, we will get in to possible solutions. If we start to jump ahead of ourselves, I will remind you to hold the thought until later.

Deal promptly and diplomatically with violations of communication rules and norms. Remind the entire group of the ground rules: "Remember, we agreed not to make any personal attacks in this discussion." If ground rules have not explicitly been set, ask the group if it wishes to set some: "I notice that we've covered only two points on our agenda. Because we have to finish by four o' clock, would the group like to set a policy of limiting discussion to 10 minutes per point? Once we've covered everything, we can return to discuss any point in more depth."

If you must single out an individual, try to do so with a compliment: "Mr. [last name], you have so many experiences to share that you have already given us a great deal to think about. Now we need to move on to the next area of discussion."

CHAPTER 8

Civic and Political Context

When you speak as a member of a community or a political body you may be entering a context in which there are conflicts of interest. For a diverse group to come to consensus, communicators have to work to build bonds. In a democratic society, we allow for the testing of ideas through vigorous debate and argumentation. We maintain social order by setting fairly strict rules constraining the form of speech. The ideal is that personal attacks are taboo, as are arguments from pure self-interest. We do not argue for restricted parking in the neighborhood around a university campus by saying, "I am inconvenienced, and my property value may be jeopardized." Instead, we state that the community needs to maintain its special character and to continue to attract residents who will be good neighbors to the university.

Passion and eloquence are not out of place in this context. Sound argument and evidence are frequently combined with appeals to common values.

Typical speaking situations in this context include public debates, community forums, legal arguments, panel discussions, political conventions, appearances before community agencies, rallies, and talk shows.

8a. Group formats

Group formats include, among others, the symposium, panel, forum, and debate.

1 Confirm the format and clarify expectations

There are many versions of group presentations, and too often, their standard labels are used interchangeably and inconsistently. You may be invited to be part of a "panel" and prepare accordingly, only to discover that the organizer has actually set up a debate. Here are the definitions most commonly used by speech communication texts:

Symposium: A series of short speeches, usually informative, on various aspects of the same general topic. Audience questions often follow.

Panel: A group of experts publicly discussing a topic among themselves. Individually prepared speeches, if any, are limited to very brief opening statements.

Forum: Essentially a question-and-answer format. One or more experts may be questioned by a panel of other experts, journalists, and/or the audience.

Debate: A structured argument in which participants speak for or against a preannounced proposition. The proposition is worded so that one side has the burden of proof, and that same side has the benefit of speaking first and last. Speakers assume an advocacy role and attempt to persuade the audience, not each other.

Do not assume that the person arranging the program uses the terms this way. Find out as much as possible about the program.

2 Prepare carefully for a group presentation

Do not be lulled into thinking a group presentation is merely a conversation. Even if you already know your topic very well, brush up on your research, plan a general outline, and bring along notes with key facts and statistics. Prepare visual aids if appropriate. Plan an introduction and a conclusion for your formal part of the session.

Be ready to adapt, however, in your best extemporaneous style. Because you are in a group, make frequent references to the other panelists: "Ms. Larsen has pointed out some of the reasons mental health care is so expensive." Also, unless the panelists co-ordinate beforehand, overlap is inevitable on related topics. When you hear your favorite example or best statistic being presented, quickly reorganize and substitute the backup material you wisely brought along. See **37** for suggestions to use in the question-and-answer exchange.

CHECKLIST

Moderating a Symposium, Forum, Panel, or Debate

If you are called on to moderate a group presentation, here are some guidelines:

- Be sure the format and ground rules are clear to all participants well in advance. Let them know who the other speakers are and what they will cover.

- Plan an introduction. Engage and motivate the audience toward the topic to be discussed. (See **31a**.)

- Make a *brief*, one- or two-sentence transition between each segment of the presentation.

- Strictly enforce time limits. Emphasize the importance of this to speakers before the program, and arrange an unobtrusive signal for when time is almost up. If a speaker goes well past the time limit, you should interrupt politely but not apologetically.

- Moderate discussion aspects of the session by keeping the participation balanced. If one topic, speaker, or audience member is consuming too much time, again interrupt politely and move the discussion along. Do not, however, take over the discussion to develop your own ideas.

- Wrap up the parts of the presentation with a conclusion. (See **31b**.) The logical closure should be an extemporaneous summary of the points that have emerged during the presentation.

---

3   Be aware of your nonverbal communication

When you speak in a group, you should still follow the guidelines for effective delivery. In fact, if you are seated, you may need to project a little more energy to compensate for the lack of visibility and movement.

Far too many speakers seem to forget is that they are "on stage" during the whole presentation. While other speakers are talking, look attentive and be courteous. Nod and respond facially in ways sufficiently subtle that you do not upstage the speaker. Above all, do not distract the audience by whispering, fidgeting, or grimacing in disbelief. Do not hurt your own credibility by looking bored or by frantically going over your notes.

The previous suggestions, combined with general speaking skills, should get you through most group situations. The public debate presents some additional challenges.

8b. Public debates

Formal academic debating and competitive tournament debating require skills beyond the scope of this handbook. Any good public speaker, though, can handle informal debates—such as those held during election campaigns or at public meetings or club functions—by remembering and applying the following prescriptions.

- *Consider the opposing point of view.* Research both sides of the topic to see what evidence you will encounter. Look at the strongest points of your opponent's case and the weakest points of your own. This helps you anticipate the arguments and prepare for them.

- *Organize your ideas, arguments, and evidence.* First, develop your own best case for your position, which will be your opening statement or constructive speech. Next, plan attacks on or challenges to the opposing position, which you will use to respond to or refute their case. Finally, compile defense material, which you will probably need to answer challenges to your position.

- *Prepare your opening speech carefully.* Pay particular attention to organizational clarity and to sound support of assertions. Follow the general suggestions for speaking to an unfavorable audience. (See **23b.3**.)

- *Address major issues during the refutation phase.* When you refute a point, explain the argumentative impact and show what damage you have done to the underlying logical structure of your opponent's argument. If you weaken an opponent's case, drive home the point by issuing a specific challenge for the opponent to repair the damage.

- *Save time for a summary of the argument.* Debates can be confusing, with points flying back and forth. So, even if you have to skip some additional specifics, use the final few minutes to focus the controversy, interpreting how it has emerged during the discussion. End with a persuasive closing statement and a clincher that capitalizes on your strongest point.

- *Maintain a calm and professional demeanor.* As with sports, poker games, or any other competitive activity, emotions can sometimes get out of hand. Do not lose perspective—getting the last word on every single point is less important than maintaining your long-term credibility. Even if another debater distorts or misleads, you should remain courteous and unflappable. Your tone may be vigorous, but it should never be hostile. Address your arguments to the audience, and refer to the other speaker by name, and not as "my opponent." Treat the person's arguments respectfully, and grant good points that are made. Always assume the honesty and good intentions of the other speaker. Never say, "That's a lie"; rather, say, "I think those figures are inaccurate. Here's what I found." Keep in mind the wisdom of the maxim, "you can disagree without being disagreeable."

CHAPTER 9

Social and Ceremonial Context

Arguably, the most ancient forms of speech are those that people developed simply to affirm their connectedness. The expectation in social and ceremonial contexts is that the participants are united. This is not a time to mention difference or to actively build consensus. Just assume consensus and celebrate it. Typical speaking situations in this context include presenting an award, proposing a toast, and nominating a candidate.

Some speeches, classified in this book as *evocative*, are designed more to fill a ritualistic function than to transmit information or change behavior. These follow standard forms, and, as with all rituals, the familiarity of the form is one source of the emotional satisfaction participants derive. Happy moments like winning an Olympic medal and sad ones like mourning a death take on added meaning when accompanied by traditional, familiar ceremony. Certain words, gestures, and acts are expected—the Olympic athlete would undoubtedly be disappointed if the medal award ceremony and playing of the national anthem were replaced by a gift certificate presented at a pizza house get-together. When you give a ceremonial speech, you are by necessity forced to tread near that line separating tradition and triteness.

9a. The language of ritual

Cover the expected bases no matter how predictable they are. Do not be *too* creative, but strive to find ways to make these ceremonial moments special and fresh. Above all, this means avoiding overused phrases and constructions. Unless you prepare carefully, you will hear yourself ad-libbing clichés you would never use otherwise:

> On this auspicious occasion . . .
> This small token of our esteem . . .
> With no further ado . . .

Information exchange is of secondary importance in these speeches; style becomes crucial. Because the two or three ideas you transmit will be fairly basic, you should expend your energy crafting ways to express them, polishing your language and timing. This is made easier by the fact that ceremonial speeches are usually short. Frequently, a memorized or partially memorized mode of delivery is best. (See **28d**.) Your language should be more elevated than in everyday speech, but not so formal as to seem stiff or unnatural.

9b. Audience analysis

In preparing all ceremonial speeches, consider two questions.

1. *What are the needs of the person to whom or about whom I speak?*
   Suppose that as company president you give a safety award each year, and so for you it is old hat. However, it is a special moment for the recipient. What can you say that he or she will remember with pride? Address the *uniqueness* of that person. Although the form of the speech may be stylized, the content should be personalized.

2. *What are the needs of the people for whom I speak?*
   In most ceremonial or ritualistic addresses, you can think of yourself as speaking on behalf of some group or community and not just for yourself. People have come together to share emotions as well as—or instead of—information. Yet these emotions may be unfocused. When you deliver a thoughtful and moving speech, you symbolize the feelings of audience members and are thus bonding them. You also help them gain perspective and find deeper meanings in their experiences. As you prepare for this sort of speech, envision yourself as a vehicle for group expression.

9c. Guidelines for various events

1 Presenting an award or honor

- Unless a surprise is part of the tradition, announce the person's name early in the speech.

- Explain how the person was selected for the honor, and by whom.

- Besides listing achievements or qualities, use a brief anecdote or description to capture some unique qualities of the person.

- If a tangible object—plaque, certificate, key to the city—is presented, explain what it symbolizes.

2 Delivering a eulogy or memorial address

- Do not accept this assignment unless you feel able to keep your composure.

- Acknowledge shared feelings of sadness, loss, and anger, but do not dwell on them.

- Highlight and celebrate the value of the one being eulogized. Some people present may have known the person only professionally or only socially, or only long ago or only recently. Touch on several aspects of the person's life. Do not be reluctant to share light, and even humorous, moments.

- Use phrases that bond the group together: "All of us who cared for Eleanor . . ." or "I see many people here who . . ." or "We all know how persistent she could be when she believed in an idea."

- Try to place the loss in some larger, more optimistic perspective. Themes of the continuity of life, appreciation of each moment, and growth through pain are timeless and universal. These philosophical concepts are still a source of comfort.

- Do not play on the grief of a captive audience to promote a specific religious belief or social or political cause.

3   Giving a toast

- If the toast is a formal part of the event, make arrangements ahead of time so that everyone will have a beverage in hand at the proper point. Be sure that nonalcoholic beverages are available so that everyone can participate.

- Refine your basic idea into a short message of goodwill, and memorize it.

- Choose the words carefully. Humor, wordplay, rhymes, metaphors, and proverbs all find their way into toasts. If no witty inspiration comes to you and if the toasts in books all seem corny and contrived, then there is absolutely nothing wrong with taking a sincere thought and stating it gracefully.

- If the toast is more than a few sentences—really, a short speech—do not make listeners hoist their glasses the full time. Start out as a speech. Then at the end say something like, "Let's raise our glasses to our new laboratory director. Sheila, we wish you luck, and success, and may all your troubles be microscopic!"

4   Accepting an award or a tribute

- Unless asked in advance to prepare a major acceptance speech, limit your remarks to a few sentences.

- Accept the honor with pride. Do not let humility and embarrassment make you seem to reject the gesture.

- Share the honor with those who deserve it. But do not get into an endless thank-you litany of the sort that tends to make to the Academy Awards presentation run overtime.

- Give a gift back to the audience. Can you offer them a genuine tribute, an insight, or even a funny story related to your relationship with them?
- End with a future-oriented statement about what the honor means to you.

5   Emceeing a Ceremony or Banquet

- Plan opening remarks that establish an appropriate mood. Whether the occasion is a solemn one, a celebration, or a regular monthly luncheon, make guests feel welcome and set the tone for the rest of the program.
- Make gracious and concise introductions. When you introduce people, direct the audience's response by asking them to hold their applause or by signaling for applause through your phrasing and inflection.
- Invite or control applause at other times during the event, if appropriate.

CHECKLIST

Sample Agenda for a Banquet or Ceremony

1. Greeting: brief statement of purpose by emcee
   - ❏ Invocation, song, patriotic ritual, group ritual
   - ❏ More extended theme-setting remarks by emcee
   - ❏ Formal welcome (from mayor, governor, etc.)
2. Introduction of honored guests at platform or head table
   - ❏ Introduction of special guests in audience
   - ❏ Reading of telegrams, messages from those not present
3. Ceremonial event (when an award is the central purpose of the program, items 3 and 4 are usually reversed)
   - ❏ Thanks to committees, planners
   - ❏ Announcements of elections, election results, and similar issues
   - ❏ Awards, presentations
4. Introduction and presentation of featured speaker or event
5. Closing by emcee
   - ❏ Quick announcements
   - ❏ Benediction, song, ritual

   Light entertainment—comedy, skits, musical interludes—may be inserted before item 2, 3, or 4.

3 Planning Your Speech

CHAPTER 10. **Your Preparation Schedule**

Have a schedule to structure the preparation of your speech.

CHAPTER 11. **Topic Selection**

Select an interesting and manageable topic and determine what response you hope to evoke with the topic.

CHAPTER 12. **Audience Analysis**

Base your speech preparation on thorough audience analysis.

CHAPTER 10

Your Preparation Schedule

One way to avoid false starts and wasted effort when preparing a speech is to give yourself plenty of time to organize your preparation. An effective plan balances the needs of creativity against the constraints of a deadline.

10a. The four phases of creativity

It has been proposed that there are four phases to the creative process: preparation, incubation, illumination, and refinement.[1] Here is how they apply to creating a speech.

1. The *preparation* phase includes gathering the materials, analyzing the topic and audience, and making the first attempts at putting the parts together.

2. *Incubation* is a phase marked by frustration, and the speech is set aside. During this phase, your unconscious mind and your peripheral awareness work on the problems.

3. *Illumination* occurs when, suddenly, the pieces fit together. Illumination may occur while you are working on the project, but it is just as likely to occur when you are driving down the freeway, taking a shower, or even sleeping. Exhilaration and relief accompany this phase. You work eagerly and fluidly, accomplishing more in a few hours than you have in several days.

4. *Refinement* comes next. After the creative burst, there follows a comparatively long period of checking details, fine tuning, and polishing. Like the preparation phase, this phase is largely cognitive and requires concentration and discipline.

This delineation of the four-phase creative process is provided to stress the importance of allocating time for *each* phase. Many creative products have never been shared with the world because the creator gave up during the refinement phase. Other fine ideas have failed to be appreciated because the speaker presented them directly after the illumination phase, without spending the needed time on refinement. The rest of this chapter supplies guidance for optimizing your planning so that none of the creative phases is slighted.

10b. A realistic timetable

At one university, a group of public-speaking instructors informally survey their students at the end of each term, asking what

[1]Based on Catherine Patrick, *What Is Creative Thinking?* (New York: Philosophical Library, 1955), 1–48.

advice they would pass on to the next group of students. Consistently and overwhelmingly, the surveyed students' response is, "Start early." To know what is "early" enough for you, you need to invest the effort to create a realistic timetable.

1 List the tasks and the time needed

Be sure that you include intellectual tasks such as analyzing your topic, and not just physical tasks like going to the library or making visual aids. For each task, jot down the most optimistic and least optimistic estimate of the time needed. When setting a timetable, always provide extra time to allow for emergencies. Speech research and rehearsal can go on when you have a headache, but the creative aspects of speech organization require physical and psychological alertness.

2 Determine the order of the tasks

This stage of preparation is what professional project managers call *determining the critical path*. Speech practice must occur after the speech outline is completed. The outline cannot be completed until you have articulated your speech purpose and goals, and so on. When you lay out the entire project in this linear fashion and add up the time estimates for each task, you will see if it is possible to reach your goals. Often, you will realize that, in order to succeed, certain preliminary steps must be taken *now*.

To take this further, suppose your speech is due in three weeks, and the critical path adds up to five weeks. If your plans are unrealistic, it is better to discover this now than two days before the speech, giving you time to scale down your plans.

3 Set intermediate deadlines

In Figure 10-1, speech planning and practice is divided into four stages: initial decisions and analysis, research, development of speech materials, and practice. For each stage, the central tasks are contained in a box with a solid border. The related but less time-bound tasks are surrounded by a broken border. Generally, time flows downward and to the right in this chart. The figure also shows the transitions between stages where deadlines fall naturally. That is, the central tasks of one stage cannot really be started until the central tasks of the previous stage have been completed. At some point, you must make preliminary decisions regarding a narrowed and focused topic, purpose, and thesis, and then get into your serious research. And, at some point, you must stop gathering material and put the speech together. If you do not have a speech outline soon enough, you cannot begin the first stage of practice. There is no point in scheduling your feedback practice sessions so late that you cannot take advantage of the feedback.

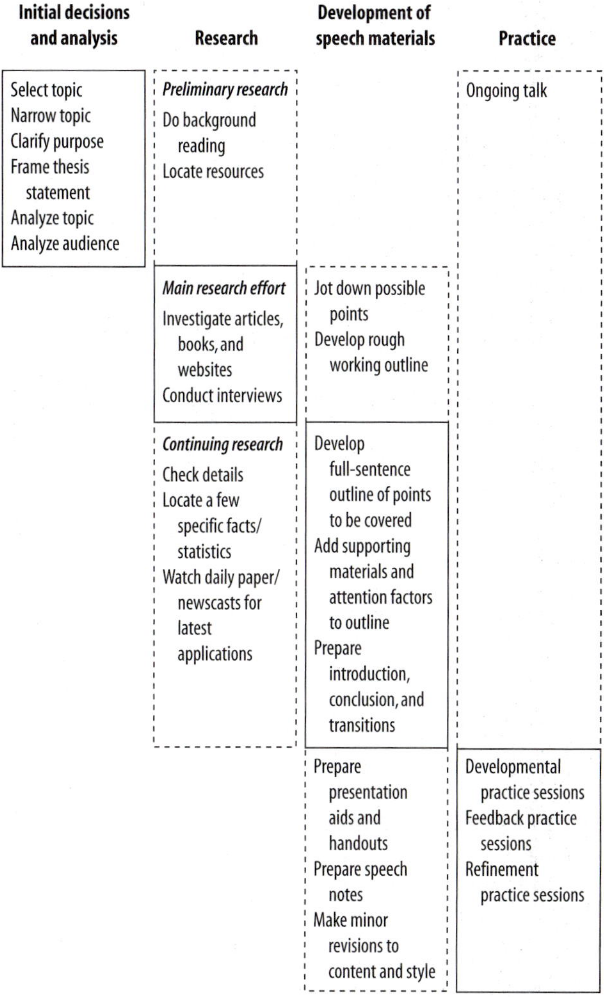

Initial decisions and analysis	Research	Development of speech materials	Practice
Select topic Narrow topic Clarify purpose Frame thesis statement Analyze topic Analyze audience	*Preliminary research* Do background reading Locate resources		Ongoing talk
	Main research effort Investigate articles, books, and websites Conduct interviews	Jot down possible points Develop rough working outline	
	Continuing research Check details Locate a few specific facts/statistics Watch daily paper/newscasts for latest applications	Develop full-sentence outline of points to be covered Add supporting materials and attention factors to outline Prepare introduction, conclusion, and transitions	
		Prepare presentation aids and handouts Prepare speech notes Make minor revisions to content and style	Developmental practice sessions Feedback practice sessions Refinement practice sessions

FIGURE 10-1   Speech Planning and Practice

Sometimes, however, you must briefly retrace your steps. For instance, important new evidence may present itself, or a feedback session may show that more visual aids are needed. Such movement should be minimal, and under almost no circumstances should you be returning to tasks "way back." We feel very strongly that you should not be making any substantive changes to the speech at the last minute. During the final practice sessions, you should have complete mastery of the organization and basic content so you can focus on refinement of phrasing, delivery, and timing, and on attainment of the desired audience response.

10c.   Oral composition

Because a speech is delivered orally, it should be composed orally. And because the meaning of a speech is dependent on the interaction between speaker and listeners, it should be created collaboratively. Keep the "speech as conversation" theme foremost even during those parts of preparation that require you to draw on your skills as a writer or performer.

Although you cannot practice "the speech" until your basic outline exists, one form of oral preparation begins with your first idea. This is the ongoing talk suggested by the large, dotted section in the Practice column of Figure 10-1. Talk to yourself about your topic. Talk to other people. Try out your ideas and words; see if they make sense. You are not, however, practicing your speech in front of other people. Work your ideas into conversations over lunch and chats with colleagues and friends. After talking to a number of people, you will find that you have begun to word the speech.

If you are fortunate, you may be able to add continuity to this oral and collaborative process by structuring it to embrace a more formal method for obtaining feedback and support. (See **33**.)

CHAPTER 11

Topic Selection

Do not settle on the first topic that occurs to you. Consider a number of different topics and examine their various facets. When you have chosen a promising one, narrow it down and crystallize your reasons for speaking about that subject.

11a.   Looking for a topic

Speakers have varying degrees of freedom in topic choice, according to the situation. At one pole is the office manager who is told to give an oral report on the effectiveness of the current secretarial assignment system. At the other is the student who is told, "Friday morning you will speak third and persuade us to do something, anything." Most speaking situations fall between these extremes. Even when the general topic is set, you need to home in on an approach that will fit you, the audience, and the situation.

1   Your experience, expertise, and interests

You bring a body of knowledge to the speech situation. Perhaps this is why you have been asked to speak. Or your background may be the springboard for discovering a slant on a topic that can be developed into a compelling and substantial speech. You should ask yourself a number of questions to help you do this.

In answering the questions that follow, do not stop to evaluate every answer as you write it down. You want to generate a list of possible topics by brainstorming. Respond to these questions in as many different ways as you can think of, even if some seem silly. Later, you will select your best topic in terms of audience and occasion.

■ *What unusual experiences have you had?* Consider places you have traveled, jobs you have held, and events in which you have participated. Do not overlook aspects of your experience that you take for granted but that might be interesting to others.

■ *What special knowledge or expertise do you have?* Each of us has developed mastery in certain areas. This may be in relation to how you make your living, or to people you meet in that context. Your course of study in school has increased your knowledge in areas that might be of interest to your potential audience. Think, too, about the talents, hobbies, and skills you have developed.

■ *What strong opinions and beliefs do you hold?* What topics stir your passions? These issues, which probably touch on your core values (see **25**), frequently make good speech topics. Besides the issues that can provoke you into heated debate, there are others that fascinate you intellectually. Explaining the basis of a pet theory or favorite area of inquiry can make an excellent speech.

■ *What would you like to know more about?* Use the occasion of giving a speech as an opportunity to research a topic that has piqued your curiosity.

2   The audience and occasion

By brainstorming answers to the questions in **11a.1**, you have created a possible subject list of great variety. To choose the one topic on which you will speak, you next need to think about who the audience members are and what they expect. This step can help you rule out a number of topics. The occasion for a speech is closely related to its context (see **part 2**).

To find the *most* appropriate topic from your list, empathy is your best tool. Imagine sitting on those hard chairs in the boardroom or classroom. What would you sit still to hear?

3   A timely and timeless topic

You may still have more than one possible topic on your list even after going through the processes in **11a.1** and **11a.2**. Other things being equal, the best topics are those that are both timely and timeless. Certain issues have always been and always will be part of human discourse. The rights of the individual versus the rights of the group and the need for security versus the need for adventure were being discussed 1,000 years ago, 100 years ago, and this past year; they will continue to be discussed by our descendants. When you tie a contemporary event to one of these enduring concerns, you link the timely and the timeless.

Neither one of these conditions by itself is an indication that the topic will be a good one. Consider the criterion of timeliness. If an event has been front-page news for two weeks, a speech on that topic may be timely. But unless you can tell your audience what it all means in more universal terms, you probably will give them little that they do not already know. The reverse is true as well: Your audience can miss or fail to be interested in the profundity of your topic if you do not tie it into the fabric of their current existence. A profound, timeless topic should have a timely application. A timely speech should point out the timeless implication of the subject.

Table 11-1 shows how topics that are too narrowly contemporary or too broadly universal may be altered to meet these criteria. Notice the different kinds of speeches to which the timely/timeless standard can apply.

TABLE 11-1   Timely and Timeless Topics

Timely (but Potentially Trivial)	Timeless (but Potentially Diffuse)	Timely and Timeless
There was a major confrontation last week when the Ku Klux Klan held a rally downtown.	Freedom of assembly must be protected for everyone.	Last week's confrontation over the Ku Klux Klan rally raised important questions about what restrictions, if any, should be placed on freedom of assembly.
I took a trip to Quebec.	Travel helps people understand diversity of human cultures.	My trip to Quebec helped me to understand my own culture by contrasting it to another.
Our company has adopted a new profit-sharing plan.	The best management philosophy is one that treats the employees like partners.	Our new profit-sharing plan will benefit the employees directly and reflect an enlightened philosophy of management.

11b. Narrowing your topic

The selection of a topic is not complete until that topic has been narrowed to accommodate the constraints of time. You have to limit yourself to the number of points that can be adequately developed in the time available. You can expedite your research and preparation by narrowing your topic from the beginning. Thus, instead of looking up all the books and articles about higher education, you can focus on those related to the financing of community colleges, or to pass/fail grading, or to coed dormitories, as the narrowed topic warrants.

1   Determine the number of ideas

The average speaker utters 100 to 150 words per minute. If you speak very rapidly or very slowly, you may fall outside this range. Chances are, though, that your rate of speaking is somewhere near 125 words per minute. Conveniently, a typical paragraph of simple sentences runs about 125 words. Thus, on average, a speaker delivers roughly one short paragraph per minute. If your material is highly technical or interspersed with statistics, dialogue, and dramatic pauses, or if you speak slowly, you had better allot two minutes per paragraph. This formula, though simple, allows you to do some realistic narrowing of your topic.

For instance, if you plan on speaking informatively for 8 to 10 minutes, you need to set aside at least 1 to 2 minutes for the introduction and 1 minute for the conclusion. This leaves 6 to 7 minutes for the body of your speech—or 6 to 7 short paragraphs.

The same formula can be applied to longer speeches, business presentations, and lectures. A 20-minute speech can be thought of as 20 short, simple paragraphs or 10 longer, more developed paragraphs.

2   Select a few main ideas

Knowing that a speech should be limited to two or three main points does not tell you *which* two or three to select. Consider the following questions, which can help you narrow your topic effectively.

Which aspects of your topic are best covered in the public, oral mode? A speech should not be used to repeat common knowledge, to discuss specialized problems of a small portion of the audience, or, of course, to indulge the speaker's ego.

Which aspects of your topic are best suited to this audience and occasion? Select those points that relate most directly to the needs, attitudes, knowledge, and expectations of your listeners. (See **12**.)

Which aspects of your topic can you present most effectively? Select those points on which you have the most knowledge, in which you have the most interest, and that best fit your speaking personality.

11c. Clarifying the reasons for your speech

Each speech has a general purpose, a specific purpose, and a set of desired outcomes. Like a speech's occasion, these aspects of a speech are also closely related to its context (see **part 2**).

1   The general purpose

What is your intention? Are you trying to change people's minds? To teach them something? To move them?

The general purpose of a speech can be classified in one of three ways:

Inform: A speech designed to explain, instruct, define, clarify, demonstrate, or teach

Persuade: A speech designed to influence, convince, motivate, sell, preach, or stimulate action

Evoke: A speech designed to entertain, inspire, celebrate, commemorate, or bond, or to help listeners relive

In reality, no speech has only one purpose. Most have a combination, but one purpose is usually dominant. For instance, a classroom lecture is used primarily to teach, but at the same time it can be used to shape attitudes. The purpose of a campaign speech is to drum up support for the candidate, but the speech can also entertain. An excellent sermon might do all three: inform, persuade, and evoke.

Within these general categories of informative, persuasive and evocative speeches, of course, there are many more specialized formats and genres. Strategic guidelines for informative speaking (**22**) and persuasive speaking (**23**) give insight into how these purposes are realized in common types of speeches, and all of part 2 addresses adapting speeches for different contexts.

2   The specific purpose

Knowing which of the three purposes—to inform, persuade, or evoke—will be predominant in your speech will help you in the next step: deciding what you really want to accomplish with your topic. In phrasing this purpose, isolate your central reason for speaking. Do not go any further until you can complete this sentence:

If there is one goal I want to achieve in this speech, it is to . . .

At this point, your topic should have a clear focus:

Not: My specific purpose is to inform the audience about politics.

But: My specific purpose is to inform the audience about the role of the two-party system in American politics.

Not: My specific purpose is to persuade the audience against drunken driving.

But: My specific purpose is to persuade the audience of the need for stiffer penalties for those convicted of drunken driving.

3   The desired outcomes

Once your goal is phrased in the terms of what *you* want to do, turn it around and phrase it in terms of what you want your *audience* to do:

If there is one action I want my listeners to take after my speech, it is to . . .

In other words, if your speech is a success, what will your audience do? This is called the **primary audience outcome**.

Not: My desired outcome is to sell this product.

But: My desired outcome is to have you buy this product.

Not: My desired outcome is to explain photosynthesis.

But: My desired outcome is to have you understand the workings of photosynthesis.

Notice the different verbs in each pair. The emphasis is on the behavior you want the *audience* to adopt.

Next, break the primary audience outcome into a series of *contributing audience outcomes*. In phrasing these components, use verbs that describe *actions*. "I want my audience to *appreciate* art" is fine for a primary audience outcome, but you must go further and ask yourself how you will know if you have succeeded. What, exactly, are people doing when they are appreciating art? If you think about the specific behaviors that contribute to appreciating art, you will come up with a list like this:

- *Go* to galleries and museums
- *Read* books on art
- *Create* pieces of art

Here is how speech purposes and outcomes can be crystallized for a persuasive speech about protecting the environment:

General purpose: To persuade.

Specific purpose: To convince the audience that changes in individual behaviors are needed to protect our environment.

Primary audience outcome: I want my audience to commit themselves actively to environmental concerns.

Contributing audience outcomes: I want my audience to

- use public transportation when possible
- minimize the use of nonbiodegradable materials
- recycle paper, glass, aluminum, and steel
- make their dwellings energy efficient
- support environmentally oriented political candidates and contribute money and time to environmental causes

11d. Developing a thesis statement

A thesis statement gives you something concrete against which to test ideas.

1 A single declarative sentence

In contrast to your "purpose" and "outcomes," your thesis sentence states your topic as a proposition to be proved or a theme to be developed. This sentence, sometimes referred to as the **central idea**, gives your speech a focus. It helps you make the transition from thinking about where you want to end up (your goal) to how to get there.

A thesis statement should not merely name your topic. It should capsulize what you plan to say about the topic. The rationale for insisting on the complete sentence is the clarity of thought that comes when you must delineate both what you are talking about (the subject of the sentence) and what you are saying about it (the predicate of the sentence). A thesis statement whose single declarative sentence is "Today I will talk about roses" makes *you* the subject and makes the fact that you *are talking* the predicate— hardly the essence of your speech content.

However, "Roses are beautiful" makes the topic (roses) serve as subject and the point being made about it (they are beautiful) the predicate. See **11d.3** for further discussion of the role of propositional phrasing in testing the relevance and completeness of ideas.

Be sure that the thesis statement includes enough information to differentiate your approach from other possibilities.

Informative Speech

Not:	My speech is on gangs.
Or even:	Young people find gangs attractive.
But:	There are a number of sociological and developmental reasons for gangs being attractive to youths.

Persuasive Speech

Not:	Something must be done about tuberculosis.
Or even:	Drug-resistant TB is on the increase and should be combated.

But: The threat of a resurgence of TB requires a major governmental program of education, research, and treatment.

2   Questions about the thesis statement

What questions will your listeners be asking themselves before they accept your thesis? They are the ones you should identify before proceeding with your research.

Consider this thesis for a persuasive speech:

Like other industrialized nations, the United States has a castelike social system based on race, sex, and age.

Audience members might ask these questions as they listen:

- Does the United States have a castelike system?
- Is the stratification based on race?
- Is the stratification based on sex?
- Is the stratification based on age?
- Is the United States an industrialized nation?
- Are these characteristics shared by other industrialized nations?

A speech about comic books might have the following thesis sentence:

With their scope, history, and influence, comic books are an interesting component of American popular culture.

For this informative speech, four questions present themselves:

- What is the scope of comic book themes?
- What is the history of the comic book?
- What influence have comic books had?
- Are comic books an interesting component of American popular culture?

The answers to these questions will not necessarily be the main points of your speech, and you might not develop your ideas in this order. However, the analysis can direct your research and prevent you from glaring oversights.

3   The kinds of propositions

In a persuasive speech, the thesis of a speech and the claim of an argument are described as propositions—the speaker *proposes* something to the audience. There are three kinds of propositions: the **proposition of fact**, the **proposition of value**, and the **proposition of policy**. When you are developing a persuasive speech, discovering which kind of proposition lies at the heart of your speech is essential to identifying your obligations and planning your persuasive strategy. See **23**.

Proposition of fact It may seem that if something is a fact, there is no need to use persuasion to establish it, but there are issues in the factual domain that cannot be verified directly. For instance, there either is or is not life on other planets. The question is one of fact, but because we lack the means to find out, we must draw inferences from the data we have. Here are some other examples:

> More than two cups of coffee a day increases the chance of cancer of the pancreas.

> Converting to solar energy can save the average homeowner money.

Proposition of value Persuasive speakers are often attempting to prove evaluative positions. Their goal is to judge the worth of something, to establish that it is good or bad, wise or foolish, just or unjust, ethical or unethical, beautiful or ugly, competent or incompetent. For example:

> It is wrong to try to avoid jury duty.

> Charlie Parker was the greatest sax player ever.

Proposition of policy Most common and most complex among persuasive theses is the proposition of policy, which advocates a specific course of action. Here are some propositions of policy:

> The federal government should legalize marijuana for private use.

> You should send your children to private schools.

KEY POINT   **Kinds of Propositions**

Propositions of fact: IS/IS NOT
Propositions of value: GOOD/BAD
Propositions of policy: SHOULD/SHOULD NOT

11e. Speech titles

Although every speech needs a thesis and a purpose, a title is necessary only when there is to be advance publicity, when there is a printed program, and, usually, when the speaker is going to be formally introduced. Unless there is a definite deadline for the title, you can defer selecting one until after the speech is composed.

An effective title should pique interest in your subject and make the audience eager to listen. Sometimes, a metaphor, quotation, or allusion that is central to the speech can be part of the title.

A title can take any grammatical form. It can be a declarative sentence, question, phrase, or fragment:

"Freedom of Speech Is in Jeopardy"

"Is Free Speech Really Free?"

"Threats to Free Speech"

"Free Speech: An Endangered Species"

> **KEY POINT** **Thesis Statement Versus Speech Title** Do not confuse the thesis statement with the speech title. The thesis statement is a declarative sentence essential for organizing and composing the speech. The title can be a word or a phrase. Its purpose is not only to indicate the topic but also to arouse interest.

CHAPTER 12

Audience Analysis

The outcome of any speech situation is a product of what the speaker actually says and how the listeners process and interpret what is said. Audience analysis therefore is much more than a step in planning a speech. It involves the constant awareness of those who are the "coauthors" of your speech—your listeners.

You speak to a particular group of people because you want a certain response from them. If you do not know the composition of that group, you cannot make intelligent decisions about what to include, what to emphasize, and how best to arrange and present your ideas. Research your audience thoroughly. Their age, gender, attitudes, and expectations are all relevant to your planning.

We approach each of these characteristics as a discrete factor and describe the techniques to be used with various kinds of homogeneous audiences. *You* have to "mix and match" these techniques as you uncover the actual composition of your potential audience.

12a. Sources of information

When you ask an audience to listen to your ideas, you are asking them to come partway into your experience. It is your obligation, in turn, to go partway into theirs.

The following are valuable sources of information about your audience. But it's important not to limit yourself to any one of them:

- *Direct observation.* If you have enough lead time, try to observe the audience, perhaps at a business meeting or while they listen to another speaker.

- *Systematic data collection.* One excellent way to become informed about your audience is to ask them about themselves. Do not discount even a simple form of data gathering, such as distributing a three- or four-item questionnaire at a meeting before the one at which you will speak.

- *Interviews/focus groups.* When you cannot get information on the whole audience, talk to some members of the group. In these individual or group sessions, try to find out not just what people think but also how they think. Ask open-ended questions and encourage respondents to expand on their answers by framing follow-up questions in a nonargumentative tone. Ask them for examples and anecdotes.

- *The contact person.* The person who asked you to speak has certain expectations about the interaction between you and the audience. Ask this contact person specific questions about his or her perceptions of the audience.

- *Inference and empathy.* When you do not have much specific information about an audience, draw on your general knowledge of human behavior and groups. Let empathy round out the image. Get outside yourself and adopt your listeners' frames of reference.

12b. Audience demographics

Obtaining each audience's vital statistics enables you to make certain general predictions about their responses. However, there is no such thing as an average audience. A speaker would be more than a little surprised to stand before a group of listeners whose composition followed exactly the distribution of the most recent census with regard to age, gender, race, socioeconomic status, and religion.

CHECKLIST

Pertinent Demographic Questions

- ❑ What is the average age of the audience members?
- ❑ What is the age range?
- ❑ What is the gender composition of the audience?
- ❑ What racial and ethnic groups are represented, in about what proportions?
- ❑ What is the socioeconomic composition of the group?
- ❑ What occupations are represented?
- ❑ What religious groups are represented?
- ❑ What is the political orientation of the group?
- ❑ How homogeneous (similar) or heterogeneous (diverse) are the audience members for each of the preceding characteristics?

Obviously, all demographic characteristics are not equally important for any given speech. Knowledge of the religious configuration of your audience will be important in preparing a speech on abortion, as will knowledge of the age distribution for a speech on Social Security reform. But religion and age might have no bearing whatsoever on another topic. Despite differences in relative importance to a particular topic, try to find out all the following demographic characteristics, if only to give you a general picture.

KEY POINT **Limitations of Demographic Generalizations**

Very few generalizations can be made on the basis of demographic factors. Social science research, even when carefully controlled and well designed, provides *probability statements* about how one group *on average* differs from another group *on average*. For example, with respect to almost any trait you might select, the differences among individual women and among individual men are far greater than the differences between the average man and the average woman. You can say that many people in an audience *are likely to* respond in a certain way; you cannot say that any individual in that audience definitely *will* respond in a given way.

1   Age/generation

Maxims like "You're as young as you feel" and "Age is a state of mind" tell us to be careful when we make assumptions based on chronological age. Current theory holds that psychological development does not stop at the threshold of adulthood but continues through life in fairly predictable stages. Works by Erikson and Sheehy offer insight into the most common crises and value realignments of people in their twenties, thirties, forties, and so on.[1] (For our purposes, *younger* refers generally to people going through adolescence, formal education, or the early phases of establishing career directions and of confirming life goals; *older* covers most everyone else.) Age may affect audience response in the following ways:

- *Younger people tend to be idealistic.* They respond positively to arguments based on change and innovation. They are impatient about social change and want to see results in the near future.

- *Younger people are strongly affected by the values of their peers.*

- *Younger people like a speech to be organized in a fluid, narrative fashion.* They prefer a rapid, exciting tempo and a delivery employing several media or channels of communication.

---

[1]See, for example, Erik Erikson, *Identity and the Life Cycle* (New York: Norton, 1980), and Gail Sheehy, *Passages: Predictable Crises of Adult Life* (New York: Dutton, 1976).

- *Older people are more conservative.* They are responsive to appeals to traditional values. They tend to have a stake in the status quo and to be reluctant to risk major changes. They are more patient in waiting for results.

- *Older people prefer a linear, highly structured speech organization, with clear previews, transitions, and summaries.* They are most comfortable with a slow, deliberate delivery.

KEY POINT   **Generational Identity** You can infer certain specific experiences audience members have had, based on their generational identity. For instance, 60-year-olds were children during the post–World War II era of prosperity, students during the idealistic 1960s, disillusioned young adults during the Watergate era, and so on. However, 80-year-olds were adolescents during the Great Depression and came of age during World War II. Think about what current events have inspired and traumatized the particular audience you are addressing. What movies, TV shows, songs, and sports figures were central to their lives? What names will be unfamiliar? What generational stereotypes might they have become weary of?

2   Gender

The issue is not how many males and females are present, but how audience members think about masculinity and femininity. These gender expectations are highly culture bound and change rapidly in contemporary life.

Traditionally, women were socialized to be nurturant, sensitive, compassionate, and emotional. So, in the past, appeals to home, family, and the safety of loved ones usually were effective with women. Traditionally, men were socialized to be dominant, aggressive, ambitious, and unemotional (except when it came to sports). So, a speech to a predominantly male group used appeals to power, success, competitive values, and logic.

In recent decades, many more women and men have become more aware of how sex-role socialization has limited their avenues of expression and growth. They are experimenting with new roles and divisions of labor in both public and private life. And men and women undergoing this process bridle when presented with stereotypical assumptions about social roles and power relationships.

3   Race/ethnicity

As with women and men, the differences between ethnic groups are not innate. The differences that do exist result from variations in socialization and experience. In the United States, we daily encounter newcomers who migrated here voluntarily to be with their families or to enhance their opportunities, or who came involuntarily as refugees. Conversations with such diverse members of our communities encourage those of us who have been in the United States longer to remember why our ancestors came: some seeking opportunity, some escaping economic hardship or political and religious oppression, some involuntarily as slaves.

This expanding ethnic and cultural diversity can be seen as either a problem or an interesting opportunity. In the past, when there were three or four predominant ethnic groups in an area, it might have been a reasonable goal to become somewhat expert on the cultural values and symbols of those groups. Today, when dozens of cultures are part of a single community or organization, this approach to audience analysis becomes overwhelming. To further complicate the challenge, it is not just that audiences are multicultural groups but also that they are composed of individuals who are themselves multicultural. It is increasingly rare to find someone whose heritage is monocultural in any real sense.

Because people's experiences, not their traits, shape them as listeners, there are no prescriptions for how to relate to predominantly white, African American, Native American, Latino/Latina, Hispanic, or Asian American audiences. Instead, you need to familiarize yourself as much as possible with the experiences of each group. The common experience of nonwhite racial groups and most other ethnic minorities in the United States has included discrimination and oppression. Members of these groups are justifiably sensitive to any communication that reduces their status or reflects old stereotypes. Forms of address, both collective and individual, are very important. Never refer to people by first names, diminutives, or nicknames unless invited to do so. And never address white males by titles such as "Mister," "Doctor," or "Colonel" while addressing anyone else more casually. Find out what group designations your audience prefers, and respect their wishes.

Beyond showing sensitivity to the relationships between members of dominant and nondominant cultural groups, a speaker can also demonstrate an appreciation of cultural diversity. People of any ethnic group can tend to look at things from the standpoint of the group's own history and culture. Taking the time to investigate other cultural views can open up a number of refreshingly different avenues to good communication. Making the effort to pronounce unfamiliar names and phrases correctly, and avoiding the most stereotypical cultural generalizations, shows your goodwill and openness.

12c.   Audience attitudes toward your topic

Reactions to the thesis of your speech can fall along a continuum that ranges from extreme disagreement to extreme agreement.

> **KEY POINT**   **Multiple Identities of Audience Members** Because speakers are not transmitting information, but rather are jointly constructing meanings with listeners, no part of audience analysis is as important as learning *how a particular group of people makes meaning*. The demographic data you collect can be useful, but only if treated within the context of this complex process. We know that age, race, and gender all contribute to a person's interpretation of the world. But so, too, do religion, social class, educational level, economic status, sexual orientation, health, physical ability, and many other factors. As the incredible diversity and constantly changing profile of U.S. society have made clear, no formula can tell a speaker how each of these variables relates to a particular topic, let alone how they all interact. In a sense, as a speaker, you have been freed from the unrealistic goal of making predictions based on static traits of your listeners. Instead, your task is to thoughtfully consider how they engage in a constant process of constructing, and reconstructing, the world. In this sort of audience analysis, you are trying to glimpse what some describe as *core values* (or *worldviews, personal construct systems, frames of reference, informal theories,* or *master narratives*). (See **25c**.) What do your listeners draw on to organize their experience and make sense of it?

Much social science research is based on asking people to clarify their attitudes on scales like this one:

Strongly disagree	Moderately disagree	Slightly disagree	Neither agree nor disagree	Slightly agree	Moderately agree	Strongly agree

If your goal is to bring about some specific act, your listeners' responses will range across these categories:

Opposed to action	Uninclined to act	Ready to act	Taking action

If the majority of your audience falls to the left on either continuum, that audience should be considered *unfavorable,* and if it falls to the right, it is *favorable.* If in the middle, it is *neutral.*

Most speakers agree that knowing the audience's predisposition toward the topic is the single most important bit of information in planning their speech strategy. If your speech deals with a controversial topic, it is crucial that you interview people who differ from you in terms of attitude and experience. Listen carefully and respectfully to their accounts of the world. At the information-gathering stage, your goal is not to plan a strategy for changing them, but rather to try to see how their views and yours might be connected. This means letting go of your predispositions and judgments about people who disagree with you. Once you determine whether your audience is favorable, neutral, or unfavorable, you can follow the specific suggestions offered in chapter **23**.

Although attitudes toward your topic are most obviously relevant to persuasive speaking, they can influence the speech to inform or evoke as well.

12d. Audience expectations

Anticipate your audience's expectations. We have stressed the importance of knowing your purpose in speaking, but what is your audience's purpose in listening? Why are they sitting there giving you their valuable time? Perhaps they are required to as part of a class or job assignment. Maybe they are present voluntarily but for a reason unrelated to you or your topic. Or perhaps, if you are fortunate, they are there because of an interest in what you have to say. In any audience, you will find combinations of these and other motivations. Knowing the predominant audience expectation is vital to the preparation of your speech. An excellent speech can fail miserably if the audience expected a different sort of talk altogether.

This is not to say that you must be bound by the audience's expectations. You can lead them to a new mind-set, but to do that, you need to discover what they know and expect.

CHECKLIST

Audience Analysis

❏ *What do they know about your topic?* Make no blanket assumptions about sophistication of your audience; rather, use the techniques of audience analysis to find it. People listen best and learn best when exposed to information that is just beyond their current level of comprehension.

❏ *What do they think about you?* Learn what your audience has heard, read, or assumed about you. You want to build on their positive expectations and overcome their negative ones. Knowing what your credibility is prior to the speech helps you decide how much you need to bolster it during the speech. (See **26a**.)

❏ *What is the history of your audience as a group?* Audiences come in many different forms, with varied levels of group cohesion. Most audiences have some common history, which may range from a long association in a business or club to a few weeks together in a classroom. Learn all you can about this collective history.

❏ *What is the program surrounding your speech?* To understand an audience's expectations of you, it is essential to learn your speech's place in the context of their immediate situation. Familiarize yourself with the agenda and where you fit into it.

4 Finding and Using Resources

CHAPTER 13

Your Research Strategy

Plan a research strategy that optimizes your effort for the time allotted. This requires you to reflect before dashing off for research. How
much time? What themes require investigation? What are your objectives? Other questions center on where you will get your information.
What can best be found in the library? Which research can be done
electronically? Whom can you approach to discuss your topic?

13a. Fit your research to your time

Chapter **10** advises having a realistic timetable for preparation.
With one day's notice, you cannot make an exhaustive study of
the literature, but you can draw from general references like encyclopedias, whether at the library, on CD-ROM, or online. With
more time, a broader effort is possible.

13b. Progress from the general to the specific

Start with an investigation of the "big picture." You do not want to
commit yourself prematurely to only one avenue of research; you
may miss signs of other paths important to your topic. As you move
further into your research, you can get more specific when you
have enough general understanding to be able to follow those trails
effectively.

There are two basic sources to tap for research: other people
and recorded information. It is usually best to start with the
recorded information, saving the use of human resources for later
when you know how best to take advantage of their expertise.
Here, too, is where the general references become your initial and
primary resource.

One of the most useful talents in the early stages of research is
the ability to skim. Because you will not have time to read everything, try to get a feel for the most important approaches and theories: look at the table of contents, skim the first and last chapters
of the book, or read the first and last paragraphs of the chapter or
article. Jot down the names of the key people who are frequently
cited, as well as recurring concepts and studies.

As you begin your research, look for summary or state-of-the-
art articles and books and sites that synthesize current thinking
on your subject. Pieces that trace the history of your topic are
also useful. Often, these sources are readily identifiable by their
titles:

"The Lasting Changes Brought by Women Workers" [*Business
Week*]

Women in the American Economy [Juanita M. Kreps, Prentice-Hall]

"Women and the Workforce" [Alice Kessler, *The Reader's Companion to American History,* via web search]

13c. Develop a terminology lexicon

As you start exploring your topic, make a list of key terms that come up. You will notice that certain phrases are widely used in the discourse. Familiarity with the language of your topic is essential as you continue your research because you need to identify key words as you search through the literature. This is particularly useful in searches for electronic information—one way to reduce an Internet search engine's "hits" from 98,000 to a more manageable number is to use precise language.

13d. Use questions to direct your research

When you've made one pass through for background research, but before you launch your main research effort, go back and analyze your topic. Consider whether you want to narrow your topic, adjust your speech objectives, or fine-tune the wording of your thesis statement. Carefully follow the suggestions in **11d.2** to list what your audience will want to know. These questions become the basis of your research objectives.

Suppose that your thesis is this:

Since the beginning of the Industrial Revolution, women in the United States have been exploited as a cheap and expendable source of labor.

Your audience will want to hear the answers to questions like these:

Are women a cheap source of labor?

Are women an expendable source of labor?

Can the labor practices appropriately be labeled as exploitation?

Has the treatment of women been rather consistent since the Industrial Revolution?

Clearly, then, your list of research objectives will include goals like these:

Find out how women's salaries compare with those of men who do the same job.

Find specific examples of women having been treated as an expendable source of labor.

Find an expert definition of *exploitation.*

Find out how women's work changed at the time of the Industrial Revolution.

Armed with this list of research objectives, you are ready to make the best use of your research time and to ask for the help you need.

CHAPTER 14

Print, Internet, and Other Electronic Resources

The vast amount of information available, literally at your fingertips, can seem overwhelming. Stay focused on your research objectives (see **13**) as you explore various electronic and print resources.

14a. The library

It is not by chance that we start our discussion of where to go for research with the library. Even with the advent of the Internet, it is still the place to find the widest variety of research tools (including access to the Internet) and the place to find professional researchers primed to give you direction and help.

> **KEY POINT** **Talk to a Librarian** Librarians are service-oriented information specialists, there to help you find the materials you need. Do not hesitate to ask them questions. They welcome the challenge of trying to understand your requirements and direct you to the answers you seek.

14b. Printed books and articles

In addition to the librarian, important library resources include the book catalogue, periodical indexes and databases, and special dictionaries and encyclopedias.

The book catalogue In most libraries, the book catalogue is a computer database. These database systems let you search for entries in a number of ways. For instance, you may choose to search by some combination of subject, author, and title. Or you can focus on topics as they are grouped in the Dewey decimal system or the Library of Congress classifications. Or you can search by keywords or *descriptors*—words or short phrases that the database uses to identify entries on related topics. Or, in some cases, you may make a *free text search,* in which the computer does not limit itself to defined descriptors, but rather looks for words and combinations of words that you have chosen within the titles and content summaries of the books in the database. The lexicon you developed in **13c** will be extremely helpful in both keyword and free text searches. Special collections may have separate catalogues; check with the librarian to see which catalogues you have access to.

Periodical indexes and databases You can locate magazine, journal, and newspaper articles on your topic using the periodical indexes and databases available at the library. Some of these are general in their coverage; others can be quite specific to a field or area of interest. Once again, do not hesitate to approach the librarian to ask for guidance in finding these sources. There also are indexes for many major newspapers.

Special dictionaries, encyclopedias, and similar resources Special dictionaries and encyclopedias are useful tools, especially for clarifying terms and concepts as they are used in fields in which you may have little knowledge. The library may have other sources of information available, including filmstrips, microforms, records, compact discs, cassettes, films, and videotapes.

14c. Electronic information retrieval

To retrieve information electronically, you can use an institutional search service that provides access to databases at remote sites; a computer terminal at the library that provides access to databases on-site or to the Internet; a personal computer to connect to an online service; a computer to access a general Internet search tool. These choices run from the highly structured (the institutional search service) to the highly unstructured (the Internet).

LEXIS-NEXIS, DIALOG, BRS (Bibliographic Retrieval Service), and Wilson OmniFile are services that provide information retrieval. A service can have hundreds of databases to choose from, each of which can cover hundreds of thousands of articles and papers. You can gain access to one of these systems via a public library, or a college or university library. Many companies have access to at least one of the major systems.

InfoTrac® College Edition is an electronic virtual library that is available 24 hours a day via an Internet connection. It consists of full-length articles collected from hundreds of scholarly and popular periodicals, a range that embraces diverse publications. Figure 14-1 shows a search conducted on InfoTrac College Edition.

Online services accessible by personal computer include online editions of encyclopedias and news magazines, stock market performance, government statistics, news on sports and entertainment.

Seeking out information may be more esoteric on the Internet, where you can use such things as Gopher servers and the World Wide Web to track down what you are looking for. There are a number of ways you gain access to the Internet and, once there, a number of ways you can move around in it. In fact, its combination of flexibility and arcane global structure can make it a daunting prospect for casual users. Tools for finding information include newsreaders to gain access to Usenet newsgroups or e-mail discussion groups, search engines to perform keyword searches on the web (e.g., Google), and subject directories consisting of links organized by subject (e.g., the Librarian's Internet Index).

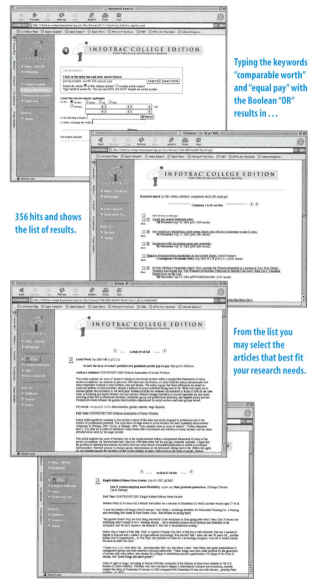

Typing the keywords "comparable worth" and "equal pay" with the Boolean "OR" results in . . .

356 hits and shows the list of results.

From the list you may select the articles that best fit your research needs.

FIGURE 14-1   A Search Using InfoTrac College Edition

1   Search effectively and efficiently

Approach the available search engines and directories with a search technique that maximizes focus and minimizes ambiguity. Use Boolean operators ("this AND that," "this OR that," "this NOT that"), if the search engine allows, to keep from being overwhelmed by tens of thousands of "hits." Many engines permit users to specify that one word in the search should be near another and use other tools (such as wildcards and required terms) to be as precise as possible at the beginning.

An excellent place to find information on the various search engines and strategies for using them is the Librarian's Internet Index (**www.lii.org**). See especially its "Searching the Internet" directory. Also extremely valuable is the UC Berkeley Library's "Finding Information on the Internet: A Tutorial" (**www.lib.berkeley .edu/TeachingLib/Guides/Internet/FindInfo.html**).

For the most efficient use of any of these electronic resources, you must create a concise research strategy by narrowing your topic after considering different avenues of approach. (See **13**.) Then you can decide what are the most likely categories and keywords to identify information related to your topic.

Table 14-1 lists some useful reference sites that could be the starting point for your Internet researching. This is just a drop in the bucket, though, and you will find many other sites through links on the sites listed, and also through links on the *The Speaker's Compact Handbook* website.

2   Carefully evaluate Internet sources

Scrutinize web-based materials with special caution. Although *any* information you gather in the course of research should be

---

CHECKLIST

Evaluating a Website

Ask yourself these questions as you look at a website:

❑ *Who is it?* Is it a personal page? If so, what credentials does the person present, and how compelling are they? If it is an organization's page, does it provide enough background information (e.g., "About us" page) for you to make a judgment about its credibility?

❑ *What's its slant?* Why was this site created? Was it to provide information, advocate a position, or just rant? If it's providing information, how is that information influenced by the underlying assumptions embraced by the site's creator?

❑ *Is it up to date?* Does the site have regular maintenance that keeps it on top of developments?

❑ *What company does it keep?* That is, whom does it link to, and who links to it? How would you assess the credibility and competence of those linked sites?

For more on evaluating websites, see the UC Berkeley tutorial and the Librarian's Internet Index previously cited in **14c.1**.

TABLE 14-1   Some Useful Reference Sites

General Reference

Internet Public Library—annotated subject directory
http://www.ipl.org

Librarian's Internet Index—annotated subject directory
http://www.lii.org

LibrarySpot—virtual library resource center
http://www.libraryspot.com

Martindale's "The Reference Desk"—subject directory
http://www.martindalecenter.com

RefDesk—index to reference sites
http://www.refdesk.com

Information Please—online encyclopedia, dictionary, atlas
http://www.infoplease.com

Virtual Library—noncommercial network of indexes
http://vlib.org

Bartleby—index to reference and literature sites
http://www.bartleby.com

Literature

Project Gutenberg—access to free electronic books in the public domain
http://www.gutenberg.org

Perseus Digital Library—Greek and Latin classics, along with early modern English
http://www.perseus.tufts.edu

Science

Eric Weisstein's World of Science—resource for math, chemistry, physics, astronomy
http://scienceworld.wolfram.com

Government (U.S.) and Law

USA. gov—U.S. government official web portal
http://www.USA.gov

GPO Access—U.S. government printing office databases
http://www.gpoaccess.gov/databases.html

Library of Congress—the National Digital Library
http://www.loc.gov

U.S. National Archives and Records Administration—archives and records
http://www.archives.gov

FedStats—links to statistics collected by the U.S. government
http://www.fedstats.gov

World Legal Information Institute—access to law databases worldwide
http://www.worldlii.org

Urban Legends and Misinformation

The AFU & Urban Legends Archive
http://www.urbanlegends.about.com

Urban Legends Reference Pages ("Snopes")
http://www.snopes.com

subjected to tests of credibility and reliability as described in **16c** and in chapter **26**, the wide-open nature of the World Wide Web invites a particularly critical eye. In contrast to the various review processes applied to getting ideas into print or onto film, all it takes to mount a website is the software and a server.

CHAPTER 15

Interviewing People About Your Topic

You are surrounded by potential sources of information in the form of other people—both as individuals and as members of informal or formal information networks. These sources can complement and supplement your library and electronic research.

15a. Finding human resources

Look for human resources at home, at school and work, and in the community.

1 Acquaintances, family, and coworkers

As you start developing ideas on your topic, begin to talk about them with the people you come in contact with every day. On many topics, what these people can offer you is not so much expertise as a lay perspective that you will not find in any book.

2 Experts

In every community there are people with specialized expertise in your topic who can often direct you to obscure sources.

- *Educators.* Dissemination of information is an educator's business. Call the appropriate department or school. They will direct you to someone knowledgeable.

- *Public officials and agencies.* People elected to public office consider it one of their duties to make information available to their constituents. If you do not know where to start, call the main switchboard of the local or regional government and outline the direction of your research.

- *Independent agencies and special interest groups.* Groups such as the American Cancer Society or the National Hot Rod Association can be excellent sources of information. When possible, interview experts with differing orientations toward your subject, especially if the subject is controversial. A useful resource for making contact with such groups is the *Encyclopedia of Associations,* available at the library or through DIALOG.

- *Potpourri.* Athletes, businesspeople, police officers, doctors, accountants can all be experts. If you do not know a person in the particular field, see if you have a link to one through a colleague or friend.

  You can also tap into an enormous pool of talent in the electronic community accessible by computer. The newsgroups and conferences available online can introduce you to knowledgeable human resources at a national, and even global, level. In these groups and on message boards, people carry on extended dialogue on many issues. Before asking a specific question, check to see if it is one that has come up many times before. Questions of this sort, along with their answers, are usually posted in a Frequently Asked Questions (FAQ) file. Links to Usenet FAQs of all kinds can be found at the Internet FAQ Archives: **http://www .faqs.org/faqs/**.

15b. Conducting interviews

As with all aspects of public speaking, in interviewing, preparation is just as important as the process itself.

1 Preparing for the interview

Ask yourself in what ways your interviewee can best contribute to your research. Devise a list of questions that are specific enough that you will not be wasting this person's time by asking for information you could have found in the encyclopedia. Prepare open-ended, but focused, questions. For instance:

Not: How many women are there in the workforce in this county? [You could have looked up the figure before.]

Not: What are the problems working women encounter? [This is too vague.]

But: I've read that in this county the average woman's salary is 32 percent less than the average man's. To what do you attribute this?

2 During the interview

First establish rapport and set a context. Explain who you are, why you need the information, and how far you have gotten. Also, confirm your understanding of the time available. If you wish to tape the interview, ask permission at this point, but be ready with a notepad in case you do not get it. Either way, take notes.

When you begin to ask questions, be sure to let the expert do most of the talking. (See the suggestions on listening in **2d**.) Use questions to summarize and direct the interview: "So far you've talked about four problems working women face—unequal pay, lack of training, sexual harassment, and inadequate child care. Are there others?"

Allow for a closing phase for the interview. Respect the interviewee's time limit, and if you are approaching it, stop—even if you have gone through only half of your questions. Summarize your perspective of the interview. Often, it is productive to ask if the person would like to make a wrap-up statement.

KEY POINT   **After the Interview**   Just as it's essential to be well prepared going into an interview, it's equally important that you do the necessary follow-up after an interview. The focus of this follow-up is twofold: ensuring that your notes or recording, or both, will be as useful as possible, and thanking your interviewee. As soon as possible after the interview, read through your notes, making sure they are legible and make sense. You can also use this review to jot down any additional details that may come to mind. If you recorded the interview, label it clearly. Whether or not you need to contact your interviewee to have information clarified or a quote verified, follow up an interview with a written thank-you note. An e-mail message is fastest and easiest, but a handwritten card or note might be appreciated more.

CHAPTER 16

Identifying and Recording Evidence

Carefully review your supporting materials: the print and electronic texts you have gathered and the interview notes you have taken. Glean from these the building blocks of your speech. Select the support for your ideas first on the basis of relevance, then on soundness, and then on interest value. Use a variety of the following methods to develop your speech.

16a. Examples

Beyond the universal appeal of a good story, examples provide audience members with a chance to check their perceptions of a speaker's message. As a speaker, you need to make decisions about whether to use real examples or hypothetical ones and about how brief or how extended these examples should be.

1   Factual examples

A **factual example** relies on an assertion that is universally accepted. Sometimes, it is directly verifiable, as in "Sandra Day O'Connor was a justice of the Supreme Court." Even if you were not at the swearing-in, there is enough corroborative evidence from many sources to satisfy you that this is a factual statement. "The earth is 93 million miles from the sun" is another assertion accepted as a fact although it is not directly verifiable through any

---

CHECKLIST

Tests of Factual Examples

❑ *Are sufficient examples given?* The more examples you give, the less likely your listeners are to dismiss the phenomenon as the product of chance.

❑ *Are the examples representative?* To be credible, examples should represent a cross section of cases.

❑ *Are negative instances accounted for?* When you reason by example, you must look into and account for dramatic negative examples. Your obligation, if you wish to carry your point, is to show how these examples are atypical and this should not detract from your conclusion.

---

of the five senses. But we do accept it, because we have constructed theoretical frameworks based on consistent results of observation and can make predictions of near-absolute certainty.

When you use examples to prove a point, though, specific logical tests must be met.

2   Hypothetical examples

Sometimes, when no factual example quite suits your purpose, or when you are speculating about the future, you might give a brief or extended **hypothetical example**. Here is an illustration of an *extended hypothetical* example:

> How should you develop an investment portfolio? Well, let's imagine that you have a monthly household income of $4,000 and that your expenses run to about $2,800. Let me show you how to calculate what portion of the remainder should go into fairly liquid, low-risk areas like the money markets or short-term T-bills and what portion can go into higher-risk areas like commodities.

Hypothetical examples do not have to be extended ones. Here is a speech segment that uses three *brief hypothetical* examples in quick succession:

> What would happen if this tax law were to pass? Well, Miguel over there couldn't deduct his business lunches. Audrey wouldn't be able to depreciate her buildings. You, Tom, with kids about to start college . . .

Be aware that the examples you pick reflect a set of assumptions about the world. Be sensitive to racist or sexist implications of your illustrations.

KEY POINT **The Appropriate Amount of Detail** When you use examples, you must decide how long or short to make each one. The factual and hypothetical examples in a speech can be kept brief when you can safely assume that the audience is already familiar with them. If a succession of quick references will not illuminate a point for your listeners, however, you need to develop the example into an illustration.

Ideally, a speech blends several short examples with a few extended ones. Properly selected, these show the audience both the breadth of your subject and some in-depth aspects of it.

16b. Statistical evidence

Statistical evidence is based on examples that have been systematically collected and coded in numerical form. An excellent source of governmental statistical information, classified by topic, state, and agency, can be found at **www.fedstats.gov.**

1 Check the accuracy

For any statistics you cite, investigate the methods and motivations of those who collected them.

CHECKLIST

Tests of Statistical Evidence

❑ *Who collected the data?* Investigate the qualifications and competence of the researchers. Was the work done by a professional pollster or the host of a call-in radio show?

❑ *Why were the data collected?* The motivation behind collecting certain information can make the data suspect. Most people have more confidence in inquiries rooted in a desire to advance knowledge rather than to sell a product or promote a cause.

❑ *When were the data collected?* Be sure your evidence is up to date. Attitudes change as swiftly as prices, and some data are obsolete by the time they are published.

❑ *How were the data collected?* Find out as much as you can about the design of the research and the details of its execution. Track it back to the original study. Check how the cases were chosen. Evaluate the method of data collection—observation, experiment, or survey conducted by phone, mail, or personal interview.

2 Avoid misleading statistics

We know that language is ambiguous, but we tend to believe that numbers make straightforward statements; there is no mystery in

2 + 2 = 4. However, numbers *can* be just as ambiguous, with statistical pitfalls to trap the unwary.

The fallacy of the average Although the average can be a useful tool for analysis, it sometimes gives a picture absurdly at odds with reality. An example of how this can mislead is the Smurge Company report that shows an average of 6 computer scanners per department when, in fact, the marketing department has 40 scanners, and most other departments have 1 or none. As this demonstrates, calculating the arithmetic *mean* is not appropriate when one or two extreme cases skew the distribution. The *median* (the number or score that falls at the midpoint of the range of numbers or scores) or the *mode* (the most frequently occurring score or number) can be more meaningful averages to use in this example, although they, too, can be abused. See Figure 16-1 for a graphic representation of the scanner distribution in the Smurge Company. In this case, although the *mean* is 6, the *median* is 2 (scores of 0 and 1 below it, scores of 3 and 40 above it), and the *mode* is 1 (the largest number of departments—three—have this score).

The fallacy of the unknown base A speaker using percentages and proportions can sometimes give the mistaken impression that a large population has been sampled. In fact, data are sometimes reported in this manner to give credence to unscientific or skimpy evidence: "Two out of three mechanics recommend this synthetic oil." Most listeners would see this as shorthand for "We polled 300 mechanics around the country, and 200 of them recommended this synthetic oil." How valid would this recommendation seem if it came to light that in reality only *three* were polled?

The fallacy of the atypical or arbitrary time frame Recently, an executive of a computer circuit board company told us that sales in February were double those of the previous month. These data could be misleading unless you know that January is always the worst month in the yearly cycle of the computer industry.

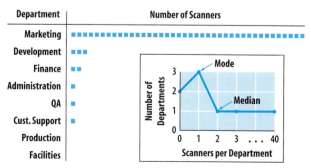

FIGURE 16-1 **Distribution of Scanners at the Smurge Company**

3   Make your numbers meaningful

The stereotypical dry, plodding speech is one that is overloaded with statistics. After a short while, the audience becomes overloaded too, and listeners start to build a mental dike against the numbers flowing over them. When you do use statistics, round them off. Say "about fifteen hundred" instead of "one thousand four hundred eighty-nine point six." Use visual representations such as charts and graphs. See **27a**. Use comparisons to make the numbers more understandable:

> For the amount of money they propose to spend on this weapons system, we could provide educational grants in aid to all the needy students in the 11 western states, or triple the government funding for cancer research, or upgrade the highway system in this state and its three neighbors.

16c. Testimony from authorities

Often, we call on statements from other people to get our point across. For instance, even if you have never been arrested or never been a public safety officer, you can give a credible speech on the penal system by making judicious use of **testimony** from experts or eyewitnesses.

CHECKLIST

Tests of Testimony

❏ *Does the authority have access to the necessary information?* A person does not have to be famous to be an authority. When you use an authority, be sure that the person had firsthand experience, direct observation, or personal access to relevant facts and files.

❏ *Is the authority qualified to interpret data?* When a person starts making interpretations, forming opinions and conclusions, and proposing recommendations, the standards of credibility become stricter. People earn the right to be considered experts either by holding specific credentials or by establishing a record of success and experience.

❏ *Is the person acknowledged as an expert on this subject?* Just because a person is an expert in one field, it doesn't follow that she is an expert in other fields.

❏ *Is the authority figure free of bias and self-interest?* We give more credence to the opinion of an authority who appears to have no personal stake—ideological or financial—in an issue. If you can find testimony from a person speaking *against* his or her interests, then it certainly will be an effective addition to your presentation.

1 Evaluate the credibility of the authorities

It is easy to find citations that say almost anything; it is much more difficult to select those that provide legitimate support for your points. This requires scrutinizing the people you quote for support.

2 Do not distort quotations

Shortening quotations to highlight the basic thrust of the message is perfectly acceptable. What is unacceptable is editing a person's statements to such a degree that they appear to support positions other than or even opposite those espoused in the actual quotations. There is the old joke about the movie critic who wrote that "the wretchedness of the acting in this film is nothing short of amazing!" only to find later that an advertisement for the movie quoted him as saying "this film . . . is amazing!"

Do not edit a quotation so radically that it loses all substance. Virtually content-free quotations are sometimes deliberately used to confuse listeners or to overwhelm them with an apparent preponderance of evidence.

KEY POINT **Finding Quotations** In addition to specific testimony, it is often effective to use the timeless words of famous individuals who have said something about your topic. There are several resources to help you locate brief generic quotations on your topic: www.quoteland.com, www.quotationspage.com, and www.Bartleby.com/quotations provide lists of famous quotations indexed by topic.

16d. A complete record of your sources

Form the habit of identifying the source for every piece of information you use and of recording complete bibliographic information for each source. With electronic catalogues your task often will be easier—you may be able to print out the bibliographic information for each of your potential sources or perhaps download it onto a portable storage medium. When you print pages from the Internet, make sure your print command will include the headers and footers from your browser, which contain the page title and the page's uniform resource locator (URL). In other situations, you will need to record it yourself. Writing down volume numbers of journals, or the cities of publication of books, or the telephone numbers of interviewees—details that you will never mention in your speech—may seem unnecessary, but routinely recording all such information will help you retrieve sources if you need to check them again.

KEY POINT **Citing Sources for a List of References** We recommend that you master one of the standard formats for citing references so that if you need to append a reference list to an outline or decide to produce a handout for your audience, the sources of your research will be appropriately laid out. Three of the most popular formats are found in *The Chicago Manual of Style (CMS),* 15th edition (2003), usually referred to simply as Chicago style; the *MLA Handbook for Writers of Research Papers,* 6th edition (2003), abbreviated and referred to as MLA style; and the *Publication Manual of the American Psychological Association,* 5th edition (2001), or APA style. MLA and APA styles are the ones most likely to be used in the context of a speech class. More information about these two styles and their organizations is available online at www.mla.org and www.apa.org. Individual variations notwithstanding, all three styles require an alphabetical listing of research sources that includes author, title, date, and publication details. In addition to the conventions for citing books, articles, chapters, and abstracts, there are correct ways to cite nearly every known type of source, including interviews, personal correspondence, photographs, TV shows, websites, and e-mail. **Appendix B** shows the APA and MLA styles for 13 types of reference citation. Keep in mind that this list is just a sampling of the types of publications and communications that can end up in a reference list.

16e. Your research notes

In the process of doing your research, you want to gather and record your information and ideas in a way that makes it as easy as possible to find things later on and to work with them creatively. The ability to photocopy whole chapters of books or to download pages and pages of text from the web does not make it any easier to review the information you have. Smaller, more manageable units will promote creative flexibility as you arrange and rearrange, structure and restructure your thoughts and data.

We talk about "notecards" in this section, but the important thing is not the media or the cardstock but the activity—and if you use an outlining tool or idea development software on a computer, these suggestions are as pertinent.

1 Notecards from print and electronic sources

As you read the book or article, jot down each discrete idea or bit of information on a separate card, being sure you add the identifying code and page number. Use only one side of each card. There are three kinds of data you might record: direct quotations or citations, paraphrased ideas, and references for later use. Do not neglect to do this for materials obtained online. Even if you have a printout, it is valuable to go through the process of paraphrasing or quoting so that you isolate and internalize the key points that drew you to the source in the first place.

If you copy entire articles or chapters, be sure to make a bibliography card for each. Many people find it helpful to photocopy the title page and copyright page of the book or periodical.

2 Notecards from interviews and surveys

The suggestions in **16e.1** relate to printed information but are easily adapted to information acquired through interviews and surveys. Make a bibliography card for each interview, citing the person interviewed, his or her qualifications, the date of the interview, and the person's telephone number or address. As you listen to the tape or review your notes, transcribe the information on cards.

3 Grouping your cards

When you have gathered many notecards, you may want to stack them under cover cards with titles such as "History," "Causes," and "Solutions." Or you may decide to put these keywords in the upper-right corner.

16f. Citing sources in your speech

In **32a** we talk about weaving supporting materials smoothly into the speech while citing the source. The form this citation takes is, like many choices in speaking, dependent on the context. The college debate or speech contest may have a strict form, developed by tradition. Otherwise, you can choose how much information you need to include about the source as you speak—according to how much you think your audience has to hear to accept the source as legitimate.

One context is your listeners' attitude toward you and your topic: in **23b** we go into adjustments you may have to make depending on whether your audience is *favorable, neutral,* or *unfavorable*. Another determinant for the density of your citations is your judgment on projecting credibility. See **26c**.

PART **5** # Organizing Your Ideas and Information

CHAPTER 17. **Exploring Your Ideas**

Look for logical groupings of ideas that could be developed as points of your speech.

CHAPTER 18. **Choosing Points That Work**

When you choose your main points, determine which ones work best to convey your ideas.

CHAPTER 19. **Arranging Points**

When you arrange your points, consider the traditional patterns of speech organization, and select or create the one that is best suited to your topic and purpose.

CHAPTER 20. **Outlining**

Use a formal outline as an organizational tool.

CHAPTER 21. **Building Sound Arguments**

Use sound reasoning to develop your speech.

CHAPTER 17

Exploring Your Ideas

You may have lots of good ideas, but you need a procedure to assess which are important and where you want to go with them—a process that cannot be given short shrift. This entails four stages:

1. Generating many ideas

2. Grouping them into clusters

3. Labeling each cluster

4. Reworking, adjusting, and culling the ideas until you have two to five major groupings that cover the most important ideas and that can be developed in your allotted time

17a. Assembling ideas and information

When you begin to prepare a speech, do not limit yourself. Jot down every item you might possibly cover, whether drawn from your research or from ideas that have been percolating. Follow the techniques of brainstorming; go for quantity rather than quality at this point. Do not judge or dismiss any idea, but instead write them all down in no particular order and don't worry about duplication. You cannot start the process of organizing until you have some raw material to organize.

17b. Identifying potential points

Look back over the brainstorming list you made and consider how you might cluster the entries. There is no one correct way to group these ideas. Almost certainly, some ideas will be omitted altogether, and others may have to be forced a bit to fit into any category. Sometimes, one or more of the ideas from your brainstorming list will serve as a category around which to group smaller points. Other times, you will group several minor ideas and then devise a heading for them.

1 A working outline

Perhaps the most traditional technique of speech organization is to arrange ideas in the hierarchical, indented outline format. At this early stage of development, however, you do not want to be constrained by the requirements of the formal full-sentence outline. The full-sentence outline has a very important role in ensuring that you properly elaborate your points and subpoints, but a less rigid form, the **topic outline,** is more useful at this point. (See **20b** for examples of full-sentence and topic outlines.)

Because you are likely to experiment with several alternative groupings of ideas, don't spend time on phrasing or format. Just try to fit ideas under one another, nesting them in various ways until you discover the pattern that seems to make the most sense.

If this is a comfortable method for you, you will have a head start on developing the full-sentence outline, but there are other, more spatially oriented ways to marshal your thoughts, which we describe next.

2   Concept mapping

Concept mapping is a visual method of showing how your ideas relate to each other. In its most basic form, you quickly draw a simple diagram made of labeled circles and squares, connecting them with lines.

Write your central idea—your topic—in a box or circle in the center of a sheet of paper. Jot some major points from your brainstorming list around the topic, leaving enough room to add more subpoints. Your ideas will start to cluster around certain points; as you write each new one down, draw a line to connect it to its related point. This doesn't have to be done hierarchically, however. Subpoints might come to you before a broader point does. You can redraw as new relationships become clear.

There are a variety of styles for doing this, under the names of *clustering, mindmapping, branching,* and *ballooning.* Figure 17-1 shows a simple concept map, one that could have been part of the organizational process that led to the comic book outline in **Appendix A**.

3   Idea notes

You can manipulate notes spatially or in linear form. For example, you can jot your ideas on Post-it® notes and stick them to a wall or desktop. You can cluster them according to themes, moving items from group to group until you are happy with the total grouping.

Another possibility is to start with your research notecards and supplement them with cards on which you've written your own thoughts. In **16e**, we suggest grouping the research notecards under subject cover cards. You can write ideas, transitions, and syntheses on additional cards and plug them in where you think they fit. As with the Post-it notes, you can easily change the organization to experiment with a variety of approaches to your subject.

You can also group and regroup your ideas on a computer, using the simple outlining facility of word-processing software or specialized idea development software.

Once you have a set of potential points for your speech, the next step is to choose the points that are most suitable for your purpose and that work best together.

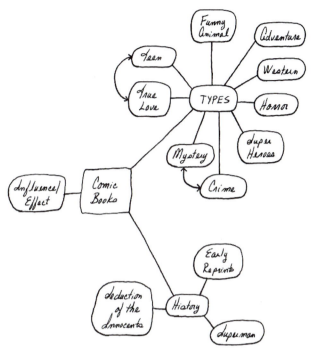

FIGURE 17-1   Simple Concept Map

CHAPTER 18

Choosing Points That Work

Experience has shown that following a few basic principles while selecting main points and subpoints from your pool of potential speech points will enhance your ability to craft a speech that is well structured, coherent, and effective.

18a. Main points that develop your thesis

Main points are those few ideas that are central and indispensable to the development of the thesis. To decide which main points to include in your speech, first look at your thesis statement. Follow the steps discussed in **11d.2** to identify the essential questions you must answer. For persuasive speeches that develop propositions of fact, value, or policy, consult **11d.3** for information on how to identify the essential questions with more precision. Once you know what a complete development of your topic requires, use the thesis statement as a standard against which to test your main points. Ask yourself:

- Is there any part of my thesis that is not developed in the speech?
- Is there any main idea of the speech that is not reflected in the thesis?

18b. Main points that are mutually exclusive

Main points should be mutually exclusive for maximum clarity. That is, each category should exclude the ideas that are covered by any other category. The challenge for the speaker lies in finding the best place for each idea.

Sometimes, when you are grouping ideas under potential main points, you will find that many fit into two or more categories. When this overlap occurs, you know that you have not yet found an effective system for classifying your ideas. Settling on a single organizational pattern is essential. If you do not know where an idea fits, your audience certainly will not.

For example, let's examine a speech on the topic of great films. Our speaker has come up with an outline that looks at great dramas with the first point, great comedies with the second, and great black-and-white films with the third. A little reflection shows that the topic was not completely thought through before the speaker began to lay out the structure of the speech. Apparently, the speaker was unable to decide whether the discussion of film should be framed along lines defined by dramatic category or by color or the lack of it. Whether a movie was shot on color or black-and-white stock does not have any intrinsic relationship to the subject (being more a matter of the history of the technology). Thus, having the three main points deal with drama, comedy, and black and white presents a problem: These three main points are not distinct categories.

Ideally, with a system of mutually exclusive main points, you will know how to classify any film and list it under one point only. If we put the sample organization to the test, however, we encounter uncertainty. *Raging Bull,* for instance, is a drama, but it could be listed under black and white, or drama. So, although each main point taken alone seems a plausible way to classify some movies, the three main points taken together do not constitute a sensible way to look at the topic.

What *would* be a sensible way to organize it? One possibility is to divide the topic into main points along a single dimension: color, or lack of it. These main points could each be broken down into two categories, drama and comedy, that are then repeated for each main point. This same topic could be divided many other ways. For instance, the main points might also form along chronology (1920s,

1930s, etc.) with each decade having subpoints that break the films out by comedy and drama. Still other classification systems might include categories for language, director, and genre.

What is most important is that you choose *one* classification scheme for your main points that gives you a rule by which to include each item under one and only one main point.

18c. Two to five main points

As a speaker, you should be able to cluster your ideas around a few main themes. Otherwise, if every thought is treated as a main point, you will have no opportunity to *develop* any of them. With many random subpoints, you never extract meaning from an unorganized barrage of information. And if you have only one main point, you basically have a topic and no organization to speak of.

Understand, too, that your audience will not be able to remember more than a few main points.

18d. Relationships among points

Ideas of equal importance or of parallel logical function are called **coordinate points**. Points of lesser significance that support, explain, or contribute steps of logical development to other ideas are called **subordinate points**.

The relative importance of main and other points must be very clear in your own mind. Every point in the speech is subordinate, coordinate, or superordinate to every other.

> **KEY POINT** **Types of Points** Subordinate points, or subpoints, should fit inside, or support, a larger idea. Coordinate points (and subpoints) should be of equal importance. Each subpoint should directly relate to the point it supports.

CHAPTER 19

Arranging Points

Once the main ideas of a speech have been selected, you need to arrange them in the order that will maximize effectiveness. In some cases, the decision is virtually made for you: many ceremonial or special-occasion speeches are so stylized that they follow a formula. (See **9**.) For the usual informative or persuasive speech, though, there is no given pattern. You, as a speaker, must select the best arrangement of ideas.

19a.   Types of patterns

Patterns arise either inherently from the subject matter or from the requirements of the thesis statement. There are several traditional patterns of speech arrangement: chronological, spatial, cause-effect, problem-solution, and topical.

1   The chronological pattern

Probably the most ancient form of extended discourse is the narrative unfolding of a story. A time-ordered format that sequences information still undergirds many contemporary speeches. *Historical* development is the most common **chronological pattern**. If you were giving a speech on the course of European music from 1600 to 1900, you might arrange it this way:

    I. The Baroque period (1600–1750)
    II. The Classical period (1720–1810)
   III. The Romantic period (1800–1900)

Also look at the outline on women workers in **20b**.

A second way to look at a subject chronologically is to analyze a process *step-by-step*. A speech on keeping fit through aerobic exercise could generate this outline:

    I. Determine the resting and working heart rate for your age.
    II. Begin each session with stretching exercises and low-level cardiovascular warm-up.
   III. Through vigorous exercise maintain your working heart rate for 30 to 40 minutes.
   IV. Allow at least 10 minutes for cool-down and stretching exercises.

Another chronological pattern might divide a topic into *past–present–future*.

2   The spatial pattern

The **spatial pattern** is often based on geography, or location. For example, the outline for a speech on crime might look like this:

    I. Crime on the Eastern Seaboard
    II. Crime in the Midwest
   III. Crime on the Pacific Coast

Other geographical arrangements might divide this topic into crime in Europe [Asia, Latin America] or crime in Manhattan [Brooklyn, the Bronx]. Geography need not refer just to areas on a map but can show up as other ways of dividing the world spatially, such as rural, suburban, urban crime.

The spatial pattern might also be applied to much smaller areas, such as the floor plan of a house. The following example of a spatial pattern for main points describes a very small area indeed—an aircraft instrument panel:

    I. Instruments needed to maintain controlled flight are on the left side of the panel.
        A. Compass
        B. Altimeter
        C. Artificial horizon
        D. Turn and bank indicator
        E. Air speed indicator
    II. Instruments providing information on the operating condition of the aircraft are on the right side.
        A. Tachometer
        B. Manifold pressure gauge
        C. Oil temperature gauge
        D. Oil pressure gauge
        E. Fuel gauge

3   The cause–effect pattern

This pattern is used to move from a discussion of the origins of a condition to the ways it manifests itself, and to show that events that occur in sequence are, in fact, causally related. A **cause–effect pattern** is well suited to a speech in which the goal is to achieve either understanding or agreement rather than overt action, as here:

    I. There has been a sharp increase in housing costs over the past generation.
        [as a result]
    II. It is extremely difficult for a one-income family to purchase a house.

Occasionally, the pattern may be reversed to an effect–cause sequence:

    I. It is extremely difficult for a one-income family to purchase a house.
        [this is because]
    II. There has been a sharp increase in housing costs over the past generation.

Of course, when using the cause–effect pattern, you must be sure that the causal relationship you propose is a valid one. (See **21d**.)

4   The problem–solution pattern

The **problem–solution pattern** is used to examine the symptoms of a problem and then propose a remedy. It is often seen in persuasive speeches that advocate a new policy or a specific course of action, as in the following:

   I. The current system of financing health care in the United States is inadequate.
      [to remedy this]
  II. A system of national health insurance would provide medical care to all citizens.

5   The topical pattern

The **topical pattern** is the most frequently used speech pattern. It is employed to divide a speech into elements that have no pattern and that are simply aspects of the topic. This is also the most difficult pattern; when subjects do not lend themselves readily to any of the arrangements discussed so far, you need to generate an original system for structuring the speech.

Often, the best structure for a speech involves listing the components of a whole or listing reasons that add up to the thesis. The following is an example of a topical pattern that lists reasons for a conclusion:

Thesis statement: Capital punishment should be abolished.

   I. Capital punishment does not deter crime.
  II. Capital punishment is ultimately more costly than life imprisonment.
 III. The risk of executing an innocent person is morally unacceptable.

19b. Organizing subpoints

After your main ideas have been set, look at the subpoints under each. These, too, need to be arranged in some effective order—topical, chronological, whatever. You do not have to repeat the pattern used for the main points; you can choose the format that makes the most sense for each set of subpoints. Notice the different arrangements in the detailed outline in **Appendix A**.

CHAPTER 20

Outlining

The speech outline is an indispensable tool of speech organization. A clear outline helps you keep track of the points you want to cover, and laying your ideas out on paper forces you to select points that support your thesis and fit together well. As the planning and practice chart in chapter **10** illustrates, you must develop a logical outline of your points and supporting materials before you can finalize the oral version of your speech. Because full-sentence outlines are so much like actual writing, they must not be used too early in the process (thus producing writer's block) or too late (thus resulting in a speech delivered in a written rather than an oral style). Oral composition and oral practice should surround this one excursion into writing.

> **KEY POINT** **The Handbook Concept of Outlining** Although some outline formats include the introduction and conclusion as main points of the speech, we do not. Rather, the outline as used here is a detailed, logical plan of the *basic* ideas in the body of the speech. Do not confuse the formal speech outline with informal research notes (see **16d**), preliminary organizational tools (see **17b**), or speaking notes (see **33b**). Also, this outline is not an essay; don't let your outline transform itself into a manuscript speech. (See **28c**.)

20a. The conventional outline format

By following certain rules of outlining, you will be able to visualize the relationships among the ideas of your speech.

1 The symbols

It is conventional to use roman numerals to label the main ideas of the speech and to alternate between letters and numbers for each successive level of subordination, in this manner:

    I. Main point
      A. First level of subordination
        1. Second level of subordination
          a. Third level of subordination
            (1) Fourth level of subordination
              (a) Fifth level of subordination

Do not skip levels. If your speech has only main points and one level of subpoints, use I, II, III and A, B, C. If your outline includes a second level of subordination, use 1, 2, 3.

2 Indentation

Each subordinate idea should be indented several spaces to align with the first word—not the labeling numeral or letter—of the point it supports. This makes the relationship among ideas visually obvious. Note how your eye is directed down the levels of subordination. Your outline should not look like a piece of prose. Your outline exists only to illuminate and clarify the structure of your ideas.

3   Two or more subpoints

English teachers are fond of saying, "Never have a 1 without a 2 or an A without a B." Generally, this is good advice. The concept of dividing an idea into parts—subordination—becomes nonsensical if a major point is "divided" into only one subpoint. Categories are useful because they encompass several related things. Suppose you outline a main point of your speech as follows:

   I. Redwood City is the best California city in which to live.
     A. It has the best climate.
  II. ....

If this is your only example, you are guilty of hasty generalization. To avoid this fallacy, outline your speech following the rule of having *at least* two supporting points at each level of subordination. The rule "No 1 without a 2 and no A without a B" is a good one to ensure depth of analysis.

20b.   The full-sentence outline

The **full-sentence outline** is a tool to ensure coherent development of your speech. Your thesis statement (see **11d**), the main points, and at least the first level of subpoints should be stated as declarative sentences. The declarative sentence is, in effect, a proposition. As such, it can be proved or disproved, accepted or rejected.

Look at the following sentence:

   I. Secondhand smoke harms nonsmokers.

If this sentence were presented to you on a true/false test, you could, with adequate knowledge, answer one way or the other. But what would you do if you encountered these items on a true/false test?

   I. Nonsmokers' rights

or:

   I. What is the effect of secondhand smoke on nonsmokers?

Obviously, an answer of true or false to either of these examples is impossible. Far too many speeches are constructed around just such vague phrases, questions, and uncompleted ideas. Listeners can identify the speaker's general topic but cannot always recognize the specific points the speaker is trying to make. Consider these examples:

  Wrong: I. What are the causes of crime?
   Right: I. Crime is caused by a combination of sociological and psychological factors.

<table>
<tr><td>*Wrong:*</td><td>I.</td><td>The history of the feminist movement in the United States</td></tr>
<tr><td>*Right:*</td><td>I.</td><td>U.S. feminism can be divided into four historical periods.</td></tr>
</table>

Besides rendering the speech more coherent for your audience, the use of declarative sentences in your outline makes you more conscious of the exact points you want to make and forces you to frame them explicitly. Once the thesis and main points are stated in propositional form, they will provide a basis against which you can test all other speech content.

The following outlines deal with a topic, the history of working women in the United States, that could fill many volumes. Here is how a *full-sentence outline* covers the topic. Observe how the thesis statement and full-sentence main and secondary points provide a basis for the speaker to decide what to include.

Full-Sentence Outline

Thesis Statement: *Since the beginning of the Industrial Revolution, women in the United States have been exploited as a cheap and expendable source of labor.*

I. In preindustrial colonial settings, the boundaries between men's and women's spheres were indistinct.
  A. Colonial women ran self-sufficient factories in their homes.
    1. Women produced candles, the major source of artificial light.
    2. Clothing and bedding were made by women.
    3. The making of soap was a major contribution by women.
  B. The rigors of frontier life decreed a more equal division of labor between women and men than was found on the rapidly industrializing eastern seaboard.
    1. Men and women shared long hours of joint farmwork.
    2. Women were often left alone for long periods to run the farm.
II. Between the Revolution and the Civil War, increased industrialization led to increased exploitation of women workers.
  A. Factories undercut home production.
  B. When the western migration caused shortages of male workers, women became a cheap source of labor for the factories.
    1. The percentage of women in the workforce increased.
    2. In 1829, women earned one quarter of what men did.
  C. Working women's efforts to improve their lot were not successful.

    1. The first women's strike was in 1824, but poor organization made it and others ineffective.
    2. Associations of working women failed because of the women's isolation and inexperience.

III. In spite of increasing unionization between the Civil War and World War II, women's position in the workforce remained inferior.
    A. Women were an unwelcome minority in trade organizations.
        1. Male union leaders did not believe in equal pay for equal work.
        2. According to men, women were barred from union offices because "no conveniences were available."
    B. Attempts by women before 1900 to organize among themselves met with failure.
        1. Women's unions were not taken seriously.
        2. Female workers were usually too impoverished to strike successfully.
    C. Important gains by working women in the first decades of the 20th century yielded little net improvement.
        1. Women's situation had improved in some areas.
            a. Unionization of the garment industry was successful.
            b. New job classifications were opened to women during World War I.
        2. Female workers still had neither security nor equality.
            a. Men got their jobs back after the war.
            b. Women received one half of comparable men's pay.

IV. During World War II and after, women were used as a dispensable and secondary source of labor.
    A. Traditional views of femininity were conveniently set aside according to economic needs.
        1. Three million women were recruited to replace our fighting men.
        2. "Rosie the Riveter" became a mythic ideal.
    B. After the war, labor, government, and industry cooperated to push women out of their new jobs.
        1. Although most women wanted to keep working, by 1946 four million were gone from the workforce.
        2. When plants began to rehire men, women's seniority was often ignored.
        3. With the unions' tacit approval, many jobs held by women during the war were reclassified as men's jobs.
        4. Many of the laid-off women were denied unemployment insurance.

    5. Articles and pamphlets exhorted women to return
to their "primary role."
        a. Women were needed to provide a haven for re-
turning men.
        b. Women were needed to nurture the nuclear
family.

For contrast, here is how a *topic outline* on the same subject
might cover the first main point.

Topic Outline

Topic: *The history of working women in the United States*

  I. Preindustrial
    A. Colonial women
      1. Soap
      2. Clothing
    B. Frontier women
      1. Indian attacks
      2. Farmwork

At first glance, the topic outline seems to be a coherent, tidy
arrangement of points. But can you form a sharp image of what
the speaker is saying about working women in the United States?
For example, the first main point of the speech is "Preindustrial."
Yet "preindustrial" is so broad that it could include the first hu-
mans to appear in America, thousands of years ago. In fact, this
point will probably deal with the work that women did between
the first European colonization and the advent of the Industrial
Revolution, but it ought to be phrased to leave no doubt.

This is only half the job, though. No matter how refined, a *subject* still needs a *predicate*. Although a speaker can delimit a subject
with precision by using sufficient modifiers and qualifiers, it still
may not be clear what she or he means to say *about* that subject.
Even if the speaker refines point I of the topic outline to describe a
specific group of women in a specific era (e.g., "Colonial life for
women, 1620–1783"), it is still not clear what idea is being developed: That there were many working women? That their lives
were hard? That they participated in all spheres of work? As these
questions are raised and answered, the speaker transforms a loose
phrase into a full sentence. If it turns into something like main
point I in the full-sentence outline, the speaker will probably decide that stories about Indian attacks, however interesting, do not
belong in this speech.

Full-sentence outlines are not extra work but rather are a
needed tool to demonstrate logical relationships in the speech.
Once you think these issues through, you can proceed to a more
spontaneous and fluid oral form of expression, confident that the
underlying structure of your speech is sound.

20c. Phrasing main points

It is not enough to have an outline with full sentences as main points. The sentences must logically encompass the main ideas of the speech. Suppose a speech outline has the following main point:

I. Many people are unaware of the origins of the paper they use every day.

If this is *really* the main idea being developed in this section of the speech, the subpoints should look something like this:

A. Ursula is utterly unaware of the origin of paper.
B. Clint is clueless about where paper comes from.
C. Ned never thought about paper for a minute.
D. and so on . . .

Obviously, the speaker does not intend to spend this whole portion of the speech exposing the ignorance of the general public. More likely, the person will talk about where paper comes from. And the main point should reflect this. The phrase "many people are unaware" does not have to be jettisoned altogether, but it can become merely a transitional lead-in, not an essential component of what is to follow.

Each main point should be cast as a *subthesis sentence* that answers two simple questions about the section of the speech being covered by the point: What's it about? and What about it?

Wrong:

Subthesis sentence:	I first would like to take a few minutes to discuss the origin of paper.
What's it about?	A speaker talking for a few minutes.
What about it?	The topic being talked about is the origin of paper.

Wrong:

Subthesis sentence:	Another interesting point is the origin of paper.
What's it about?	The origin of paper.
What about it?	It is interesting.

Right:

Subthesis sentence:	The origins of paper can be traced to the use of papyrus in ancient Egypt.
What's it about?	The origin of paper.
What about it?	It can be traced to papyrus in ancient Egypt.

Do not include in the outline transitional phrases that might be part of your oral presentation. They make for pseudosentences. Also, do not include your supporting evidence in the phrasing of a main point; keep statistics, testimony, and examples at the subordinate levels. Your main points should express the more general ideas of the speech; these are supported by evidence or data.

> **KEY POINT** **Phrasing for Impact** Once you have framed your main ideas so that they are logically and grammatically complete, take time to recast your points in language that highlights them for your audience when you speak. In this final phase of refining the outline, you move from one aspect of composition—organizing points logically—to another—sometimes called "writing for the ear."
>
> Listeners are not as quick to see the relationships between points when the perspective and the focus keep changing. Whenever possible, strive for grammatical consistency of structure, person, number, and voice. Ideas that are phrased in concise, colorful, parallel language are more likely to be remembered by both speaker and listeners. (See also **29**.)

CHAPTER 21

Building Sound Arguments

Reasoning is the process by which we come to understand something previously unknown, through analyzing and integrating those things we already know. Any remotely intelligent group of listeners will not be moved by hearing *what* you think; they want to know *why* you think it. Consequently, the reasoning that should be the foundation of every speech can also be seen as "the giving of *good* reasons."

To develop a logical line of thought and test its validity, you need to understand a little more about how reasoning functions to link key points of a speech together. You also need to become familiar with standard patterns of reasoning and with a few of the common fallacies. Only then can you decide how best to use reasoning in putting your speech together.

21a. Identify where reasoning is needed

In all persuasive speeches and some sections of evocative and informative speeches a challenging task confronts the speaker: You must develop lines of argument through reasoning to explain why you reached your conclusion. This *conclusion* can also be called a claim. Claims are any statements that you need to substantiate because they are not taken for granted by your listeners. Your thesis sentence is a claim, your main points are claims that support that claim, and even some of your subordinate points have to be reasoned through before they become acceptable.

1   The link from evidence to a claim

Suppose you have a conclusion or claim that you want your listeners to accept, and you have some evidence or data that you believe support that claim. Clearly, everyone who confronts the same facts and figures does not automatically come to the same conclusion that you do. What links the data to the claim, or *warrants* its acceptance, is the process of reasoning. For example, suppose two different people are confronted with the fact that more people go to the doctor in countries with national health care programs than in countries with privately funded health care. Person A concludes that this is an argument in support of adopting national health care in the United States. Person B concludes that it is an argument against national health care.

As Figure 21-1 shows, there is no connection between evidence and claim except through the reasoning link that you provide.

2   Familiar patterns

In the health care example, Person A is drawing on a pattern observed in the past—namely, that people who cannot afford a service they need will seek out that service when it becomes affordable. This is perfectly reasonable and logical; we all can think of plenty of commonsense examples.

Person B is also being logical and reasonable in linking the evidence of increased medical visits to the claim that national health care would be undesirable. This person is drawing on another observed pattern of human behavior—that people who see a resource as free and unlimited may use it inappropriately and wastefully. There is also plenty of support for this view.

The issue here is not what the facts *are*, but what the facts *mean*. For our purposes, the significance of these opposing views is to show that there are many sensible ways to interpret the same piece of evidence. A speaker who uses evidence to support a claim cannot simply present the evidence and hope it speaks for itself.

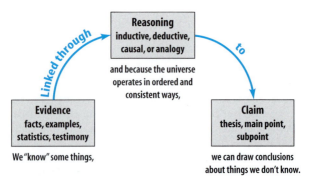

FIGURE 21-1   **Reasoning Links Evidence and Claim**

The speaker must explain the relevance of the evidence and justify the link to a particular claim.

21b. Inductive reasoning

You use an inductive pattern of reasoning when your argument consists of combining a series of observations that lead to a probable conclusion. Dozens of times a day, we draw inferences that go beyond what we observe directly. We could not function unless we trusted regularities in events, unless we believed that much of what has happened before will happen again: We step in front of oncoming traffic because we believe from previous experience that the cars will obey the traffic signals. Figure 21-2 depicts the process of inductive reasoning.

1 Adequate data

Inductive reasoning consists of collecting enough instances to establish a pattern. Remember the logical tests in **16a.1**. A typical line of inductive thought can be portrayed as follows:

Orchid 1 has no fragrance.

Orchid 2 has no fragrance.

....

Orchid *n* has no fragrance.

Therefore, it is probable that all orchids have no fragrance.

The extent to which you can generalize from such observations is linked to the extent of your sampling. If you smelled only a few orchids or only the orchids in one corner of one hothouse, you would be less able to make a general conclusion than if you had smelled orchids in different hothouses throughout the country.

Be cautious in drawing inferences from limited data. How many cases did you examine? Were they selected fairly? Are the contrary instances accounted for? (See **16b** and **21f**.)

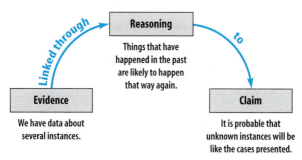

FIGURE 21-2 **Inductive Reasoning Draws Inferences from Observations**

2   Strong probability

The conclusions drawn from induction are always *probable* rather than *absolute*. An inductive conclusion can fall anywhere along this continuum:

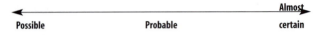

The degree of certainty depends on the methods used in making our observations and on the number of observations made. How strong must this **probability** be before you can consider the conclusion of an inductive argument to be valid? A 51 percent probability? or 75 percent? or 99 percent? It depends. There is no mathematical or logical answer to the question.

Would you leap off a 20-foot wall for $1,000? Many would say yes. It is *possible* that you could be killed, but it is probable that you would escape with no worse than a sprained ankle or broken leg. Would you jump from the roof of a three-story building for $1,000? Most people would say no. It is *possible* that you would be unharmed, but not very probable. In both cases, you set the acceptable level of probability by weighing potential risks against potential gains. In inductive reasoning, the acceptability of a probable conclusion always depends on cost–benefit analysis. (See **24a** and **24d.2**.)

21c.   Deductive reasoning

You use a deductive pattern of reasoning when your argument demonstrates how the relationships among established premises lead to a necessary conclusion. Unlike induction, in which the emphasis is on collecting observable data, **deduction** consists of manipulating verbal statements, or premises, according to formal rules. Deduction, then, does not involve bringing new data into play. Rather it is rearranging things you already know to discover something meaningful about how they fit together, as in scientific breakthroughs, gossip, and the English murder mystery. In our everyday lives, we have that "Aha!" experience when we suddenly discover the pattern underlying separate facts and realize their implication. Figure 21-3 depicts the process of deductive reasoning.

Because the correctness of deduction lies in whether it adheres to certain rules, experts in deductive reasoning learn complex symbolic formulas by which they test arguments. For the purpose of this book, we need only touch on the basic concept of deduction: If we know certain things about how two terms (concepts, events, characteristics) are related, we can discover other relationships that are logically entailed or implicated:

Term A is related in a known way to Term B.

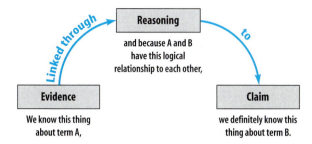

FIGURE 21-3   Deductive Reasoning Finds the Patterns in What You Already Know

We know certain things about B.

Therefore, we can draw certain conclusions about Term A.

To use deductive reasoning in a speech, you need to transpose this into a series of steps:

Step 1: Establish that a relationship exists between two terms (the **major premise**).

Step 2: Establish the actual condition/status of one of the terms (the **minor premise**).

Step 3: Show how a conclusion about the other term necessarily follows.

1   Begin with an absolute statement

Step 1 in deduction—establishing the *major premise*—takes many forms. It always involves an absolute relationship between two terms. Here are examples of four common relationships.

- One term may be an intrinsic characteristic of the other: All ducks have webbed feet.

- One term may be a category that includes the other: The Food Stamp program is part of the social welfare system.

- One term may be inevitably linked to the other: If corporate taxes are cut, then investment will increase.

- The two terms may be the opposite of or exclude each other: Either that fabric is natural or it is synthetic.

2   Derive a necessary conclusion

When you have established one of these basic major premises, you have set up a formula that will serve as the linking device at the top of your arc of reasoning. When you move to Step 2, you establish something about one of the two terms—in what logicians call the *minor premise*.

A piece of evidence like "Daffy is a duck" might mean many things, or nothing, in some lines of argument. But in the context

of the first major premise illustrated earlier, it is the minor premise, and the resulting, relevant implication is that Daffy has webbed
feet.

Feed in the data you have, follow the rules of deductive logic,
and certain conclusions are inevitably entailed:

> This blouse is made of a synthetic fiber, *so it is not made of a
> natural fiber.*

> Corporate taxes were not cut, *so investment must not have
> increased.*

The beauty of deduction lies in its certainty. If your listeners
accept the premises, they *must* accept the conclusion. The problem
with deduction is that, for its conclusion to be absolute, its premises must be absolute. The requirement of having an all-or-nothing
beginning premise is so restrictive that true, formal deductive reasoning is rather rare. (See **24b** and **24d.2** for more on using the
deductive pattern.)

21d.   Causal reasoning

You use **causal reasoning** to demonstrate that one event results
from another. It is the backbone of all speeches that deal with policy and problem solving. In most cases, if a person says, "I don't
favor your policy (or program, or solution)," what that person is
really saying is, "I disagree with you that *X* causes *Y*." This means
that you must carefully scrutinize the relationship between two
events to satisfy yourself that it is causal. Figure 21-4 depicts the
causal reasoning process. (See **24c** and **24d.2** for more on using
causal claims in your speech.)

1   Test the validity of the relationship

A causal relationship is stronger than mere correlation or coexis-
tence or coincidence. Two events may occur together or in

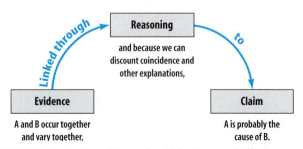

FIGURE 21-4   **Causal Reasoning Links Cause and Effect**

sequence without one causing the other. For instance, morning sickness and weight gain often occur together, but neither causes the other; they are the result of a third condition, pregnancy. To be sure that the relationship is a causal one, apply these tests.

Do the alleged cause and alleged effect occur together? To prove that a causal relationship exists, at least two formal comparisons must be made, as with a control group and an experimental group. Otherwise, mere coincidence or correlation cannot be ruled out. It is not enough to show that the alleged cause is present with the alleged effect; you must also show that, in the absence of the alleged cause, the alleged effect does not appear:

> If a rash appears every time you eat tomatoes, and never appears when you haven't eaten tomatoes, this is strong evidence that tomatoes cause the rash.

> To prove a causal relationship, you must show both concurrent presence and concurrent absence.

Do the alleged cause and the alleged effect vary together? Another test of causation is to determine whether the magnitude of change in the cause matches that in the effect:

> If one bite of tomato gives you a small rash, and consuming many tomatoes gives you a big rash, this is one more bit of evidence to suggest that tomatoes cause your rash.

2   Do not oversimplify

In the worlds of physics and chemistry, there are some clear, straightforward causal relationships:

> Adding silver nitrate solution ($AgNO_3$) to sodium chloride (NaCl) will cause silver chloride (AgCl) to precipitate.

This type of relationship between cause (C) and effect (E) could be represented as

$$C \to E$$

However, in the areas of politics, psychology, medicine, economics, and the like, more complex patterns usually exist.

Some effects have multiple causes

If smoking were the single cause of lung cancer, then every smoker would have lung cancer, and every victim of lung cancer would be a smoker. Obviously, this is not the case. Yet research does show smoking to be one causal factor contributing to lung cancer.

Some causes are also effects, and some effects are also causes in a long causal chain When we designate a cause of a certain event, we can look at the immediate cause or a more distant factor. A doctor might say that the cause of a particular death was a cerebral hemorrhage. What, though, was the cause of the hemorrhage? Perhaps a fractured skull, which was caused by going through a windshield, which was caused by the impact of a car with a tree, which was caused by excessive drinking, which was caused by worry over being unemployed, and so on:

$$C \rightarrow (E/C) \rightarrow (E/C) \rightarrow (E/C) \rightarrow E$$

It is sometimes important to point out the cyclical nature of certain causal chains. For example, ignorance about a particular group may lead to prejudice, which in turn results in lack of contact with that group, which perpetuates ignorance. This sort of analysis is far more interesting than positing a single cause of racial disharmony.

Some effects result from a one-time cause, and some from ongoing causes Effects that are labeled undesirable can be dealt with in two ways, either by treating the effect directly, or by blocking the cause that produces the effect. To decide which strategy makes the most sense in a given context, you need to determine whether the cause is one-time or ongoing, as in a neighborhood with bare dirt for landscaping, shattered windows, broken furniture in the yards, and residents in need of medical care—if you find that a tornado whipped through the area, you may push for emergency relief, but if you learn that the area is chronically depressed you may choose to advocate structural economic reform. A mistake in evaluation, whereby the effect of an ongoing cause is treated as if it resulted from a one-time cause, will lead to the eventual reappearance of that effect.

21e. Reasoning by analogy

You use **reasoning by analogy** to draw conclusions about unknown events, based on what you know about similar events. Figure 21-5 depicts the process of reasoning by analogy.

Reasoning by analogy is a natural and powerful way to make links. People intuitively look to similar examples when they want to understand something. Suppose the president's foreign policy advisors are trying to decide whether to intervene in a foreign country's internal struggles, or a judge is pondering whether to admit expert testimony on battered wife syndrome, or you are

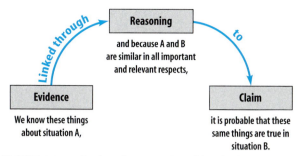

FIGURE 21-5 **Analogy Compares Two Things in the Same Category**

wondering whether to take the freeway or back streets to work. In all these cases, from the most cosmic policy issues to the most mundane everyday decisions, people ask themselves, "What is this like that I already know about?"

Although reasoning by analogy is so innate—or *because* it is—you need to choose your analogies carefully.

Be sure that when you reason by analogy the two cases are similar in all relevant and important respects. No cases are identical, and simply pointing out differences does not automatically discredit an analogy. If they differ in relevant and important ways, the differences are probably significant enough to reject the comparison. (See **24d.2** for more on using reasoning by analogy in your speech.)

KEY POINT **Use the Correct Type of Analogy** Do not confuse a literal analogy, which is a form of reasoning, with a figurative analogy, which is used only in a descriptive function. Reasoning by analogy *requires* a comparison of two members of the *same* category. Figurative analogy compares the members of different categories:

> Convincing my boss, Fred, to adopt a new procedure takes as much persistence, luck, and timing as starting my 1972 Fiat on a January morning.

> Going to war in Vietnam was like tap-dancing on quicksand.

These analogies may have stylistic impact, but they cannot support a conclusion because they compare a human relationship with a human–machine relationship, and a war with an athletic impossibility.

21f. Common reasoning fallacies

Some people commit reasoning **fallacies** knowingly, with dishonest intent. Others commit them due to a lack of practice or skill in doing their own thinking. The good public speaker wants to avoid the appearance of either. Once you have built your speech around sound, logical arguments, go through it to detect any constructions that even hint of sloppy thinking. One glaring fallacy in your speech will make all your other conclusions suspect. It is not necessary to learn all the fallacies—over one hundred have been categorized—but you should be familiar with the most common of them.

1   Attacking the person (ad hominem)

The **ad hominem fallacy** substitutes character assassination for solid refutation or persuasion:

> Anyone who advocates abortion on demand is a murderer anyway. It certainly wouldn't surprise me to find them taking kickbacks from the clinics that would receive government funds.

2   The slippery slope

The **slippery slope fallacy** consists of making the false assumption that taking the first step in any direction will inevitably lead to going dangerously far in that direction. The image is of someone sliding down a slope without being able to stop.

> If we let the government ban the sale and possession of assault rifles, banning all firearms is next.

> If we let the government abandon support of the arts, artistic freedom will die.

3   The semantic fallacy

The rich, connotative nature of words, which so enhances communication, can also abet fuzzy thinking. When midstream shifts of definition are obvious, they can be funny, as in "blackberries are red when they're green." More subtle and dangerous **semantic fallacies**, or shifts in definition, can occur in various critical parts of an argument:

> The free enterprise system, which we all cherish, could not exist without competition. This bill to protect small businesses threatens our whole economic structure. There can be no true competition when one group is given special protection.

In the underlying value premise, the word *competition* is used in the general sense of a market mechanism. In claiming that the bill endangers competition, the speaker uses the term in a much narrower sense, as in "a specific contest between individuals." The semantic fallacy is especially difficult to identify and frustrating to respond to because the syllogistic form of the argument appears to be valid. The problem of identification arises from the slight slippage of definition as a term is used with different meanings in different premises.

4   False dichotomy

A **false dichotomy** is reasoning based on an *either-or* statement when the two alternatives are not really mutually exclusive or when other alternatives exist. Many speeches set up artificial choices:

> Either we stand up to naked aggression, or we lose the confidence of our allies.

This basic premise so oversimplifies a complex issue that no conclusions can be drawn from it. Do not set up a deductive argument with a false dichotomy as its major premise.

5   Hasty generalization

A **hasty generalization** entails making a premature inductive "leap." (See **21b**.) It is glorified in the pomp surrounding Groundhog Day, when data from an isolated event are blindly accepted as gospel in relation to a much wider range of events.

This statement makes a faulty leap:

> The savings and loan scandal proved that every elected official has a price.

Time may not allow you, as a speaker, to include all the data that led you to some conclusion. It is especially important, then, to have the unused data at your fingertips so that you can respond to any accusations of hasty generalization that may arise.

6   Confusing sequence with cause (post hoc)

The Latin label for this fallacy (*post hoc, ergo propter hoc*) translates as "after the event, therefore because of the event." It is natural to try to understand the world around us by looking for cause–effect patterns wherever possible. So strong is this motivation that we are frequently guilty of imitating Chanticleer the rooster, who firmly believed that it was his predawn crowing that caused the sun to rise each day.

To avoid the **post hoc fallacy**, never assume causation based on time sequence alone. Test every causal hypothesis against the criteria in **21d**.

7   Setting up a straw figure

The **straw figure fallacy** consists of creating a weak argument, attributing it to the opposing side, and then proceeding to demolish it. The false implication is that all the opponents' arguments are as flimsy as the "straw figure" and could be dismissed with equal ease if time permitted.

Opponents of affirmative action policies are sometimes heard to raise these objections:

> We can't hire people from underrepresented groups without regard for their qualifications. It's not right to hire a mathematician to teach English just because she's a woman.

This claim is misleading because proponents of affirmative action do not advocate disregarding qualifications. The speaker has used an extreme example instead of taking on the complexity of the issue.

8   Extending an argument to absurd lengths (*reductio ad absurdum*)

The **fallacy of the absurd extreme** makes a potentially sound argument appear groundless by extending it to a point at which it can be ridiculed. Often, this extension goes beyond reasonable interpretation of the original point. In challenging current methods of criminal sentencing, a speaker might say:

> The average criminal is condemned to a bleak cell while top government wrongdoers lounge around in "country club" facilities. The logic is that the latter have already been punished by loss of reputation and professional standing. This seems to say that punishments should be harsher on those who have the least to lose. By this reasoning, the senator who commits murder might get off with a citation and public embarrassment, while an unemployed ghetto dweller who shoplifts should be put on bread on water, with regular sessions of torture.

Pointing out these outrageous inequities does not constitute a legitimate attack on the basic concept that the impact of punishment on an offender can be one valid criterion for decisions about sentencing. This kind of fallacy relies on the humor of the cock-eyed image it creates. Disarmed by a ludicrous example, listeners lose sight of the real issue.

9   Circular reasoning

Circular reasoning assumes as one of its premises the very conclusion it sets out to establish. Often, circular reasoning comes out of definitional word games:

- No sane person would consider suicide, because it's insane to want to take your own life.
- We need a court of equity to resolve labor-management disputes, because collective bargaining results in settlements that aren't equitable. What do I mean by an equitable settlement? I mean the kind of settlement that is arrived at by a court of equity.

6 Getting Your Ideas Across

CHAPTER 22

Informative Strategies

A large part of speaking is explanation—stating an idea and then re-stating it in a way that develops the basic notion. Unfortunately, some explanations confuse rather than clarify when the speaker has lost sight of which details are the essential ones. It is a real challenge to select the most significant details and present them in the clearest order. How can you most economically create the mental picture that will aid your listeners' understanding?

22a. Help your listeners grasp information

Base your speech structure and content on an understanding of how people acquire, process, and retain information.

1   Avoid information overload

When you speak on a topic that you know a great deal about, there is a tendency to want to bring your audience up to your level immediately. When you give out too much information in too short a time, the result is information overload. The informative speaker has to manage a large mass of information and deliver it at the right pace and in the right-sized chunks so it can be useful and meaningful for listeners. Bear in mind the information-processing principle known as *seven, plus or minus two*. Research suggests that this is how many points the average person can comprehend at one time, so select just a handful of points to develop.

2   Use an organizing framework

Have you ever tried to put together a jigsaw puzzle without look-ing at the picture on the box? What you have is a jumble of unre-lated pieces. Once you see the big picture, you have some idea of how things are supposed to fit together. Do not plunge directly into the specifics of the topic before giving your audience some sense of the whole.

3   Move from the simple to the complex

Even at the risk of temporary oversimplification, it is advisable first to lay out the most basic concepts and later to introduce qualifiers, exceptions, and interesting tangents. Think of each listener as the newcomer to town who first wants to learn the basic route from home to work, and only after mastering that wants to learn about shortcuts and scenic detours.

4   Move from the familiar to the unfamiliar

Any group can learn about any subject if you start where members are and move along at the proper rate. Teachers will attest that learning proceeds best when they are able to adjust the focus of their instruction to a point just beyond the current knowledge level of the group. If the instruction duplicates what the group already knows, the material will not be challenging. If the focus is two or three levels beyond them, group members will get discouraged.

22b. Common techniques of clear explanation

If you employ the following, you substantially ease your listeners' path to comprehension.

1   Organizers

Provide your listeners with cues as to how they should structure the information.

Signposts One organizer is the signpost. Signposts, like their physical counterparts, point the way you are going and can serve as a reminder of where you've been:

> First, I'll show you how to make a simple white sauce, and then move on to three more elaborate sauces that start with the basic recipe.

> So, from this short description of one novel and three of her poems, you can see once again the two themes that permeate Sylvia Plath's work.

Enumeration Numbering is an obvious organizational cue:

> The many steps in building an apartment complex can be grouped into these three phases:
>
> > One: Finding attractive sites with the proper zoning.
> > Two: Negotiating for the purchase of a piece of property.
> > Three: Contracting with architects and builders.

Acronyms An acronym is a word that is formed from the first letters of a series of words and that can be pronounced like a word. For instance, radar is an acronym formed from RAdio Detecting And Ranging. Other examples are SETI, for Search for Extra Terrestrial Intelligence, and GIGO, for Garbage In, Garbage Out.

Slogans, catchwords, and memorable phrases Like acronyms, these types of cues give your listeners a framework for remembering your points:

> So, look at those files in your drawer that you haven't used in a year, and assess their real value. Keep in mind Peg Bracken's advice about leftover food: "When in doubt, throw it out."

Try to do something decisive with each piece of mail as you open it. Apply the "Four D's": Drop the item, Delay the item, Delegate the item, or Do the item.

2   Emphasis cues

Underline and highlight key points with phrases like "this is very important," "if you don't remember anything else," and "here's what it all comes down to."

You can also emphasize points by vocal or physical cues. When you want an idea to stand out, speak more loudly, or occasionally more softly. Pause before and after the big idea. Step forward. Let your facial expression forecast the seriousness of a point.

3   Examples

When an audience is feeling confused, nothing reassures them like a concrete example. You might begin with a simple, even whimsical, example:

> A "win–win" negotiation has occurred when both parties achieve their important goals without perceiving that they have had to make a major sacrifice. Phil and Dave are roommates, and they both think the other needs to do more around the apartment. After talking about it, they agree that Dave will do all the cooking and Phil will do all the cleaning. Each thinks he got off easy.

Next, you could move to a more complex and realistic example:

> Or suppose that you have a used car for sale and your neighbor wants to buy it but does not have all the cash now. You offer to carry an interest-free note due in six months if your neighbor will take care of your pets and plants for three weeks while you are on vacation.

Finally, you might give an example that is sophisticated, subtle, and complex enough for your audience to apply it to situations they may actually encounter:

> Now, let's see how these principles apply to a typical real estate negotiation. On this chart you will see the seller's and buyer's prioritized needs and bargaining chips.

4   Analogies

Compare the known to the unknown. For instance, you might use this simple analogy to explain a complex process:

> A nuclear power plant is like a steam locomotive. The fireman shovels coal into the furnace, where the heat it gives off turns the water in the boiler into steam. The steam travels through

pipes to pistons, where the energy is converted and carried by driving rods to the wheels, pulling long trains of cars down the rails. Substitute a nuclear pile for the coal, a turbine for the pistons, and an electrical generator for the drive wheels, and you have a nuclear power plant.

To reinforce points and reach more listeners, draw analogies from many areas: sports, movies, nature, history, other cultures, and so on.

5   Multiple channels

Your message will be clearer if you send it through several channels. As you describe a process with words, also use your hands, a visual aid, a chart, or a recording. Appeal to as many senses as possible to reinforce the message. A good rule to follow is this: If a point is very important or very difficult, always use at least one other channel besides the spoken word to get it across.

6   Repetition

People learn and remember what they hear repeatedly. If a principle is important, say it over again, in the same words or different words. Repeat it. Paraphrase it. Reinforce it. Refer back to it. Then mention it again.

CHAPTER 23

Persuasive Strategies

When you try to change others' attitudes or behavior, you need to base your persuasive effort on some guiding principles. This requires an understanding of how and why people change their minds.

23a.   Your goals

A strong grasp of purpose is especially important in **persuasive speaking**. When you try to change people, and not simply educate or inspire them, you are more likely to encounter resistance. It helps to know exactly what your goals are—and what they are not. (See **11c**.) You want to aim for a realistic target.

Some authorities distinguish between persuasive speeches that seek to change actual behavior and those that merely try to influence beliefs and attitudes. Although an attitude is a predisposition to respond in a particular way, holding a certain attitude does not guarantee certain behaviors associated with the attitude. People may say they believe in recycling but never drum up the energy to separate their trash. Generally, if you want action, you should set your goals in terms of behavior and tell the audience what to *do* (or *not do*), not what to *think*. (See **11d.3** for different kinds of propositions in persuasive speeches.)

23b. Audience types

Consider your audience's attitude both toward your topic and toward you. (See **12c.**) The following continuum classifies audiences according to their predisposition toward your topic:

Unfavorable			**Neutral**	**Favorable**		
Strongly	Moderately	Slightly	Neither agree	Slightly	Moderately	Strongly
disagree	disagree	disagree	nor disagree	agree	agree	agree

Here are some suggestions on how to deal with favorable, neutral, or unfavorable audiences.

1   Favorable audience

A speaker facing a favorable audience rarely needs to establish credibility. Your listeners, perceiving your position as identical to theirs, approve of you already. Furthermore, a favorable audience will not raise internal counterarguments for you to deflect or defuse. But if you accept the challenge of speaking to a favorable audience, you can solidify or strengthen their attitudes, or you can cause them to move from theoretical agreement to positive action.

Use emotional appeals to intensify support There is a difference between intellectually agreeing with a position and making a commitment to it. Even once committed, the difference between commitment and action is usually a function of emotional arousal. Out of the vast number of positions you might agree with, there is a much shorter list of issues that you really care about. These issues appeal to your most basic needs, touch on your core values, or have a personal effect on your life.

To get your speech topic on your listeners' short list, appeal to basic values (such as patriotism, humanitarianism, and progress), to basic needs (such as survival, security, and status), and to basic emotions (such as fear, pity, and love).

A major task in speaking to a favorable audience is the creation of personal involvement. First, be very specific about how their lives are affected, and then show them that their actions can make a difference:

> Your 10-dollar check can feed a Sudanese refugee family for a week.

If you can take that extra second to switch off the lights as you leave the room, you can save yourself 50 dollars a year.

Get your audience to make a public commitment Invite your listeners to offer suggestions, sign a petition, raise their hands to volunteer, lend their names to a letterhead, or talk to others. People who have made a public commitment—oral, or written, or physical—are less likely to change their minds.

Provide opportunities for action Make it easy for listeners to take action by offering several specific choices. For example, with people who have shown up at a rally for a candidate, do not say, "Stop by campaign headquarters sometime." Instead, say, "I'd like everyone here either to walk a precinct or to spend an evening making phone calls. Sign-up sheets are being passed around now." With a favorable audience, do not settle for urging members to do "something." Tell them what you want them to do, and make the execution easy and attractive: If you want them to write letters, give them addresses; if you want them to reduce their sodium intake, give them low-sodium recipes.

Prepare your audience to carry your message to others Audience members can become persuaders in their own right. Each of them may later discuss your topic with coworkers, neighbors, or friends who are neutral or hostile toward it. Give your listeners ammunition for these interactions, and make that material memorable and quotable. Provide your audience with ready answers to refute standard counterarguments. (See **23c.3**.) Here's an example:

> You may meet people who tell you that the administration's economic policy is designed to help the average worker. Just ask those people why the greatest tax relief goes to the rich. Have them explain to you why a person who earns $300,000 a year will have a 50 percent reduction in taxes, but a person making $30,000 a year will see a reduction of only 6 percent. They may say, "Ah, but we are creating new jobs." Ask them this . . .

This also serves to inoculate your listeners against the persuasiveness of those counterarguments.

2   Neutral audience

Audience members can be neutral toward your position because they are *uninterested,* they are *uninformed,* or they are genuinely *undecided.*

For an uninterested audience stress attention factors With this sort of audience, draw on all the attention techniques described in chapter **30** with special emphasis on concrete illustrations of the impact of your subject on their lives. Be sure the facts and statistics you use are relevant to your listeners' experience. Sprinkle your speech with humor and human interest. Make a special effort to have a lively and animated delivery and style to stimulate them.

For an uninformed audience, stress clarification Before you can expect people to agree with you, they must have some comprehension of the issue. The main concern is clarity: Use explanation, definitions, examples, and restatement. (See **16a**.) Visual aids can be helpful. Keep your language simple and your organization straightforward.

A direct persuasive appeal should be saved until the very end of the speech.

For an undecided audience, establish credibility Present new arguments that blend logical and emotional appeals to establish your credibility. The undecided neutral audience is both interested in and informed about your topic but finds the arguments for each side equally compelling.

Let them know that you understand their ambivalence. Grant the complexity of the issue, and admit that there is truth on both sides. As you present the arguments for your side, stress any recent evidence or new interpretations that might justify a decision. Be sure that you acknowledge and respond respectfully and thoroughly to the main arguments against your position. In short, a well-documented, logical presentation works best for the undecided neutral audience. Appeals to emotions, needs, and values are effective only if used sparingly and clearly interwoven with the logical argument of the speech.

3   Unfavorable audience

An unfavorable audience is by no means a belligerent one—*unfavorable* is defined to encompass anything on the disagree side of neutral, starting with "slightly disagree." However, the more intensely the audience disagrees with you, the more members will be predisposed to reject both you and your message. Any idiosyncrasies of appearance and style of delivery will allow them to dismiss you as being on the fringe.

Set realistic goals Do not try to do too much with an unfavorable audience. Attitudes change slowly. If most of your audience strongly disagrees, do not expect your 10-minute speech to change them to strong agreement. Even if it means modifying your thesis statement, set a goal that you have a reasonable chance of achieving, such as easing those who strongly disagree over to moderately disagree, or those who moderately disagree over to neutral. Do not make a call for action when action is highly unlikely.

Stress common ground However great the difference between you and your audience on any particular issue, there are bound to be places where your opinions and experiences overlap. When you think about the unfavorable audience you face, ask yourself what goals and values you share. Even the intensity of a disagreement between you and your audience over, say, school busing reveals a common concern for children's education.

Use sound logic and extensive evidence The unfavorable audience is skeptical of your position and will reject most emotional appeals as manipulative. Your only chance to persuade these listeners is to build an iron-clad case supported by impeccable, unbiased evidence. With this audience, you must clearly indicate every step of your reasoning. Discuss and defend even those assumptions that seem obvious to you. Spell out the logical links that hold your argument together. Do not overstate your points; be careful not to claim more than the data allow. Say, "These examples suggest . . . ," rather than "These examples prove . . ."; say, "Smoking is one contributing cause of cancer," rather than "Smoking causes cancer."

Use factual and statistical evidence, and always cite your sources completely. (See **16**.) If you mention the results of a survey, for example, tell when, where, and how it was conducted and where it was presented or published. Confront directly the arguments that are foremost in your listeners' minds. Be willing to concede minor points that do not damage your basic case. State the remaining counterarguments fairly and answer them forcefully, but never stoop to ridicule.

Establish a credible image The careful establishment of good character, good sense, and goodwill is essential in a speech to an unfavorable audience. (See **26c**.) Plan every detail of your speech content and delivery to project an image of a calm, reasonable, fair, well-informed, and congenial person. The judicious use of humor can bolster this image while releasing tension and putting the issue in perspective. Direct the humor at yourself, your position, a common enemy, or the ironic aspects of the confrontation. Never direct it at your listeners and their beliefs.

Although you do not want to seem combative, you should remain firm in your position. It is fine to stress common ground and grant minor points, but do not waffle or be overly conciliatory.

23c. Organizational patterns

The speech organization patterns discussed in chapter **19**—topical, spatial, and chronological—grow out of analysis of the speech content. Other patterns can form from retracing the reasoning that led you to your conclusion—inductively, deductively, causally, or analogically. (See **21**.) Yet another way of ordering points is to consider how your speech unfolds for your listeners. So, if none of the familiar formats seems strategically adequate, here are some alternative arrangements.

1   The motivated sequence

Developed by Alan Monroe several decades ago, the **motivated sequence** is one of the most widely used organizers for persuasive speeches.[1] This psychologically based format echoes and anticipates the mental stages through which your listeners progress as they hear your speech.

Attention:	The speaker must first motivate the audience to listen to the speech.
Need:	Listeners must become aware of a compelling, personalized problem.
Satisfaction:	The course of action advocated must be shown to alleviate the problem.
Visualization:	Psychologically, it is important that the audience have a vivid picture of the benefits of agreeing with the speaker or the evils of alternatives.
Action:	The speech should end with an overt call for the listeners to act.

Here is an example of a speech that follows the motivated sequence:

Thesis Statement: *We need a light rail system in our county to reduce excessive commuter traffic congestion.*

Attention

Introduction: I was on my way to work, having left home earlier than usual so I could be there in plenty of time for my first important presentation. I heard screeching brakes. It turned out to be only a fender-bender a quarter-mile ahead of me. Nevertheless, I sat in my car, and sat, and sat, while my mood progressed from irritation to outrage to despair. I arrived at work an hour and a half late, just as the meeting was breaking up.

Need

    I. Excessive reliance on automobile transportation to the county's major employment areas is causing severe problems.
       A. Major traffic jams
       B. Pollution
       C. Stress to commuters

[1] Raymie E. McKerrow, Bruce E. Gronbeck, Douglas Ehninger, and Alan H. Monroe, *Principles and Types of Speech Communication*, 14th ed. (Needham Heights, MA: Allyn & Bacon, 2000).

Satisfaction

> II. A light rail system should be constructed to alleviate these problems.
>   A. (Definition of light rail)
>   B. (Proposed route)
>   C. (Proposed funding)

Visualization

> III. The new system would be a vast improvement.
>   A. Scenario with the light rail system: free parking, time to relax, drink coffee, read
>   B. Scenario without the light rail system: increased traffic, gridlock, daily stress

Action

Conclusion: Support the county initiative for a light rail system. Urge your friends to vote for it. Write to members of the county board of supervisors on this issue. Ask your employer to commit to providing free shuttle service from the proposed light rail station to your place of business.

This organization is rather similar to a standard problem–solution speech, but the presence of the visualization step makes all the difference. Instead of merely providing a logical need satisfaction in Main Point 2, this speaker has added another psychologically powerful step in Main Point 3. The two narratives should be developed in detail to drive home the case for the listeners.

It is essential that the attention step be engaging and that the action step be concrete.

2   Strongest points first or last

Ideally, all of the arguments and support for your thesis statement should be strong. In reality, however, you will find that you must use materials of varying strength. These should not be arranged randomly. People will remember best what you say first (the **primacy** principle) and what you say last (the **recency** principle). In light of this, arranging your arguments either from weakest to strongest (climax) or from strongest to weakest (anticlimax) will be more effective than placing your best points in the middle (pyramidal).

The research on which one is stronger—primacy or recency—is far from conclusive. Our best advice regarding what to say first and last is that you consider the importance of your topic to your listeners, their attitude toward it, and your credibility.

3   Dealing with opposing arguments

Generally, it is a good idea to address counterarguments in addition to presenting your own viewpoints. On widely debated topics, these ideas will already be on listeners' minds, and they expect a response. Even on less familiar subjects on which you may have the first word, you probably won't have the last. At the end of a straightforward "pro" speech, your audience may agree with you. But if listeners later become aware of powerful opposing arguments, they may discredit your entire position.

Speakers often inoculate their audiences by presenting a few counterarguments and answering them. Then, when these points are brought up later, the listeners will say, "Oh, yes, I was warned about this." Inoculation has created "antibodies" to resist the opposing position. In most cases, answer counterarguments after developing your own position. The only exception is when you know audience members are so preoccupied with an opposing position that they may not listen to you. In that case, respond to the point immediately.

CHAPTER 24

Reasoning

In laying out your speech, you make sure that your evidence is sound (see **16**). Next, you need to recast the arguments into a form that fits speaking to an audience. For example, instead of stating a conclusion or claim after the evidence, when speaking to an audience, stating that claim may well be the first thing you want to do. Then you develop that thesis or main point by retracing your reasoning in an audience-friendly manner.

24a.   The cost–reward analysis of an inductive argument

A speaker who is using induction (see **21b**) must convince the audience that the conclusion is probable enough to warrant their acceptance. The issue is one of "enoughness." Are your examples sufficient in both quantity and quality? The so-called inductive leap is an apt image. You lead the listeners to a certain point with your data and then ask them to jump across an imaginary chasm to the conclusion you see.

Suppose you know of a new drug rehabilitation program that has been found to be quite effective in pilot studies in three different communities. Because there are only three cases in your sample, you cannot state your conclusion at a high level of probability, but imagine that both proponents and skeptics of the program agreed that there was about a 75 percent chance of its success. A member of your audience might well ask, "Why should we spend $650,000 for just a three-out-of-four chance we might help a bunch of junkies?" You cannot change the odds, but you can influence your audience's assessment of the costs and rewards. Tell them how the program, if it works, will benefit the whole community: It will decrease crime, put former addicts back into the workforce, and lower the temptations for adolescent drug use. Also minimize the costs: "I know $650,000 sounds like a lot, but it's only 85¢ per citizen." When the listeners reassess the costs and rewards, and see them as you do, the 75 percent odds may look more attractive.

Consider another example.

Suppose the conclusion that nuclear power plants are safe could be granted a 95 percent level of probability. Even so, you might not feel the evidence is sufficient to make the inductive leap. In this case, you would minimize the rewards—most of the energy we would get can be obtained through other sources—and maximize the risks by describing just how awful a nuclear accident would be. Your argument would be: "I'm not willing to subject my family to a 5-out-of-100 chance of this sort of destruction just to have a few extra electronic luxuries."

In the case of the drug program, a low probability met the test of enoughness for the speaker. In the case of the nuclear power plant, even 95 percent was not enough. The difference lies in the perception of risk and reward. No level of enoughness is too high or too low—no inductive argument is innately logical or illogical. The validity is negotiated between you and your audience.

24b. The premises of a deductive argument

One of the advantages of structuring ideas deductively (see **21c**) is that you must state the relationships among the concepts. When you clearly state the major premise on which your argument rests, you call to your listeners' minds certain values and assumptions. The audience can then apply these concepts when you move on to specific cases in developing your minor premise.

In the following logical arguments, notice how the major premise serves in each case to direct the listeners' awareness to a statement that the speaker might otherwise have left implicit.

Major premise: Anyone who has been elected to high office has had to make a number of political compromises along the way.

Candidate J has served as governor and U.S. senator.

Therefore, Candidate J has made a number of political compromises.

Major premise: It has always been the goal of our social welfare system to help recipients become self-sufficient.

> Certain current programs encourage dependency and discourage initiative.
>
> Therefore, these programs should be changed.

Sometimes, speakers have so internalized a point of view that they leave out parts of their argument. On controversial topics with diverse audiences, neglecting to lay out every part of the argument is dangerous. In excellent speeches, speakers take the time to articulate and justify their premises.

24c.   Causal claims

Pure, simple causal arguments (see **21d**) are rare. More common are lines of reasoning that lead to probable causal claims, like the following:

> X was present in these cases, and Y occurred.
>
> X was absent in these cases, and Y did not occur.
>
> Changes in the amount of X have often led to corresponding changes in the amount of Y.
>
> *Claim:* Therefore, it is probable that X causes Y.

Probable to what degree? To the degree that your examples are sufficient and representative, and that conflicting examples are minimized or explained.

With this sort of causal argument, follow the advice in **16b**. Do not overstate your claim. Say, "This is a major cause," and not "This is *the* cause." Say, "There is strong evidence of a causal link between . . ." and so on.

24d.   Showing links between evidence and claims

It is not enough to present only a cluster of evidence or a cluster of reasons for a claim. The reasoning process must be made transparent through organization and word choice so that listeners can then decide if it's well conceived and executed.

1   Organization of points

Controversial claims can be found at all levels of a speech; the thesis statement, main points, and subpoints all require substantiation. There is no one correct way to display your lines of reasoning in a speech outline, but it is very important that you phrase points to show the connections. Do not simply group "reasons," as in the first example. Show reasoning, as in the second example.

Wrong:

> I. Having a longer school day does not improve learning.
>   A. They tried it at Riverdale High School, and test scores were unchanged.

    B. They tried it at Glenbrook High School, and test scores actually went down.

    C. At Creekside High School, test scores have gone up even though their school day has not been lengthened.

    D. Braeburn High School shortened their school day, and test scores did not change.

Better:

  I. Having a longer school day does not improve learning.

    A. In cases in which the school day was lengthened, test scores did not improve.

      1. Unchanged at Riverdale High

      2. Went down at Glenbrook

    B. In cases in which the school day was not lengthened, test scores were not lower.

      1. Improved at Creekside

      2. No change with shorter day at Braeburn

Summary transitional statement: If there were a causal relationship between the length of the school day and learning as measured by test scores, we would logically expect that scores would be higher where the school day is longer and lower where the school day is shorter. I have just demonstrated that this is not the case. Sometimes, the opposite is true. So you can see why I conclude that having a longer school day does not improve learning.

In order for your audience to accept your reasoning, you must differentiate between points and support for the points. Do not use sources in place of reasoning. In the first example that follows, a speaker attempts to support a causal claim by saying that experts have agreed with the claim. But the listeners do not know *why* these people came to the conclusion they did. In the second example, the reasoning behind the causal claim is explained, with experts used to back up specific points.

Wrong:

  I. The use of sexist language perpetuates discrimination against women.

    A. Dr. Deborah Stone says sexist language causes problems.

    B. Professor Lydia Sorenson says sexist language is the root of many social problems.

    C. Linguist Chris Nupriya states that language affects behavior.

Better:

  I. The use of sexist language perpetuates discrimination against women.

    A. Language shapes social perception.

   B. Speech that leaves women out can lead to people over-
looking them.
     (Cite experts and studies.)
   C. If people subconsciously exclude women from certain
roles, they discriminate against women.
     (Cite experts and studies.)

2   Word choice

In addition to setting up a speech structure that highlights your
reasoning, you should use words, phrases, and transitional sentences that spell out what your evidence means and how the parts
of your argument are linked. Never merely jump from one point
to the next. Use phrases that are specific cues to the kind of reasoning you are using. (See **21b, c, d,** and **e.**)

For inductive reasoning
Show the strength of your examples:

> One case that supports my claim is . . .

> Across many levels of income and many parts of the country,
> the same pattern holds true. For example . . .

Acknowledge the probable nature of your data by using qualifiers:

> Many/Most . . .

> Virtually every study in the literature . . .

> From these cases, I feel quite confident in concluding . . .

Demonstrate costs and rewards:

> I'm willing to bet my tax dollars that this program will work . . .

> This is a gamble we can't afford to take . . .

> The risks, though they do exist, seem minimal compared to
> the rewards . . .

For deductive reasoning
State your premises:

> Underlying my position is one of the fundamental tenets of
> our constitutional form of government.

> The argument for my claim rests on one basic assumption that
> I hope you will agree with. It is . . .

> Either . . . or . . .

> If . . . then . . .

Spell out your reasoning:

> Because I've shown you X and Y, . . .

> Therefore . . .

From this it follows that . . .

It seems logical to conclude that . . .

For causal reasoning

Show how the cause and effect are related in a predictable way:

> In state after state where spending on education went up, crime went down.

> This is no coincidence. When X occurs, then Y occurs.

Qualify your causal claims if necessary:

> There may be many causes, but the one I have identified is a major causal factor.

> It is highly probable that smoking causes these health problems.

Explain the mechanism of the cause:

> The reason all these experts have concluded that X causes Y is that . . .

> I've shown you all these cases in which being abused as a child seems to lead to being an abusive parent. Let me explain how that happens.

For reasoning by analogy

Stress the points of similarity:

> In Ecuador, as in neighboring Colombia and Peru, . . .

> For 8 of the 10 other universities in our conference, adding women's sports to the athletic program has led to more alumni support.

> In a parallel case, . . .

Spell out the link:

> If it worked in New Jersey and Idaho and Georgia, it will work in the rest of the country.

> Let's not wait too long on planning for earthquake safety. We put off dealing with flood control, and the results have been tragic.

CHAPTER 25

Motivational Appeals

Understanding the humanity of your audience means reaching them as total persons—packaging your logical case so that it touches the listeners' feelings, needs, and values.

25a. The emotional impact you want

Everything you say has the potential to trigger some sort of emotional response in your audience. You can strengthen your speech by selecting main points, supporting material, and language that can engage your listeners' feelings. Positive emotions—hope, joy, pride, love—are surefire motivators. Negative emotions like fear, envy, disgust, and contempt can also motivate; witness the popularity of roller coasters and horror films. The motivational effects of negative emotions are less predictable, however, and can sometimes boomerang. Moderate levels of fear appeal can enhance persuasion, but higher levels may work against the desired effect.

25b. The needs of your listeners

The best-known way of classifying human needs is the hierarchy devised by Abraham Maslow[1] shown in Figure 25-1. In this hierarchy, the lower-level needs have to be met or satisfied before an individual can become concerned with the needs on the next-higher level. For instance, on the topic of physical fitness, you could appeal to your audience at any of the following levels:

- The effect of exercise in reducing risk of cardiovascular disease appeals to the *survival* need.
- *Security* might be drawn in by mentioning how physically fit people are more likely to be able to resist or evade attackers.
- The need for *belonging* can be linked to becoming trim and attractive, as well as to making friends through physical activity.
- *Esteem* needs can be tied into the current popularity of fitness and the social desirability of an active image.
- Fitness can be related to the need for *self-actualization*—the highs of exercise, and the mental and physical challenge of reaching one's potential.

The significance of **Maslow's hierarchy of needs** is apparent. You must analyze your audience well enough to determine which need is most salient. Listeners whose jobs are in danger and who are struggling to feed their families want to know which local economic program will create jobs. Being absorbed with their security needs, they are not likely to respond at the self-actualization level. It is counterproductive to aim your emotional appeals too high, and unethical to aim them too low.

25c. The values of your listeners

We hold a certain **value** if we believe that a particular thing is either good or bad, in the broadest sense of those terms. Specifically,

[1]Abraham Maslow, *Motivation and Personality,* 2nd ed. (New York: Harper & Row, 1970), 35–58.

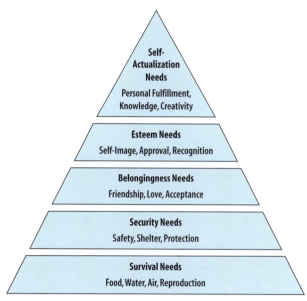

FIGURE 25-1 **Maslow's Hierarchy of Needs**

we *evaluate* concepts, people, objects, events, or ideas every day as we label them just or unjust, wise or foolish, beautiful or ugly, and so on.

1 General values

Although values are individually chosen, the choice is not often a totally conscious and rational one. Culture has a strong influence, shaping values through families, schools, media, and peers. Moreover, values are rarely formed in isolation; rather, they are organized and structured into related clusters. By knowing the culture of your listeners, the influences on them, and perhaps

---

KEY POINT **Contemporary American Values**[2]

- A comfortable life
- An exciting life
- A sense of accomplishment
- A world at peace
- A world of beauty
- Equality
- Family security
- Freedom
- Happiness

- Inner harmony
- Mature love
- National security
- Pleasure
- Salvation
- Self-respect
- Social recognition
- True friendship
- Wisdom

[2] Sandra J. Ball-Rokeach and Joel W. Grube, *The Great American Values Test: Influencing Behavior and Belief Through Television* (New York: Free Press, 1984), 90.

some of the other values they hold, you can make an educated guess as to how much particular values might shape their attitude toward your speech topic.

2 Core values

Obviously, not all members of a culture give equal importance to the common values. Any particular issue can touch on many values, on both the pro side and the con. Examples of this value conflict become apparent around election time. Suppose there is a proposed bond issue to build a fine arts complex. A person may be drawn toward approving the bond as a result of holding the values of a world of beauty and a sense of accomplishment. But this person may also have reservations about taking on a greater tax burden because of a belief in the values of a comfortable, prosperous life and family security. The resolution of this conflict depends on how this person has prioritized these values.

Values that are central to identity are called **core values**. Other values, though important, are not as central. Understanding this, you should try to make reasonable inferences about your listeners' core values and stress them in your speech.

3 Sense of community

Understandably, when people first encounter an issue, they tend to ask, "How does this affect me and my immediate circle, now and in the near future?" One of the most powerful ways that public speakers can use motivational appeals is to draw people outward and refocus their awareness on larger frames of reference.

This broader awareness is there and available to be tapped. Accounts of starving polar bears stranded on melting ice in the Arctic gave people new understanding of global warming. Pictures of fish disfigured by discarded pop-top rings contributed to beverage companies' changing the design for opening soda and beer cans. As a speaker, you can create powerful word pictures to remind listeners of their interdependence with other people and creatures, and to transport them into the past and the future. You can use your words to show people the historical and cultural meanings of endangered animals and places. You can take listeners into the future and reveal the effects of our environmental policies or our national debt on unborn generations. Link your speech topic to your audience's values in ways that tie into the broadest sense of community and situate the present in relation to the past and the future.

25d. Inappropriate use of motivational appeals

A speech with too much emphasis on feelings can embarrass and offend the audience. If listeners perceive that the speaker is playing on their emotions to the exclusion of sense and logic, they can become infuriated. It is always a mistake to underestimate the intelligence of an audience. Aside from the issue of effectiveness (advertisers and politicians show us that many times these appeals can be effective), there is the question of ethics. (See **3**.)

CHAPTER 26

Credibility

Your content and delivery determine, to a great extent, whether your listeners believe what you say. However, your audience is also influenced by who you are—or, more accurately, who they think you are. Your **credibility** is that combination of perceived qualities that makes listeners predisposed to believe you.

For centuries, scholars have been fascinated by credibility—from classical discussions of *ethos* to contemporary investigations of concepts like *image, personality,* and *charisma*. Aristotle observed that audiences are most inclined to believe a person they see as having good sense, goodwill, and good character. Modern social scientists have tried to isolate the characteristics that distinguish the most credible speakers from others. Their lists include competence, dynamism, intention, personality, intelligence, authoritativeness, extroversion, trustworthiness, composure, and sociability. You can enhance your credibility, and thus the chances of meeting your speech objective, by projecting these qualities. You can build your image prior to the speech, and you can take steps to improve your credibility as you are speaking.

26a. Assess your speaking image

Before you can work on improving your credibility, you need to see where you stand now. Is your overall credibility high or low? Do people agree with you because of, or in spite of, your personality?

CHECKLIST

Your Speaking Image
1. Are you perceived as competent?
2. Are you perceived as concerned about your audience's welfare?
3. Are you perceived as trustworthy?
4. Are you perceived as dynamic?

Which components of credibility are strongest for you? Which need to be developed? If possible, have some friends or acquaintances help you with this appraisal. It is very hard to see ourselves as others see us.

26b. Build your credibility before the speech

Provide the contact person with information about your qualifications Do not be overly modest when asked for information for advance publicity. Send a résumé that lists your background and achievements. Include clippings, testimonials about your speaking, a list of your books and articles, and a photograph if appropriate. If there are aspects of your background you would like to have stressed for a particular speech, be sure to say so.

Manage your image during all contact with the group In your class, service organization, or work group, you know that you have a certain image, based on previous interactions. But with an unfamiliar audience, virtually all of your interactions with them will affect your credibility. Your friendliness, professionalism, and confidence in negotiating arrangements and even in making small talk prior to the speech will be very influential.

26c. Bolster your credibility during your speech

As you prepare your speech, think about ways to communicate your competence, concern, trustworthiness, and dynamism. The opening minutes of the speech are especially important because first impressions are being formed (see **31a**). But many credibility boosters can be woven throughout the entire speech as well.

1 Present your credentials

Most inexperienced speakers find it difficult to "blow their own horn." Do not be reluctant to provide information about your qualifications to speak about your topic:

> The most common error I see in the 20 to 30 loan applications I look at each week is . . .

> I've had a special awareness of the barriers the physically handicapped face since 1991, when my brother Dave returned from the Gulf War.

Judgment and tact are important in deciding which qualifications to mention and how to work them into the speech. Our culture frowns on bragging and name-dropping, yet false humility is out of place. You can include many statements of your qualifications without seeming boastful if you present them matter-of-factly and include only relevant qualifications.

2   Demonstrate your understanding of your topic

To communicate your expertise, you must show listeners you have done your homework. Mention the nature of your research when appropriate:

> The seven judges I interviewed all agreed on one major weakness in our court system.

> I read the minutes of all the committee hearings on this bill, and not one expert mentioned . . .

Use concrete examples, statistics, and testimony. Be sure you have your details straight. One obvious error early in the speech can ruin your credibility. The people listening will wonder what other information is wrong.

3   Be sure your material is clearly organized

Appearing competent depends on being in command of the material and seeming to know where you are headed. Listeners may regard you as uninformed rather than unorganized if you wander from topic to topic and apologetically insert, "Oh, one thing I forgot to mention when I was discussing. . . ."

4   Present an objective analysis

To demonstrate that you are fair, trustworthy, and of good character, acknowledge the limitations of your evidence and argument, where appropriate:

> I'm not saying television is the only cause of these problems. I realize that's an oversimplification. But I do think that TV has had a pronounced effect on the imaginative thinking of the last two generations.

Also be sure to acknowledge opposing evidence and opinions:

> Some studies indicate that an alcoholic can return to social drinking, but . . .

Acknowledge self-interest when it exists to prevent the audience from thinking you are trying to hide something.

> It's true I'm a real estate agent and I stand to profit by having folks invest in real estate. But that's not my main reason for urging you to invest.

If they discover later that you are more partisan than you made it sound, your credibility will suffer.

5   Express your goodwill toward the audience

Let them know that your speech is offered to serve their interests:

> I'd do anything to save your families the headaches and heartaches that go along with having a relative die without a will.

Taking up cycling has added so much to my life that I'd love to see some of you share in that fun.

26d. Effective delivery

Too many expert and well-prepared speakers lose credibility because they cannot *transmit* these qualities to their audience. Dropping cards, reading in a shaky voice, fumbling with whatever is at hand—all suggest lack of competence. An unexpressive face and voice might be interpreted as disdainfulness and detract from perceived goodwill. Hesitancy and uncertainty are sometimes falsely seen as shiftiness or dishonesty. To be seen as a believable source of information and opinion, continue to work on all aspects of delivery covered in chapters **34** and **35**.

CHAPTER 27
Presentation Aids

Depending on circumstances and context, presentation aids may help you be more effective in communicating your message. A **presentation aid** is an object that adds another communicative dimension to your vocal content and delivery. Generally, presentation aids are visual, but they can be aural or audiovisual.

27a. Determine what aids are appropriate

What can be represented by presentation aids? And should they be? The first step is to decide whether an aid will help you meet your speaking goal. Then you can move to deciding what form aids will take and what tools you'll use to create and present them.

There are places in a speech where a visual or audio aid can help you make a point more clearly and quickly than spoken words alone. Conversely, poorly used aids can obscure your ideas and slow the pace of your speech. Presentation aids should support your message, not be your message. And sometimes a speaker can fall into the trap of spending more time preparing the aids than preparing the speech.

Another consideration is the context. In some settings, especially in the business world, a speaker is expected to have a slide show. To do without would violate the norms of the situation and jeopardize the speaker's credibility. In other settings, like a graduation speech, the expectation is that there be no aids. Finding out this sort of information is an important part of the speech planning process.

1   Is a presentation aid needed?

Complex data to compare? Well, there's a possible subject for an aid. Need to intensify an emotional point? Another aid possibility. A recurring theme? Yet another aid possibility.

The two most obvious reasons for using presentation aids are to explain an unfamiliar, complex, or technical idea, and to reinforce a particular message. (The approach you use will depend on whether you use discrete or continuous aids. See **2** and **3** below.) A geneticist might use a wire-frame model of the DNA double helix when talking about how that remarkable molecule duplicates itself. The speaker wishing to impress upon an audience the importance of stiffer drunk-driving penalties may choose to reinforce a recitation of traffic fatality percentages with a pie chart. To help the audience understand the differences between Ragtime, Stride, and Boogie Woogie piano styles, another speaker may choose to play three short audio clips of Jelly Roll Morton, Fats Waller, and Meade "Lux" Lewis to highlight the syncopated scriptedness of Ragtime, the jumping left-hand movements of Stride, and the accelerated bluesiness of Boogie Woogie.

Don't decide which technology you'll use before you've determined what you wish to show. Figure out what concepts you want to show first, then decide what you'll need to make those concepts concrete and immediate, and *then* determine the best ways to present them.

2   What technology will best suit your purpose?

If you've concluded that presentation aids would be useful in your speech, the next questions you ask yourself are: What am I going to use to make them? and How am I going to present them? To answer these questions, you first have to investigate the physical environment of your speaking venue. Then you can start choosing what aids would work in the space, primarily related to visibility and volume. (See **27b.1**.) You also need to consider how much time you have to prepare your aids; how much time displaying or playing your aids will take; how portable the aids are; what technology is available to you for creating the aids; and what technology is available at your speaking venue for you to exploit.

A multitude of approaches   You may decide to have text highlighting your main points, along with a few graphs and photographs to clarify certain points. There are many possible approaches to producing these aids: posters, a flipchart, slides. Or you may wish to add impact to a particular point with text, or image, or sound. There may be a quotation that gets to the heart of the matter. Or a photograph that captures the essence of your point. Or an audio clip that brings the point to life.

> **KEY POINT**   **Match the Medium to the Message** Consider how
> many items or images you want to show. If there are just a few, it
> would be simpler to create a poster or model than to go to the effort
> of creating a two-slide presentation with a noisy projector and a
> darkened room for just a minimal part of your talk.

Presentation software Microsoft's PowerPoint is but one of many
choices. Other presentation software packages available are
Corel Presentations, an application included in WordPerfect Office;
Freelance Graphics, an application included in Lotus SmartSuite;
Keynote from Apple; ProPresentations from Harvard Graphics; and
a variety of specialized packages used by religious organizations,
law firms, medical providers, and the like. Once you've made the
decision to use presentation software, you must decide what physical form the output will take. With the same file you can have the
slides blown up, printed, and mounted as posters, or printed on
transparency sheets for use with an overhead projector, or not
printed at all but projected directly from the software program.
Whatever the form of the output, pay particular attention to the design suggestions in **27b** and **27c**.

3   Visual representations

The object or a model of it While demonstrating the simplicity of a
new lens-to-camera attachment system, a speaker can use the actual camera and lens. With a large audience, however, this sort of
demonstration might not work because of the smallness of the
camera. In this case, the speaker might use a larger-than-life-size
models. Other objects are obviously too large to use, like the USS
Carl Vinson, so a scaled-down reproduction is necessary.

Pictorial reproductions A speaker can also use pictorial reproductions, including photographs, sketches, plans, pictures, slides,
overhead transparencies, computer animations, film clips, and
videotapes. If the mechanical device that attaches the lens to the
camera is complex, the speaker might use a schematic drawing to
show the interaction of all the pieces. Again, object size and audience size are important factors in determining which to use and
which technology would best serve to prepare and present them.

Pictorial symbols Representation of abstract concepts generally
calls for pictorial symbols, including graphs, charts, diagrams,
and maps.

When speaking on the declining state of the economy, you
might choose to use a line graph showing the buying power of the
dollar over the past two decades. A speech on local politics might

use a map showing city council district boundaries. Figures 27-1 and 27-2 show some common pictorial symbols.

Each kind of chart or graph is best suited for a particular kind of information. In general, **line graphs** are better for showing trends than **bar graphs**, and **pie charts** are better for showing relationships of parts to a whole than line graphs. Table 27-1 describes the preferred use of each type, along with some examples. Using the wrong type of graph may convey implications that are not present in your data. Figure 27-2 shows U.S. car production data for 2002, using two different graphs. The line graph is the wrong one to use for this information because the connected dots imply some trend among the state totals that does not exist. The bar graph allows the viewer to see the totals and make comparisons without confusion.

27b. Make your aids clear and manageable

The time spent preparing aids will be wasted if they are mismatched to the situation or difficult to use.

1 Size

The place in which you will be speaking and the size of the audience determine to a great extent the type and size of your aids. It helps to look over the facility in advance if possible. Stand at the back of the room and envision the scene. Screens for projected presentations, slides, and filmstrips should be large enough for the size of the room, and projectors should have focal lengths great enough to fill the screen. With a videotape, make sure that the monitor can be mounted high enough to be seen by people in the back row or that there are enough monitors for everyone to get a good view. Check that your sound equipment is adequate for the size of the room and the ambient noise of the environment.

If you already have a rough mock-up or draft of one of your aids, like a poster or a model, place it where you expect it to be when you speak and walk around the space. Obviously, if the aid is too small, you need to enlarge it. Lines on charts should be thick and bold. Captions should be concise and large. Model parts should be large enough to be distinguishable. If the room is too large for a poster, flipchart, or **whiteboard** to be effective, consider using a slide projector, overhead projector, or digital projector. Reduce any aid that is too large for the size of the room, or that is so unwieldy you will have to wrestle with it.

2 Simplicity

Visual aids should contain just enough detail to allow your listeners to distinguish easily one part from another. Do not crowd maps, charts, graphs, models, and photographs with so much data that your audience cannot tell which part you are referring to. If

Pie Graph

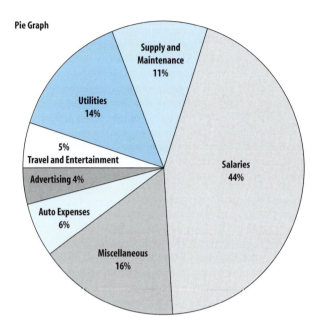

Annotated Map

Slogan or Memorable Phrase

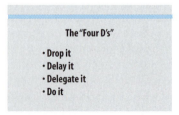

FIGURE 27-1 **Pictorial Symbols**

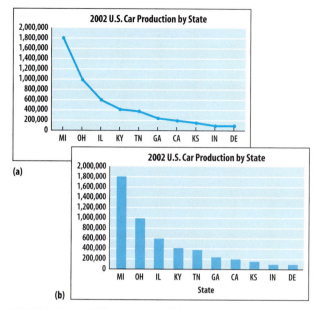

FIGURE 27-2 **(a) Improper and (b) Proper Choice of Graph to Match Data Type**

there are too many lines on a line graph, audience members are at risk of taking a "wrong turn" while following one line across. With photographs, try to find one that shows the object by itself or more prominently than other objects.

Keep the wording on any visual aid simple and familiar. Label parts and ideas with as few words as possible, and use color to delineate different aspects of the object or symbol. Also follow these suggestions to ensure that the overheads and slides (and posters) you create are effective:

1. Use simple typefaces. Do not mix more than two typefaces on a sheet. Avoid ornate or showy type, and stay away from drop shadows, outline fonts, and other decorative type modifications that add visual "noise."

2. Use uppercase and lowercase letters in the titles and text. Sentences printed exclusively in capital letters are harder to read.

3. Use a lot of "white space." That is, do not crowd too much information on one sheet. Keep the information simple; use your speech to fill in the details.

4. Maintain continuity throughout the slides. Settle on a design theme and carry it out for each slide. For instance, if you use a border or background, put it on all slides; if you use bullets for a list on one sheet, do not use numbers or dashes for a list on another slide.

TABLE 27-1 **Uses of Charts, Graphs, and Tables**

Type	Preferred Use, *with examples*
Bar Graph/Pictogram	To make comparisons, especially differences in quantity or frequency. ■ *Number of users for different computer operating systems* ■ *Sales by region*
Line Graph	To show trends or changes over time, or to show how one thing is affected by another. ■ *New subscribers to a service, per year, over a 5-year period* ■ *Heart rate affected by level of exercise*
Pie Graph	To show relationships between parts and the whole, relative proportions, percentages. ■ *Project costs by department* ■ *World production of heroin, by continent*
Flowchart	To show a process, series of related decisions or actions. ■ *Steps to troubleshoot and fix a problem* ■ *Flow of information through an organization*
Table/Grid	To show large amounts of data in one place (Table) or to juxtapose and compare discrete elements (Grid). ■ *Actuarial table of male and female life expectancy* ■ *Rubella infections by age and location* ■ *Comparison checklist of features among different products*

27c. The benefits and perils of presentation software

Presentation software can be considered a mixed blessing to the speaker. On the one hand, it is possible to create slides and handouts that are consistent and attractive. On the other, it is possible to be put in a position in which you are narrating your outline rather than giving a speech.

1 Templates and special effects

The templates that come with the presentation software application are designed to keep your slides simple. That is, if you use the typefaces in the sizes that come as the default, it will be difficult for you to clutter up a slide with too many words and ideas. This is good; avoid the temptation to finesse your way around the constraints of the type size. Instead, look for better ways to organize your material, and pare down your language to the minimum. (See **18** and **19**.)

You can use animation effects or "builds" to expose certain elements of a slide in a particular order for dramatic effect or to keep the focus on the most immediate point. If you do take advantage of this capability, do so with restraint; the efficacy of the effect will diminish with overuse. Similarly, exercise restraint with the sound effects that come with the package—"zoop"-ing sounds may be fun with 5 slides, but with 30 they become irritants.

2 Visual consistency

Used properly, presentation software can help you maintain a consistent look throughout your slides. While templates work for keeping the type consistent, the program's settings for color schemes, slide backgrounds and patterns, and so on, work to keep other elements consistent. Even with this help, though, you need to review your slides to make sure no discrepancies have crept in. Look at the captions. Are they all in burgundy 14-point bold Helvetica? Or has one somehow ended up in green 14-point Arial Narrow? How about the placement of elements? Click through the slide show quickly to see if elements seem to jump from place to place in relation to other instances. Also, check other features, like transition effects and builds, for consistency. Sometimes, especially if a presentation is being created from a number of earlier ones, these may get mixed up, so that you end up with most slides using a "fade through black" transition and a few using a "wipe right."

3 Clip art

Avoid the temptation of using clip art because you feel people expect it or there's "white space" to fill. Use it because it adds a dimension to your message or hammers home a point with an apt visual symbol. Because the popular software packages have such wide exposure, the use of a familiar clip art image—for example, of businesspeople standing around a table or the ubiquitous business handshake—makes your message seem less than unique. Additionally, too many images peppered around your text can be distracting. Images in different styles (a line drawing of a person followed by a cartoon image of a person, for instance, or a low-resolution bitmap image followed by a sharp PostScript image) can be distracting as well.

Figures 27-3 and 27-4 show two text-based slides, the first of which violates many of the design guidelines in **27b** and **c**. In Figure 27-3 the creator has tried to fit too much into the text, making it a "read along" slide. Inconsistent clip art fills the empty spaces and does nothing to advance the message. The modification done to the

- We are positioned to become the leader in service order management and provisioning software
- We have strong, capable and competent technical and project management
- We are in a large, rapidly growing market:
  - Provisioning software market estimated at $6.3 billion by 2006
  - Industry business environment creating need for more sophisticated provisioning software
  - General migration towards packaged solutions
- We can offer a differentiated product and solution:
  - High quality customer list
  - Unique solution for provisioning complex services;
  - Strong domain knowledge
  - Powerful competitive position; technological superiority
  - Strong industry and technology partners

FIGURE 27-3 **Overworked Text Slide**

Opportunities!

- ⧓ Positioned to become the leader in service order management and provisioning software

- ⧓ Strong, capable and competent management

- ⧓ Large, rapidly growing market

- ⧓ Differentiated product and solution

FIGURE 27-4 **Effective Text Slide**

slide title text makes it hard to read. The second slide provides a better approach. Instead of full sentences, it uses key phrases, making the message clear while supporting, rather than supplanting, the speaker. The type is large and readable and is not fighting with extraneous elements for the viewers' attention.

PART 7 Crafting Your Speech

CHAPTER 28

Modes of Delivery

Decide early if your speech will be **impromptu** (off-the-cuff), **extemporaneous** (given from notes), **manuscript** (written out and read), or **memorized** word for word. Settle on the predominant mode you will use, but be aware that no speech is purely *one* mode.

28a. The extemporaneous mode

Extemporaneous speaking is the most common mode of delivery. You should use it in all but a few special cases because it makes for a more conversational and flexible presentation. In this mode, you prepare extensively, constructing the progression of ideas with the aid of an outline, planning your content thoroughly, and practicing until you are comfortable and conversational. But you never commit yourself to a rigid, exact sequence of words.

Prepare an extemporaneous speech in four steps:

1. *Begin with a fully developed outline.* Follow the recommendations in chapters **17** through **20** to arrange your material in a logical and effective manner.

2. *If you have used a full-sentence outline, convert it to a keyword or key-phrase outline.* The sentences of a full-sentence outline are written English, not spoken English, and if you use them for the wording of your speech, the result may be dull and lifeless. For this reason, we suggest that you convert the full-sentence outline to a **keyword or key-phrase outline** that enables you to improvise as you proceed through Step 3.

3. *Word the speech.* Working from this brief outline, practice putting your ideas into words. The second time through, some clumsy phrases will have disappeared as you play with sentence structure, rhythms, and so forth. Third time, fourth time, fifth time through—your topic is becoming more and more familiar, giving you the freedom to relax and to allow yourself to really experiment with construction. You will also discover that one way of expressing a set of thoughts is not necessarily better than another.

4. *Convert your brief outline to speech notes.* See **33b** for directions on how to transfer your content to easy visual cues.

28b. Speaking impromptu

No one should give an important speech in the impromptu mode, but sometimes a person needs to give a speech unexpectedly. On these occasions, follow these four simple steps.

1   Keep your composure

Remind yourself that you speak all the time in conversations without extensive preparation. You should have realistic expectations for yourself and not fall apart if you fail to deliver your most polished performance. Do not apologize. Speak slowly and confidently.

2   Select a theme

Very quickly list several possible approaches to the topic. Do it mentally or, if time permits, with pencil and paper. By thinking beyond the most obvious approach, you may discover a way to link your topic to a subject you are conversant with.

3   Select an organizational framework

You will not have time to make an extensive outline, but you can hook your topic to a simple framework like one of the following:

> Past–present–future
>
> Pros and cons
>
> Concentric rings, progressing from immediate concerns to universal concerns (e.g., the home, the school, the community; or locally, regionally, nationally, internationally)
>
> Domains, or different spheres touched by the topic (e.g., political, social, or economic spheres; or practical, theoretical, or moral implications)

After you have organized your main points, find one way to support or develop each idea, such as an explanation, example, story, fact, or statistic.

If time permits, jot some notes. Even a few keywords on a napkin can reassure you and keep you on track once you have started to speak.

4   Plan your first and last sentences

By having introductory and concluding sentences, you avoid the aimless rambling so characteristic of impromptu speaking. When you know your task is to start with Sentence A and finish with Sentence B, you have a reference against which to judge ideas that occur to you as you are speaking.

28c.   Manuscript speeches

Limit your use of manuscripts to the following situations:

- The time allotted is specific and inflexible (e.g., the broadcast media)

- The wording is extremely critical (e.g., some sensitive and emotionally charged topics)

- The style is extremely important (e.g., a major speech of tribute)

There is a widespread misconception that speaking from a manuscript is the easiest and safest mode of delivery ("I'm not an experienced speaker, so I'd better write it out"). However, a bad manuscript speech is much worse than a bad extemporaneous speech. Stilted phrasing, monotonous vocal delivery, and lack of eye contact are all perils facing a novice speaking from a manuscript.

A poorly delivered manuscript speech is marked by a singsongy cadence, gasping for breath between overlong sentences, and the occasional quick glance up from the page. To avoid these distractions, practice reading and rereading your manuscript out loud until you are comfortable with it. You should neither sight-read nor memorize the text, but become familiar with its flow and rhythm.

Start with a full-sentence outline for good organization, but for the actual wording of the speech "talk" the speech out and onto the paper. You need to check your composition against your ear more than your eye. As you write and rewrite, keep saying it aloud, listening for the rhythms of oral style. (See **29**.)

CHECKLIST

Manuscript Readability

❏ Print out the manuscript on a printer, on heavy paper, triple spaced, with wide margins.

❏ Use capital and lowercase letters in standard sentence format. Make sure the letters are dark and legible.

In some speaking situations, you will not have your manuscript in your hands, but will be reading it from a teleprompter or similar machine.

CHECKLIST

Manuscript Delivery

❏ Retain a conversational style of speaking.

❏ Be familiar enough with your content to sustain eye contact.

❏ Memorize the wording in a few places (e.g., first and last sentences) where audience contact is crucial.

28d. Memorized speeches

By definition, giving a memorized speech entails a manuscript speech—without the manuscript. The only times you should give a memorized speech are when the speech is to be short, and the situation is inappropriate for holding a manuscript. These occasions are most often ceremonial: giving a toast, presenting a plaque, or accepting an honor.

1. *Memorize the structure of the speech before memorizing the speech word for word.* Learn a few keywords that help you internalize the main sequence of ideas.

2. *Read the speech aloud several times and then work on learning it paragraph by paragraph.* Always keep your mind on the meaning. Do not try to learn sentences in isolation, but rather work on whole paragraphs at a time, reinforcing their logical and conceptual unity.

3. *As you practice, visualize giving the speech.* Avoid thinking of your speech as lines of text in a social vacuum. You do not want to be startled and lose your concentration when you realize that you are actually facing a roomful of people.

4. *Do not go into a trance when delivering the speech.* Once again, be comfortably familiar with your material so that you can maintain eye contact and establish a rapport with your audience.

5. *If you go blank, switch to the extemporaneous mode and recall the structure of the speech rather than groping for the next word.* Speaking along the general lines of the point you know you were trying to make, you can collect your thoughts and click back into what you have memorized.

CHAPTER 29

Language and Style

Competent speakers consciously develop their ideas through language to achieve an effective speaking style. In the context of speaking, **style** is simply your choice of words and the way you string them together. "Good" style involves choosing and combining those words so that your audience can easily understand and assimilate your content. Good style uses clear, appropriate, vivid, and varied language.

29a. Oral and written styles

Although oral style and written style use the same components, there are some important ways in which they differ. A speaker is more likely than a writer to use repetition to ensure comprehension. Oral style employs more signposting, internal summaries,

TABLE 29-1 **Differences Between Written and Oral Styles**

Written Style	Oral Style
As mentioned above . . .	As I said a few minutes ago . . .
One cannot avoid individuals with this characteristic.	We can't avoid people like that.
A hypothetical case might be a situation where government . . .	Imagine this. Suppose Uncle Sam . . .
It is unlikely that such will result.	Well. Maybe.
Subjects were randomly assigned to either a control group or one of three experimental treatment groups, pretested for initial attitudes toward the topic, then posttested after each experimental group had received a persuasive message containing one of three levels of fear appeals.	Here's how we did our research. First, we randomly assigned the subjects to four groups. Next, we gave all four groups a pretest to see what attitudes they held toward the topic. Then, three of the groups heard persuasive messages. One had a high level of fear appeals, one a medium level, and one a low level. Last, we posttested the attitudes of all four groups, including the control group that received no message.

and internal previews to make the organization clear. (See **32**.) Shorter sentences and words of fewer syllables are characteristic of oral style as well. And sentence fragments are acceptable, as are contractions. Even in a formal setting, a speech will still be more colloquial than an essay on the same topic. Table 29-1 illustrates some key differences between oral and written style.

29b. Clear language

To construct clear messages, you must do two things. First clarify your own thoughts. Know exactly, not approximately, what you want to communicate. Second, consider who the receivers of your message are and what the words are likely to mean to them.

1   Be precise

To avoid fuzzy communication, seek out the word that means precisely what you wish to convey and use it in a structure that illuminates its meaning. Do not say a person was "indicted" for robbery if in fact you mean "arrested" (much less serious) or "convicted" (much more serious). Learn important distinctions and honor

TABLE 29-2   Specific, Concrete Language

Do Not Say	If You Mean	Or If You Really Mean
We need to attract individuals.	We need to attract customers.	We need to attract grocery shoppers.
This will cause problems.	This will be expensive.	This will cost us $2,500 we don't have.
Our committee has studied it.	Our committee researched and discussed it.	Our committee read documents, heard testimony, and deliberated for several hours.

them. Be sure you know what an unfamiliar word means before rushing to use it. Be careful around words that sound similar but have no similarity of meaning. *Allusion* means "a passing mention," and *illusion* means "a false perception." Some other troublesome near-homophones can be found in **Appendix C**.

2   Be specific and concrete

The more specific and concrete your words, the less is left to your listeners' imaginations. Table 29-2 gives examples of specific, concrete language.

3   Be concise

Express yourself with the fewest words that effectively convey your meaning. Avoid wordy, euphemistic language. Sometimes, speakers use long words, extra words, and convoluted constructions for the reasons listed in Table 29-3.

Most often, though, wordiness results from lack of discipline. It takes time and effort to find the best wording. The clear speaker makes every word count.

29c.   Appropriate language

Different audiences and topics require different approaches. Based on your audience analysis, you must decide how formal to be, which part of your personality to project, and how specialized your language should be. Your age, status, and personality also determine what language is appropriate for you. The vocabulary and stylistic level suitable for, say, a senior executive differs from those for a teenager or a poet-in-residence.

Language is not fixed. New words and phrases are always coming into our language, and others fading out. Meanings change, as do standards of appropriateness.

TABLE 29-3 **Motives for Bloated Language**

Motive	Uneconomical	Economical
To hide meaning, as with doublespeak.	We sustained losses through friendly fire.	We shelled our own troops.
To avoid responsibility, as with the passive voice.	It has been determined that your services are no longer needed.	I have decided to fire you.
To soften unpleasant messages, as with euphemism.	Jesse has gone on to his reward.	Jesse died.

1 Level of formality

Just as you dress differently for formal and casual events, so should you tailor vocabulary and usage to fit the situation. In general, the more formal the occasion, the more serious the tone, the more subtle the humor, the more elaborate the sentences, the greater the number of figures of speech, the greater the departure from everyday word choice.

More formal occasions include debates, presentations of policy statements, and ceremonial speeches. Less formal occasions include business conferences, roasts, rallies, and after-dinner speeches.

2 Jargon and slang

Both jargon and slang can be used to create a bond with a specialized audience. At times, **jargon,** the special vocabulary of a particular group, can also allow you to get a point across more quickly. **Slang**—popular, nonstandard catchwords and phrases—when called into play at opportune moments, can enrich the texture of your language. But the perils they introduce are substantial. You may confuse your audience with technical terms or sacrifice your credibility by using slang expressions that are offensive or out of date.

3 Substandard usage

The speaker's competence as perceived by the audience has a large bearing on the speaker's credibility. Although acceptable usage varies, many words and constructions are rated substandard by consensus. The speaker who consistently uses double negatives or who gets sloppy with noun–verb agreement will find that a large percentage of the audience does not give serious consideration to the speaker's points. Of course, you can sometimes break the rules for dramatic effect, like capping your opposition to a proposal with "Ain't *no* way!" **Appendix C** gives some examples of standard versus substandard language.

KEY POINT **Not All Nonstandard Language Is Substandard**
Sometimes, when people try to "standardize" the language others use, they are actually trying to change the content or to mold the identity of the speaker. Women should not have to talk like men. People of color should not have to talk like their compatriots of northern European descent. You will not feel comfortable or seem authentic if you abandon your own idiom. Strive to find a way to maintain your own cultural, ethnic, and individual identity while still speaking in a credible way.

4   Respectful and inclusive language

Referring to a group or individuals by the name they prefer is a sign of respect. Make a reasonable effort to learn which reference people prefer. You can make a commitment to flexibility. It is worth the temporary inconvenience of changing a language habit if that change is highly symbolic and important to your audience.

Some guidelines for the use of inclusive language can be found on the websites of various universities and publishers; for example:

> **www.hcc.hawaii.edu/intranet/committees/FacDevCom/ guidebk/teachtip/inclusiv.htm**
>
> **www.uhv.edu/ac/style/inclusive.asp.**

29d. Vivid, varied language

Your message may never get past your listeners' short-term memory if you do not infuse it with vigor and a sense of newness. Energize your language with the following verbal devices.

1   Imagery

When you describe something, put the senses and the imaginations of your listeners to work:

Not: The life of the long-haul trucker is rough.

But: The long-haul trucker pulls to the side of the road, and even though the truck is stopped, his arms up to his elbows still throb to the rhythm of hitting four hundred miles of highway expansion joints. The harsh roar of the engine leaves him with an infuriating ringing of the ears.

2   Stylistic devices

Enliven your language through figures of speech and arrangements of words and phrases.

Simile and metaphor   You can add vigor to your speaking by connecting objects or ideas to vivid images. A **simile** makes a comparison between two things ordinarily dissimilar: "When she came in from shoveling off the walk, her hands were like ice." No one would mistake a hand for some ice, but in this case they share the characteristic of extremely low temperature. A metaphor equates two unlike things: "Her hands were ice cubes."

Personification You can bring objects or ideas to life by imbuing them with human qualities. We know that no room is really "cheerful," that winds do not actually "whisper," and that, being legless, the economy cannot possibly "limp." Nevertheless, all of these images are potent because we find it easier to identify with reflections of our own behavior.

Hyperbole For emphasis, you may deliberately overstate a point in a way that is clearly fanciful:

> This paperwork will be the death of me.

> The governor has repeated this same promise to you a million times.

Repeated words or structure By repeating keywords or phrases, you make your listeners feel that your points are snowballing to a certain conclusion. Use parallel structure to add emphasis. You can also use repetition to introduce consecutive ideas. For instance, a speaker can build a sense of urgency by repeating the phrase "We must act now to . . ." as each problem is presented. Or you might end several sentences with the same words as in this example:

> What remains? Treaties have gone. The honor of nations has gone. Liberty has gone.
>
> *—David Lloyd George*

Alliteration and assonance These devices repeat the same sound. Whether it is with consonants (alliteration) or vowels (assonance), this repetition can make an idea more memorable, or at least charge it with a sense of poetry.

At his brother's grave, Robert Green Ingersoll said the following:

> He who sleeps here, when dying . . . whispered with his latest breath: "I am better now." Let us believe, in spite of doubts and dogmas, and tears and fears, that these dear words are true of all the countless dead.

Antithesis When you want to contrast two ideas, certain sentence structures can dramatize the differences. Antithesis uses forms like these:

> Not . . . , but . . .

> Not only . . . , but also . . .

Upon the receipt of the 2001 Nobel Peace Prize, Kofi Annan in his Nobel lecture combined antithesis, alliteration and assonance, and repetitive structure:

> Today's real borders are not between nations, but between powerful and powerless, free and fettered, privileged and humiliated.

3   Original language

The power of figurative language lies in the images stimulated in the listener's mind. After too many repetitions, the original impact is lost. "Fresh as a daisy" once summoned a picture of a clean, bright, dew-studded blossom. At the first turn of the phrase "it went in one ear and out the other," its aptness produced pleasant surprise. Now both expressions are likely to be processed as just extra, empty words; they have become clichés.

Certain fad words attract a cult following and are used to the exclusion of many good (and fresher) synonyms. Invest the time needed to select original combinations of words and phrases that capture the image, mood, or thought you want to get across.

4   Varied rhythm

Although oral style is characterized by simpler, shorter phrases with less variation in word choice, you are not compelled to homogenize your sentences into dullness. The "singsonginess" associated with doggerel can creep into a speech if you fail to pay attention to how you are stringing your sentences and phrases together. Be sparing in your use of parallelisms and repetition. Consider this plodding passage:

> The association's annual convention should be user supported. The convention is attended by a core of regulars. The average association member doesn't benefit from the convention. These average members shouldn't have to bear more than their fair share.

This passage is tedious because the sentences have the same length and structure. Recasting the sentences will create a more fluid and graceful paragraph:

> The association's annual convention should be user supported. Who attends the convention? A core of regulars. The average association members, who don't benefit from the convention, shouldn't have to bear more than their fair share.

CHAPTER 30

Capturing Attention and Interest

When you give a speech or presentation, your words are competing for attention with every other sight and sound in the room and with every daydream in the mind of each listener. The better you understand the psychology of attention, the more likely you will receive the compliment most appreciated by speakers: a sincere and simple "That was an interesting speech!"

30a. How to enliven your speech

The following techniques will help you catch and keep your listeners' attention.

1 Concrete, real-life examples

Examples are always more interesting when they are specific and real. Never say "a person" or "one" if you can give a name. Use well-known figures, members of the audience, or even hypothetical characters. And give place names, brand names, dates, and details.

2 Your listeners' self-interest

Most times, when people say, "So what?" they are really saying, "What's it to me?" Do not assume that the benefits of your particular approach are obvious; motivate your audience to listen by spelling out the rewards. Do careful audience analysis and tap into as many of your listeners' needs and values as possible. (See **25**.)

> You don't have to be a vegetarian or a gourmet cook to benefit from these menu ideas. By serving just a few meatless meals a week, you can save 30 to 100 dollars on your monthly grocery bill and also provide a healthier diet for your family.

3 Storytelling

A well-constructed story commands the interest of nearly everyone. Notice how excellent feature articles and documentary films share many of the qualities of good fiction or drama. A speech, even if it is an annual report, can captivate an audience if it unfolds in a narrative fashion with suspense, conflict, intriguing characterizations, lively bits of dialogue, and a moment of climax leading to the denouement. Your speech need not promise to make your listeners rich or famous if it takes them outside their experience in an engaging way.

4 Humor

Humor is both powerful and tricky. An infusion of humor into any speech can ease tension, deflate opponents, enhance the speaker's image, and make points memorable.

What is important is the ability to spot a potentially humorous idea in your speech and to craft it into a genuinely funny moment. Look for the humor in your everyday experience. The boring, frustrating, and mundane aspects of life all have their humorous elements. Take note of the everyday things that make you laugh on your job, in your relationships, on television, and in the paper.

Developing your use of humor is not a matter of collecting jokes and gags. Topically organized books of humor or websites like **www.humorlinks.com** or **www.joke-archive.com** can sometimes yield just the gem you need to catch people's atten-tion. Be selective, though, choosing only material that is relevant, appropriate, and fresh.

5   Variety

Change attracts attention. Sameness is dull. If your content or delivery becomes totally predictable, audience members' interest will start to wane. Vary your forms of support—do not rely on only statistics or only testimony. Draw examples from many domains.

Whenever possible, give the speech a sense of movement. Use images of activity. Use vivid verbs, and stay in the active voice as much as possible. For instance, instead of saying, "Five new businesses can be seen downtown," say, "Drive down First Street and you will see five new businesses."

In your delivery, too, remember the importance of vocal variety and physical movement. Who wants to listen to a deadpan speaker monotonously delivering a presentation while standing on a particularly adhesive spot on the floor? (See **34b** and **35**.)

30b.   How to involve your audience

If you have done a thorough audience analysis, you should have been able to build many references to the audience into the speech, and there are always more opportunities to adapt to your audience once you start your speech. Here are some adaptations you might try.

Use the names of people in the audience "Suppose Ms. Silver's [you nod toward a listener] hardware business is expanding so rapidly that she decides to take out a loan to enlarge her store."

Refer to the person who introduced you and to the other speakers "As Dave was saying . . ."

Refer to details in the immediate setting or from shared experience "And all of that expensive atom-smashing machinery was housed in a room not half the size of this one."

Use audience participation techniques "Can I have a show of hands?" "How many people here . . ."

Make liberal use of the word *you* "You've probably seen . . ." "Now, I'll bet you're saying to yourself . . ." "You could undoubtedly give me a dozen more examples." "In your city here . . ."

CHAPTER 31

Introductions and Conclusions

A carefully composed introduction and conclusion can crystallize your relationship to your listeners.

31a. The introduction

A speech introduction prepares your listeners to deal with you and your topic. Both speaker and audience need a period of adjustment before getting to the meat of the speech—the audience to get used to a speaker's appearance, mannerisms, and style of talking; you to settle into your role.

1   Project confidence before starting

It is important to realize that your speech really starts before you utter the first word and that that first word is crucial to the success of the speech. The moment the attention shifts to you, you need to begin to develop a rapport and prepare your audience to listen to you. Stand up and, if necessary, move confidently to the position from which you will speak; then pause to engage audience members. Look at them and acknowledge nonverbally the fact that you and they are together.

2   Engage the audience's attention immediately

You don't want to risk leaving your opening sentences to the inspiration of the moment. You need strong basic material that will carry the speech forward. Start with a sentence that leaves no doubt that you are beginning. Avoid false starts and apologetic or tentative phrases such as "Is the mike on?" or "Well, here goes nothing." Tone is almost as important as content here. Your immediate purpose is to command the attention of your audience. (See **30**.)

Your **attention-getter** (a few sentences to capture the audience's attention and invite them to listen) can be a joke, relating a story, an apt quotation, a startling statement, or a provocative question. Be imaginative, and even a little dramatic; but do not go too far. Avoid contrived and gimmicky openings such as flicking off the room lights and asking, "Are you in the dark about . . . ?" Your attention-getter should also be consistent with your personality and the situation. Adopting an unnatural style is doubly troublesome; not only will you be uncomfortable, but your audience will sense that you are not being yourself.

With this in mind, consider the following possible attention-getters for the comic book speech in **Appendix A**. A humorous or light introduction of the topic may suit you best:

> Did you ever want to leap a tall building in a single bound? I did. Did you ever want to be more powerful than a locomotive? I did. Did you ever want to be faster than a speeding bullet? I did. As you can tell, I was warped early by the influence of comic books.

Or perhaps you are more comfortable with a dramatic attention-getter:

> On a May afternoon in Washington, Frank Salacuse and John Snyder wrapped up their negotiations and shook hands. Both were happy with the result. Snyder walked away with $17,500, and Salacuse's syndicate now had a mint copy of *Marvel Comics*, no. 1, a comic book with the 1939 price of 10 cents on its cover.

A straightforward conversational approach to the topic can still get attention:

> In the 10 years I've been collecting comic books, I've learned that they are more than escape or entertainment. As I read the 13,000 comics in my collection, their contribution to popular culture becomes clearer and clearer.

As this third example illustrates, attention-getters need not be unduly catchy or clever. However, it is essential that you begin your speech with a few well-planned sentences that say, in effect, "I know where I'm going and I want you to come with me—it will be worth your while."

3   Turn attention into interest

Before you can ask your audience to concentrate on the substance of your message, you need to orient them psychologically. This psychological orientation has two parts: establishing a good relationship with your listeners and motivating them toward your topic.

Establish a relationship Speakers can seem distant from the audience because of their role and status. Use your introduction to create a personal bond with your listeners. You can do this with, among other things, references to everyday, common occurrences. You want to set a tone of collaboration with your audience.

CHECKLIST

Connecting with Your Audience
- ❏ Establish credibility.
- ❏ Establish common ground.
- ❏ Refer to the setting or occasion.
- ❏ Flatter your audience.
- ❏ Refer to the person who introduced you or to some other person present.
- ❏ Use humor.

Motivate your audience toward your topic This motivational step is one of those most often overlooked in speech making, but it is the pivotal step of the introduction. You need to reassure your listeners that there are good reasons for them to be warming seats, that your topic has a link with their own experiences and is thereby worthy of their attention.

4   Provide a logical orientation

Now that your audience is *motivated* to listen, you must be sure they are *prepared* to listen. In the logical orientation, you show your listeners how you will approach and develop your topic—in effect, giving them an intellectual road map. In this phase of your introduction, you show the larger whole into which your speech fits and the way you have partitioned your topic. Give your audience a perspective on your topic by using one or more of the following approaches.

Fit your topic into a familiar framework Consider this statement:

San Jose is located 54 miles southeast of San Francisco, about 30 miles inland from the Pacific Ocean.

Here, the unknown is linked to the known in a geographical sense. You can also relate your topic to some schema, chart, organizational structure, or process with which your audience is already familiar. In this case, your listeners presumably know where the Pacific Ocean and San Francisco are, so they can start to think about San Jose.

Place your topic historically The historical context helps listeners learn about the events that led up to your topic. One of the most famous speeches by an American, Abraham Lincoln's "Gettysburg Address," used this simple form of introduction:

> Fourscore and seven years ago our fathers brought forth on this continent a new nation, conceived in liberty and dedicated to the proposition that all men are created equal. Now we are engaged in a great civil war, testing whether that nation or any nation so conceived and so dedicated can long endure. We are met on a great battlefield of that war. We have come to dedicate a portion of that field, as a final resting place for those who here gave their lives that that nation might live. It is altogether fitting and proper that we should do this.

Place your topic conceptually Just as you can place your topic in time or space, so can you locate it in the world of ideas. By showing your listeners how your speech fits in with familiar theories, concepts, and definitions, you prepare them to listen. For example:

> You're familiar with the law of supply and demand as it relates to goods and services. Let me review this basic market mechanism with you, because I want to ask you to apply these same essential principles to our system of information exchange.

Provide new definitions and concepts If you use unfamiliar terms and concepts in your speech, or use familiar terms in unfamiliar ways, prepare your audience.

Here is how you might introduce an unfamiliar term:

> *Operations Support Systems* for a telecommunications service provider are software applications that deal with four broad areas: billing and customer care, provisioning, planning and engineering, and network management.

Here is how you might define a familiar term used in an unfamiliar way:

> Often, when people speak of a system of restitution for criminals, they refer to a program in which prisoners contribute wages to a collective pool of some sort. The restitution system I will be talking about involves direct compensation from individual criminals to their victims.

Orient the audience to your approach to the topic The second step in a logical orientation—once you have shown how your speech fits into some larger context—is to preview the structure of your speech. If you give your listeners a framework on which to attach your points as your speech unfolds, you make it easier for them to comprehend your topic and thesis.

In most introductions, you will explicitly state one or more of the following: your topic, thesis, title, or purpose—for example, "I would like to persuade you to change your vote on this bond issue." At times, you also want to tell what you are *not* talking about—essentially explaining to your audience how you have narrowed your topic.

Here is an example, derived from the comic book outline in **Appendix A**, of a speaker spelling out what the speech will not cover:

> I am not going to tell you which comic books are currently the best investment. Nor am I going to explain how to treat and store comic books so that the acid in the paper won't turn them into yellow confetti. I *am,* however, going to tell you some things about comic books that will help you better understand their place in American popular culture.

You must also decide whether to give an exact **preview** of the points you are going to cover or merely a general overview of your topic. Explicit previews are useful in the majority of speeches and essential for speeches with fairly technical or complex topics. The speaker gives the listeners a reassuring road map to carry through the speech, one that they can refer to if they start to get lost.

5 Make your introduction compact

Generally, the introduction should take up 10 to 15 percent of your speaking time. To avoid an introduction that is disjointed and overlong, organize it in a natural narrative style. Often it is more important to fulfill the *functions* of getting attention and providing psychological and logical orientation than to progress mechanically through the three steps. Whenever possible, select material that fulfills more than one function.

In addition to combining parts of the introduction, it is often appropriate to omit steps altogether. A presidential speech can begin, "My fellow Americans, tonight I want to talk about the serious problem of international terrorism." Attention, credibility, and motivation to listen are assumed.

31b. The conclusion

Many speakers make the mistake of not leaving sufficient time for a proper conclusion. Just as you led your audience into your topic step-by-step in the introduction, so must you lead them out again in a conclusion, tying all the threads together and leaving the audience with a sense of completeness or closure. Like the introduction, the conclusion should be precisely planned, almost to the point of memorization. Social scientists tell us that people are most likely to remember what they hear last, so you should choose your words carefully.

1   Provide logical closure

Although you have already demonstrated the interconnectedness of your points and ideas in the body of the speech by the use of transitions and internal previews and summaries, you still need to tie it all together for your audience at the end.

Summarize the main ideas   In all but the shortest of speeches, include a fairly explicit restatement of your thesis and main ideas. A conclusion can reinforce the pattern that has been implicit all along. This can be used for either inductive or deductive lines of reasoning, when the final relationship among points needs to be spelled out. (See **21**.)

Reconnect your topic to a larger context   There can be an integration of the parts of a speech that goes beyond mere summary. In the introduction, you drew your speech topic out of some broader context. After developing your ideas, you may want to show how they tie back to the original larger picture.

2   Provide psychological closure

Making your main points fit together logically for your audience is not enough. Members should walk away psychologically satisfied with your speech—you need to have touched them. When you plan your conclusion, think not only about what you want your listeners to understand and agree with but also about how you want them to feel at the end of the speech.

Remind the audience how the topic affects them   In the introduction, you make the topic personal to your audience. During the speech itself, you make your examples and manner of speaking appropriately personal. At the end, you bring the topic home again and show your listeners why they have a stake in what you have described. Here is an example:

> Whether you work for a large organization or have your own small business, whether you keep your own books or deal with a cadre of accountants, these two systems will affect you. Understanding the basic logic of each is necessary if you are to make sound decisions.

Make an appeal   Part of the psychological wrap-up of a speech can be a direct **appeal** to your audience, especially in a speech to persuade. Ask them directly to behave in a certain way, or ask them to change their attitudes. An appeal can be strengthened by a statement of your own intent: "I plan to give blood tomorrow morning, and I hope to see you down there."

3 End with a clincher

It is as important to plan your last sentence as it is your first. Every speech needs a sentence that leaves no doubt that the speech is finished.

One type of effective clincher ties back to the technique of the attention-getter. This involves answering the provocative question you asked initially or reintroducing your opening joke or story and taking it one step further in light of your thesis:

> Frank Salacuse's syndicate spent $17,500 for its comic book, but all *you* need is a pocketful of change and transportation to the nearest newsstand or grocery store to rediscover a unique facet of Americana.

Another type of clincher is a proverb, aphorism, quotation, or snatch of poetry. Martin Luther King, Jr., ended his historic "I Have a Dream" speech by evokingthe words of an old spiritual: "Free at last, free at last, thank God Almighty, we are free at last."

The delivery of your clincher is as important as its content. Do not mumble your final sentence in a throwaway voice or spend the last few speaking moments gathering up your notes. Be familiar enough with your clincher that you can deliver it while maintaining eye contact with your listeners.

31c. Common introduction and conclusion pitfalls

1. *Don't* begin with "Before I start, I'd like to say. . . ." You have already started. (See **31a.1**.)

2. *Don't* begin with an apology like "I'm not really prepared" or "I don't know much about this, but. . . ." (See **31a.2**.)

3. *Don't* use an attention-getter that has no real link to your topic. Avoid the temptation to stretch a point so you can start with an unrelated joke you think is hilarious. (See **31a.2**.)

4. *Don't* make your introduction disproportionately long. (See **31a.5**.)

5. *Don't* use stock phrases like "Unaccustomed as I am to public speaking" or overworked apocryphal stories. Ask a friend to give an honest critique of your trove of expressions and anecdotes. (See **29d**.)

6. *Don't* startle your audience by bursting out of a yogalike trance into an explosion of oral energy. This is a favorite of high school orators. Engage your audience before you start. (See **31a.1**.)

7. *Don't* read your introduction or your conclusion. Or, if you have memorized them, be sure they do not sound

mechanical. These are times when you should maximize eye contact and keep your inflection natural and conversational. (See **34b**.)

8. *Don't* end with an apology: "I guess I've rambled on long enough," or "I don't know if I've made this clear," "I'm not usually this hyper; it must be the coffee."

9. *Don't* trail off. Do your audience the courtesy of wrapping things up and using a clincher. (See **31b.3**.)

10. *Don't* introduce a new point in your conclusion. The body of your speech is the place for that. (See **18a**.)

11. *Don't* make the conclusion disproportionately long. It is a summary and ending.

12. *Don't* end in a style or mood that is at odds with the tenor of the rest of the speech. You do your listeners a disservice if you have kept them laughing up to the very end only to hit them with a stark recitation of doom.

13. *Don't* use the phrases "in conclusion" or "in summary" in any part of the speech other than the actual conclusion. You will lose part of your audience while they reorient themselves to the fact that the speech is continuing when they thought it was winding down. (See **32**.)

CHAPTER 32

Polishing Your Speech

When you have completed research, selected and organized your points, and added an introduction and conclusion, a final step remains: smoothly and gracefully tying all the components of your speech together. This helps avoid choppiness and provides listeners with a unified presentation that is easier to follow. Figure 32-1, at the end of the chapter, illustrates how the speech components flow together.

32a. Weave in supporting materials smoothly

When you have chosen appropriate definitions, facts, examples, statistics, and testimony, you still have to present these materials effectively. You want to emphasize their quality, make them clear and understandable, and organize them appropriately in relation to the points they support.

1   Vary the lead-ins

Do not introduce all your illustrations, statistics, and so on, with the same phrase: "Some figures about this are . . . some figures about that are. . . ." There are many possibilities for lead-ins:

> To support this idea . . .
>
> _____ put it well, I think, when she said . . .
>
> What causes this situation? One answer to that question was offered by _____ when he wrote last year . . .
>
> There are several examples of this. Let me share just two . . .

To introduce a direct quotation (in contrast to a paraphrase), be sure to indicate to your listeners the boundaries of the quoted material. This can be done by saying, "and I quote . . ." followed by, "End of quotation," or in some cases a subtle change in your voice or posture is enough.

2   Cite specific sources

By giving credit for your supporting materials, you build your own credibility by showing the range of your research. You are also providing information your listeners are almost certain to want. Very few audiences will settle for "studies show . . ." or "one researcher found . . ." or "a friend once told me . . ." To evaluate these statements, listeners need to know more about where the information came from.

This does not mean that you are required to present regulation footnotes in oral form, citing volume and page numbers. Nor do you need to recite an authority's complete biography or necessarily explain a study's design intricacies. Although you should know the *who, why, when,* and *how* of every bit of data you use, you will probably mention only a couple of these in introducing the evidence.

3   Give adequate citations

The form an oral citation takes is, like many choices in speaking, dependent on the context. In some cases there is a rigid and stylized form, as in the college debate or speech contest. Otherwise, you can choose how much information you need to include about the source according to how much you think your audience has to hear to accept the source as legitimate.

Here are three examples of citation density. The first introduces the information with no citation at all. The second presents the name of the source, which indicates that you are not picking numbers out of the air. The third example is fairly dense, giving your listeners enough information that they can jot down and use to check your source if they so wish.

No citation

Only 17 percent of all bicycle accidents are car–bike collisions, and in only 10 percent of those collisions was the car overtaking the bike from the rear.

Light citation

According to transportation engineer John Forester, only 17 percent of all bicycle accidents are car–bike collisions, and in only 10 percent of those collisions was the car overtaking the bike from the rear.

Dense citation

In his 1993 book, *Effective Cycling,* published by MIT Press, transportation engineer John Forester notes that only 17 percent of all bicycle accidents are car–bike collisions, and in only 10 percent of those collisions was the car overtaking the bike from the rear.

If you must be dense in your citing, make it as conversational as possible. Avoid the "big parenthetical speed bump" that interrupts the flow of a sentence, as in "Transportation engineer John Forester notes (*Effective Cycling,* MIT Press, 1993) that only. . . ." It may take a few more words to come up with a smooth version, but the result will be more natural to the ear.

32b. Use signposts to link points

Transitional sentences, phrases, and words serve as bridges between points. They also signal how two ideas are related. Clear and evocative transitions are more important in speaking than in writing because the spoken message is ephemeral. In this book, for example, we show the relationships among ideas by indenting, capitalizing, and using punctuation and different typefaces. As a speaker, however, you do not have access to these devices. You need to use verbal signposting techniques to show how your points relate. (See **22b.1**.) You can help your listeners follow the overall structure of your speech by the generous use of signposts like these:

My next major point is . . .

To show you what I mean, let me tell you two stories.

What, then, is the solution to this three-part problem I have outlined?

Do not worry about using too many signposts. Your audience will appreciate them.

1   Transitions that reflect logical relationships

The transitions you choose should illuminate the basic organizational structure of the speech. Without even knowing their content, you can tell what pattern these speeches follow:

Thesis Statement: ....

   I say that for three reasons. First,
 I. ....
   This situation is also due to
 II. ....
   Last of all, we can attribute the problem to
 III. ....
or

Thesis Statement: ....

   Initially,
 I. ....
   Next,
 II. ....
   Finally,
 III. ....

The transitions alone tell you that you are hearing an effect-to-cause speech in the first case and a chronologically arranged speech in the second.

 Points can be related in a number of ways. Table 32-1 lists common transitional words and phrases that can be used to tie main points to one another, main points to subpoints, subpoints to one another, supporting evidence to arguments, and introductions and conclusions to the body of the speech.

2   Internal previews and summaries

Sometimes, transitions between main points should take the form of **internal summaries** or **internal previews** that pull together two or three main points.

Internal Preview

 Once your résumé has been prepared, the next step in job seeking is to prepare a list of specific job openings. The three best sources here are newspaper and web listings, your campus placement service, and word-of-mouth recommendations. We will examine the pros and cons of each of these.

Internal Summary

 Because the problems in our department were affecting morale, and because we had found they were caused by poor communication, we instituted an unusual training program. Let me tell you about it.

TABLE 32-1   Transitional Words and Phrases

Relationship	Transitional Words
Chronological	First, second, third Next, then Following
Cause–effect	So, since, thus Therefore, hence Consequently, as a result Due to, because
Part-to-whole	One such, another The first (second, third) of these For instance, for example Illustrative of this, a case in point
Equality	Similarly, additionally Another Of equal importance
Opposition	But, though, however On the other hand, conversely In spite of Nonetheless, nevertheless

Internal Summary and Preview

I've told you why we need to reduce our dependence on the automobile, and I hope I've convinced you that a light rail system is the best alternative for our city. Now, you're probably asking two questions: What will it cost? and How will it work? I want to answer both these questions. First, the question of cost.

KEY POINT **Premature Summaries** Do not say "In summary" anywhere but in the conclusion. Carefully qualify your internal summaries by using phrases like "So, to summarize this first idea . . ." or "Let me review the points so far."

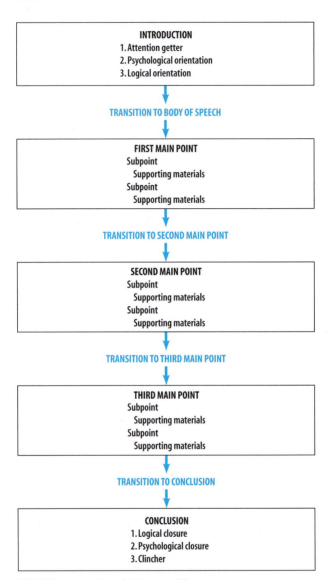

FIGURE 32-1 **Speech Structure Chart**

CHAPTER 33

Practicing Your Speech

Start practicing your speech aloud well before the presentation. Using the three stages of practice sessions enables you to finalize your points, get feedback from others, and polish the delivery. Whenever possible, form a support group of other learners, colleagues, or friends. See **2c** for a discussion of constructive feedback.

33a. The three stages of practice

Your practice sessions need a timetable: you should plan your practice sessions, write down a schedule of steps and phases, and adhere to it. Table 33-1 shows possible timetables for different kinds of speeches with different amounts of advance notice. This can be used as a guide to help you create a schedule for your speeches.

1   Stage 1: Flesh out your outline

During these early developmental sessions, you transform your outline of ideas into a speech by adding the elements of language and delivery to the logical framework of your outline.

Begin by internalizing your outline. Read it over a number of times, becoming familiar with the flow of the logic. Sit at your desk or a table and talk your way through the outline. Try to explain the ideas to yourself.

At this point, pick a quiet spot and start to put together the speech as it will actually be given. Stand up and give the speech out loud in your speaking voice. Visualize the speech situation and mentally put yourself there.

Sometime during this stage, you will have made the first draft of your speech notes. These will evolve. They are mutable according to how things shape up as you tinker with the wording.

2   Stage 2: Get feedback

After you have become comfortable with your material but before doing the final polishing, you should seek feedback on your speech. If you solicit feedback on content, style, and delivery before you have finished shaping your basic speech, you will miss getting help on those parts that have not yet been crystallized. If the feedback comes too late in the schedule, you will not have the time to incorporate it comfortably.

Practice in front of others Just as people are good sounding boards for the development of your ideas, as stated in **10c**, so are they the best source of feedback. As you rehearse your speech for colleagues, family members, or friends, imagine that you are in front

TABLE 33-1 Example of Practice Schedules

Type of Speech	Commitment Made to Speak	Preliminary Analysis, Research, and Outline Completed	Stage 1: Early Practice Sessions (Development)
Major policy address	Several weeks before	1 week before	1–2 weeks before: Discuss ideas with colleagues. 5–6 days before: Talk through speech once a day.
Classroom speech	10 days before	4 days before	4–10 days before: Talk about speech with friends. 4 days before: Read outline several times; practice aloud twice.
Routine oral report in a business meeting	24 hours before	Evening before	Afternoon or evening before: Talk through basic ideas with friends or colleagues. Evening before: Practice aloud one to three times.

of your actual audience, and do not leave things out. Do not talk about your speech. Give your speech.

Ask for honest feedback on content and delivery, but do not necessarily take any single person's comments as the last word. He or she has quirks and prejudices just like everyone else. This is why a group of people is preferable, giving you a sampling of responses.

You should not ask, "How'd you like my speech?" Answers like "It was nice" or "I thought it was okay" do not help you much. Lead your critics with a few questions and seek clarification of their answers. Here are some questions you can begin with:

- "What did you see as the single most important thing I was trying to say?" If they do not come up with your thesis sentence, then you must look at your structure again.

- "What were the main ideas I was trying to get across?" They should answer with your main points.

It is important to get answers to these two questions before moving on to finer points of development and delivery. Everything else is insignificant if your reason for speaking is not being understood.

Videotape your practice session A video is the next best thing to a human critic. When you view your performance on playback, try

Stage 2: Middle Practice Sessions (Feedback)	Stage 3: Final Practice Sessions (Refinement)
4 days before: Give speech on videotape, review with advisors, repeat.	Beginning 3 days before: Practice aloud once a day; read notes or outline once a day. Day of speech: Practice aloud once; review notes just before speaking.
3 days before: Give speech to friendly critic, receive feedback, practice aloud one other time.	Beginning 2 days before: Practice aloud one to three times a day; read over outlines and notes several times. Day of speech: Practice aloud once; review notes just before speaking.
Morning of meeting: Give report to colleague if possible.	Day of presentation: Practice aloud once; review notes just before leaving for meeting.

CHECKLIST

Questions to Elicit Useful Feedback

❏ "Did my ideas flow in a logical sequence?"

❏ "Did the speech hold your attention? What parts were boring? Confusing?"

❏ "Did I prove my points?"

❏ "Did my introduction show you where I was going?"

❏ "Did the conclusion tie the speech together?"

❏ "Did I sound natural?"

❏ "Did I have any distracting mannerisms?"

to get outside yourself and see the image as that of a stranger. In this case, you may temporarily shift your focus from your message and your imagined audience to yourself as a speaker. Become the audience and ask yourself the same questions raised previously. A hazard to avoid here is being too self-critical. Seeing yourself on tape can be devastating if you notice only the aspects that need improvement. Look also for things you are doing right. This is where it can be helpful to watch the video with a friend or coach who can give you a more balanced perspective.

3   Stage 3: Make refinements

By this time, you should be committed to a basic version of your speech while maintaining the flexibility of the extemporaneous mode. You should not be making radical changes.

Make the final practice sessions as realistic as possible. If you are going to use presentation aids, they should be ready early enough that you can include them in your final practice sessions. The same holds true for the final draft of your notecards. Check yourself against your time limit. Practice your speech, standing up, at the rate and volume you will be using. Speaking with rudimentary mechanical amplification to a large audience, for example, will use more breath than will the conversational volume used in early practice. You need to unabashedly boom out your speech in the final practice sessions if that is what it will take to be heard when you actually give the speech.

Continue reading through your notes and outline, but do not think of these activities as a substitute for the formal practice sessions. Save the hours just before the speech for one final run-through and for getting into the proper, relaxed frame of mind.

33b. Speech notes

Speech notes are not the same as your outline; they serve different functions. An outline is used to ensure logical organization. **Speech notes**, in contrast, are used as a guide and a safety net while you are actually speaking.

Like your outline and wording, your notes should go through several drafts. Do not feel committed to the first thing you write.

1   Keywords, key phrases, and material to be cited directly

Unlike your outline—in which your points must be parallel, mutually exclusive, and in full sentences—your speech notes do not have a rigid, regulation form. A point can be represented by a word, a sentence fragment, or an actual sentence or two. See Figure 33-1. What goes into your notes depends on what you find you need during practice.

While practicing, you may also find that you want more than just a keyword reminder to get through an important but tongue-twisting sentence or to ensure that you remember an especially eloquent turn of phrase that has a delicate rhythm. Your notes may also contain material that you will be citing exactly such as long quotations or complicated statistics.

Keep in mind, however, that your notes should remain *notes*. If you make them too extensive and detailed, you risk moving out of the extemporaneous mode and into the realm of the manuscript speech. Your notes should be referred to, not read from.

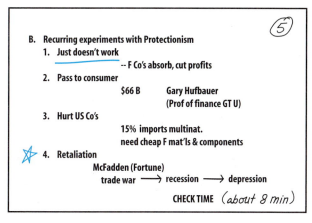

FIGURE 33-1   Speech Notes

2   Format

There are many contexts in which your speaking can occur (see **part 2**), and these will dictate to some degree the format your notes take. The invited speaker at a world affairs forum may use $4'' \times 6''$ cards. An attorney in court does not look out of place referring to a legal pad while speaking. A project manager can glance at the PowerPoint note page on her laptop screen covering the content of her slides. For all of these instances, however, the advice in **33b.1** still applies.

CHECKLIST

Formatting Suggestions for Speech Notes

❑ Words and phrases should be large, well spaced, and uncluttered.

❑ Include visual cues (large card numbers, underlining, indenting, stars, highlighting, different colors) to make it easy for you to find what you want at a glance.

❑ Add time notations to keep on track (writing, "If more than 8 minutes, skip to [card 6/point 4/slide 10]").

❑ Mark optional sections of the speech, if appropriate (highlighting in yellow to mean: "Include this if the audience seems uncertain about my point. Otherwise, omit it").

If you choose to go the notecard route, a few medium-sized cards can easily become an extension of your hand as you gesture and move about. They will not be distracting to your listeners if you seem comfortable with them. Whatever medium you choose for your notes, do not be coy about using them—refer to them honestly. A surreptitious peek will not fool your listeners into believing that you are speaking without aids.

Do not go to the other extreme and get lost in your notes. You should be able to look down, see what is next, and then talk about it. If you find yourself burying your nose in your notes, you have not prepared them correctly.

Speech notes with presentation software Presentation software gives you the option of entering notes to accompany the slides you create. Here is where you can put the tongue twister, the precise data, or the quotation mentioned in **33b.1**, but don't be constrained by the default font settings to make everything too small to read easily. Also, feel free to mark up the output with the other visual cues as illustrated in Figure 33-1. If you don't want to have to deal with 8½″ × 11″ sheets, use a paper cutter to lop off the top part of the printer output with the image of the slide—assuming you have prepared your notes with adequate keywords to cover the content.

33c. Timing your speech

In a speech class, there may be penalties for not reaching a minimum time limit. In most other settings, no one is going to be upset if you take only 15 of the 20 minutes you have been given. However, taking 40 minutes when you have been allotted 20 can disrupt the schedules of other speakers and audience members.

Often, you cannot tell for sure how much time your speech will take until you have gotten well into the practice sessions. In extemporaneous practice, you will experience variations in length as you work with the form of your ideas and the style and rhythm of your speaking. Most inexperienced speakers practice at a speaking rate faster than the one they find necessary for clarity during the speech itself. The more realistic your practice, the less likely you are to incorrectly estimate your time.

To clock your speech, do not glue your eyes to the sweep hand of your watch. Merely note the time when you begin and when you finish. A sweep hand can induce unnatural behavior, such as speaking at twice your normal rate for the last minute if you think you are running long, or slowing your delivery to a tired shuffle. There are more sensible ways to solve problems of length. The first step is to time the parts of your speech. You can have a helper jot down the times of your main points on your outline as you practice, or you can time yourself with a tape recorder.

Look at the relative proportions of the parts of your speech: introduction, body, conclusion. Generally, the body should make up 75 percent of your speech. Does an extended story make the introduction too long? Look, too, at the relative proportions of your main points. Are you spending half your time on only the first main point? Is it worth it?

When your delivery time becomes consistent, mark the cumulative times of the parts in your notes. For example, you might print "2 min" at the bottom right of your notes on the introduction, "5 min" after the first main point, "8 min" after the second, and so on. (See Figure 33-1.) This will make it easier if you need to adapt your speech to audience feedback or a last-minute change in the program.

Some people have internal clocks that are accurate enough that they do not need external cues. If yours is not that well developed (and most of ours are not), feel free to take off your watch and lay it where you can see it, or have a colleague in the audience give you prearranged time signals. Avoid excessive reliance on the clock, though. Become comfortable with your presentation by practicing and timing your speech.

> **KEY POINT**   **Practice Out Loud** Sitting and thinking about your speech, or reading over your outline or notes, is no substitute for rehearsing the speech aloud. Oral practice is essential to get comfortable with phrasing and to check your timing. Do not let "speaker's" block make you put off working orally until the last moment.

8 Presenting Your Speech

CHAPTER 34

Vocal Delivery

As important as preparation, organization, content, and style are, the essence of the speech is still your spoken words. What a waste of time and brainpower if what you have to say cannot be heard or understood. You must be aware of the mechanics of transmitting sound: articulation, breath control, projection, and so on. At the same time, your most important goal is to develop a style of vocal delivery that sounds natural and conversational.

34a. Speak to be heard and understood

1 Volume

For the inexperienced speaker, the appropriate **volume** level will sound too loud. This is understandable, because speeches must be louder than normal conversation.

The only thing that will make loud speaking more comfortable and natural is, of course, practice. In the early stages, you have to ignore the feedback on volume that you receive from your own ears and rely on a friend or perhaps a tape recorder set some distance away. What you are aiming for is a louder voice that retains the rhythms and inflections of your normal conversation. You want to be loud, but not to yell like a drill instructor. As you practice, you will discover that this requires more air for each phrase and that you need to develop breath control to permit you to keep your breathing pauses in normal patterns.

Create a mental image of propelling your voice to the far corners of the room. You will then find yourself doing things that naturally aid projection, such as keeping your head up and opening your mouth wide.

2 Rate

In general, you will need to speak more slowly than you do in daily conversation. To be sure you have timed the speech realistically, practice at the rate and volume you will actually use. An average **rate** of speaking is around 125 words per minute. The need to speak a little louder and a little more distinctly will require extra breath. It will be more natural to pause to breathe between phrases than to rush through the last few words of a sentence and gasp for air.

3 Enunciation

The audience can miss information because of distance from the speaker and distracting noise. Thus it is important to work on crisp, precise **articulation**. Use your tongue, teeth, and lips to pronounce every sound. Be sure you say "govern*m*ent" rather than "goverment" and "hundred" rather than "hunnerd." Do not mumble, run words together, or swallow whole phrases. (See **34d.2** for a discussion of chronic articulation problems.)

You can enunciate properly and still sound natural. It merely takes some practice incorporating precision into your normal conversation instead of creating a separate "speaking persona."

4   If you have an accent

If you have a regional accent or if you are not a native speaker of American English, you may be concerned about being understood. Do not try to eliminate or hide your accent. Your manner of speaking is part of your unique personality. The differences can add interest and charm to your presentation. To ensure comprehension, follow these suggestions:

1. Do not start out with the most important material. Use your introduction to let the audience adjust to the pronunciations and patterns of emphasis that differ from their own. Usually, this will take just a few minutes.
2. Speak more slowly and distinctly than you do in conversation.
3. Be alert to feedback. If you see confused faces, repeat ideas slowly. Unclear vocabulary or mispronunciation of a keyword may mystify your listeners. Try several synonyms for important words.
4. Consider using more presentation aids with key phrases.

If you are a nonnative speaker of English, you may find these two simple tips useful in increasing your intelligibility:

1. Prolong your vowel sounds. In contrast to many other languages, spoken American English carries more meaning in vowels than in consonants. It will sound odd to you, but make a conscious effort to extend your vowels. Maaaaake eeeeeach laaaaaast a loooooong tiiiiiime.
2. Also blend the end of one word into the beginning of the next so that each phrase sounds like one long word. This reduces the perceived choppiness of much accented English.

For more detailed suggestions, refer to

Porter, Patricia A., and Margaret Grant. *Communicating Effectively in English: Oral Communication for Non-Native Speakers*, 2nd ed. Belmont, CA: Wadsworth, 1992.

Raifsnider, Barbara. *American English Pronunciation Program for Speakers of English as a Second Language and Native Speakers with Strong Regional Accents*. New York: Living Language, 1999.

34b. Vocal variety

Your voice should not simply transmit words; you can use it to underscore and reinforce your message. The speaker who has a clear speaking voice devoid of vocal tics wastes these good qualities if there is no variation in pitch, rate, or volume.

Suppose your speech on air pollution contained these two sentences:

When the pollution levels are high, my hair feels gritty, and I have to wash it more often.

Every time pollution reaches the Alert level in our city, more people with chronic respiratory problems die.

Delivering these sentences in the same tone of voice could imply that they are of equal importance. Vocal variety, or changes in emphasis through pace, volume, and pitch show your audience what is significant and can signal humor, seriousness, irony, and a range of emotions.

34c. Standard pronunciation

Some regional differences in the ways people pronounce words are inevitable and cause no problem for public speakers. If, however, a person says "warsh" instead of "wash" or "ax" instead of "ask," many listeners will consider this substandard and draw conscious or unconscious conclusions about the speaker's educational level, competence, and intelligence. This sort of linguistic snobbery can be unfair, but it is easier to change some pronunciations than to change everyone else's attitudes.

1   Identify words that you habitually mispronounce

Look over the list in **Appendix C** and see if you make any of the identified pronunciation errors. If you find one or two words that you mispronounce, you can easily work on correcting them. If you find five or more, you may need help in the form of coaching or coursework. Due to factors in your background or perhaps a lazy ear for the finer distinctions of speech, you probably are also mispronouncing several other words. Here, too, feedback from your practice audience can alert you to errors of which you were unaware.

2   Check the pronunciation of unfamiliar words

Your reading vocabulary and your speaking vocabulary are different. There can be words you frequently see and understand yet rarely hear spoken. Without exposure and feedback, you might develop your own way of mentally pronouncing them and mistakenly add a sound or reverse sounds. If you give a whole speech about the Electorial College (instead of Electoral), your listeners might wonder just how knowledgeable you really are. Or they may be confused or amused if you constantly refer to the need for a counselor to listen "emphatically" when you think you are saying "empathically," a word that means something entirely different. Check words you encounter in research, but do not use regularly, to be sure you have them right.

Refer to these sources for questions of pronunciation:

Dauer, Rebecca M. *Accurate English: A Complete Course in Pronunciation.* Englewood Cliffs, NJ: Prentice-Hall/Regents, 1994.

Prator, Clifford H., Jr., and Betty Wallace Robinett. *Manual of American English Pronunciation,* 4th ed. New York: Holt, 1985.

Silverstein, Bernard. *NTC's Dictionary of American English Pronunciation.* New York: McGraw-Hill, 1994.

Yates, Jean. *Pronounce It Perfectly in English* (with 3 cassettes). Hauppauge, NY: Barrons Educational Audio, 1995.

34d. Distracting vocal characteristics

Your reason for speaking is undermined when your listeners begin to pay less attention to what you are saying and more to how you are saying it: "That's the fifteenth time she's said 'quite frankly'" or "Why doesn't he clear his throat?" Your voice and speech style should be unobtrusive vehicles for your ideas.

Distracting speech habits are difficult to identify and even more difficult to change. Vocal mannerisms become so familiar to you and your closest associates that they are overlooked and cease to distract, but to a new audience they are blatant. Follow the suggestions in chapter **33** for receiving feedback. Use video, audiotape, and critics to get some objective perspective on your performance.

1 Problems of voice quality

The resonant, musical voice you view as an ideal may be beyond your reach, but there is, of course, no one perfect voice for effective speaking. Although the quality and timbre of your voice are determined to a great extent by your larynx and by the size and shape of your nasal cavities, you can still have a pleasing voice unless you are hampered by one or more of the following problems.

- Harshness, hoarseness, or stridency, giving an impression of anger or gruffness.
- Breathiness, thinness, or weakness, resulting in a soft, childish-sounding voice that lacks authority and power.
- Nasality or denasality, producing either whiny or stuffed-up qualities.

2 Problems of articulation

Many people have speech problems that are not severe but that are still sufficiently distracting to impede good communication. Listen closely to your speech for irregularities in the way you produce consonant sounds or blends of consonants. Many articulation errors take the form of *substitutions,* such as "*d*ese" for "*th*ese." Also common are sound *distortions:* the hissing or whistling *s,* and the lazy *l* or *r.* Less frequently encountered articulation errors are *additions* ("ath*a*lete" for "athlete," "real*a*tor" for "realtor"), and *omissions* ("doin'" for "doing," "reg*l*ar" for "regular").

3 Irrelevant sounds and phrases

Do not be afraid to pause between sentences or thoughts when you speak. But avoid filling those pauses with distracting and meaningless sounds and phrases. When a speaker is nervous, a 1-second pause can seem like a 10-second stretch of dead air, and the temptation to fill it with something can be great. Consider these questions:

- Do you use **vocalized pauses:** "uh," "um," "err"?
- Do you fill pauses with other nonspeech sounds: lip smacking, tongue clicking, throat clearing, snuffling?
- Do you unconsciously insert a giggle after every sentence?
- Do you repeat to excess certain words or phrases in nonsensical places?

Here is a list of words and phrases that lose their original meanings when allowed to spread throughout a speech:

okay?

y'know

see

like

I mean

or whatever

and so on and so forth

et cetera

in other words

you might say

4 Repetitious inflection patterns

There are logical and natural places in sentences to vary the pitch of your voice. For instance, in English, the pitch usually goes higher at the end of a question or deepens for an emphatic statement. In normal conversation, we use a variety of inflections without having to think about it. In public speaking, however, there can be a tendency to deliver every sentence with the same inflectional pattern regardless of the sentence's meaning or grammatical structure. This happens when the speaker is not thinking about the content of the speech, is nervous, or is reading from a manuscript or recalling a memorized text. A singsongy, hypnotic pattern of inflection can easily lead to drooping eyelids in the audience.

5 Self-improvement versus professional help

Self-improvement When you identify a problem and your motivation to correct it is strong, you may devise a simple plan of action. Books and recordings are available to provide exercises in breathing and projection. These also have exercises, like tongue twisters, that make apparent the muscle groups used to produce certain sounds properly. You can start with such books as these:

Hahner, Jeffrey C., Martin A. Sokoloff, and Sandra L. Salisch. *Speaking Clearly: Improving Voice and Diction,* 6th ed. (with pronunciation CD-ROM). New York: McGraw-Hill, 2002.

Modisett, Noah F., and James G. Luter, Jr. *Speaking Clearly: The Basics of Voice and Articulation,* 4th ed. Minneapolis: Burgess, 1996.

Wells, Lynn K. *The Articulate Voice,* 4th ed. Boston: Allyn & Bacon, 2004.

For a deeply ingrained habit, you may choose to map out a program of behavior modification. This approach, which has been quite successful in helping people to lose weight or quit smoking, is based on the premise that habits that develop gradually are best eliminated gradually. New behaviors are substituted for old ones, and the new behaviors are rewarded.

CHECKLIST

Steps to Behavior Modification
1. **Assess your present behavior.** Quantify the frequency of the distracting habit.
2. **Set a specific, realistic goal.** If you say "okay?" after nearly every sentence, perhaps 20 times in a 10-minute speech, resolve to cut down to 10 times.
3. **Do not simply estimate your progress.** Have a friend tally the occurrences, or tape each speech yourself. Keep a written chart of your progress.

Professional help Some problems of vocal delivery are difficult to diagnose or solve without professional help. In seeking help, consider the nature and seriousness of your vocal problem, as well as the time and money you are able to commit. Then consult the appropriate professional person, such as a speech therapist, a voice coach, or a public-speaking consultant.

CHAPTER 35

Physical Delivery

Much of how your listeners respond to you is a result of what they see rather than what they hear. Do people dismiss you because you look 10 years younger than you are? Or do shaking knees and fidgeting fingers contradict your confident words? Poor posture and a grim expression can reveal the lie in "I'm so happy to be here!" When practicing and delivering your speech, be aware of the visual image you are creating. As with vocal delivery, the goal is to be natural and to avoid any actions that will distract your audience from your message.

35a. Appearance

As you get ready for your speech, consider what your hairstyle, grooming, and clothing might communicate to your audience. You should show that you took care in preparing, that you consider the event important enough to expend some energy in trying to look good.

Ideally, your clothes should provide a tasteful and unobtrusive frame for your personality and your remarks. Be aware of regional, cultural, and occupational norms. There is no need to be drab, but remember that your audience could be distracted by gaudy colors, busy patterns, eye-catching jewelry, unorthodox combinations of apparel, and any clothing they associate with seduction or courtship.

35b. Distracting mannerisms

Distracting mannerisms fall into two categories: those you have all the time (tucking your hair behind your ear, cracking your knuckles), and those you have only when giving a speech (noisily fanning and squaring up your notecards, rocking back and forth on your heels). Few acts are inherently distracting—it is the repetition of some act that becomes distracting. As with vocal mannerisms, you are probably unaware of the frequency of the act until someone points it out. Thus, the biggest step toward eliminating the problem is becoming aware of it. Sometimes this awareness is sufficient to resolve it, or you may want to adapt the behavior modification techniques described in **34d.5**.

35c. Posture

As a general rule, you should stand when speaking. This focuses audience attention on you and gives you a better view of your listeners. There are exceptions, of course—as a member of a panel discussion, you may be constrained to follow the lead of the moderator. If, however, you can learn to be comfortable speaking without a lectern—with your weight evenly distributed, your notes grasped casually in one hand at waist level, and no props of any kind for support—then you can easily adapt to any setting. Appropriate variations might include leaning across the lectern to show deep involvement or sitting on the edge of a desk or table to signal the shift to an informal mood. Draping yourself across the lectern, lounging at the side with one elbow extended, or standing in an off-center posture are incompatible with the energetic and controlled image of a polished public speaker.

35d. Movements

You can give a perfectly good and proper speech standing behind a lectern. However, most speeches can be aided by movement at appropriate times. Taking a few steps to the left or right or moving closer to your listeners can add variety and emphasis to your speech. You also establish contact with the segment of the audience that you move toward. Moreover, physical movement during a speech is a constructive way to release tension.

Make your movements purposeful. Pacing nervously around the room is distracting. If you are going to move at all, be decisive. Take at least two or three normal paces diagonally or directly forward.

The timing of your movement can reinforce your ideas. Generally, it is not effective to move around when explaining complex material or when delivering your most emotional examples or powerful arguments. Physical movement works best at transitional points, where it signals a change in mood, content, or form.

35e. Gestures

What you should do with your hands in a speech is exactly what you do with them in normal conversation. For some people, using their hands in this manner means hardly using them at all. For others, it means gesturing a great deal. Whether you gesture a little or a lot, you do it to describe, to point out, to enumerate, to emphasize, to entreat, and so on.

There is no need to plan what gestures go with your speech. If you are absorbed with your topic and with communicating it to your listeners, your gestures will emerge spontaneously at the appropriate points. But this will happen only if your hands are free to move.

Too many speakers immobilize their hands completely, out of both the panicky need to cling to something and the desire to prevent uncontrolled movement. Do not lock yourself into any of these gesture-inhibiting stances:

The bear hug: Arms across the chest—one of the most common ways of getting a grip on yourself

The flesh wound:	One arm hanging useless at the side, the other hand serving as a tourniquet above or below the elbow
The choirboy/girl:	Hands clasped at waist level, with fingers entwined
The fig leaf:	Demurely crossed hands, strategically placed

Actually, all of these are perfectly acceptable *transitory* postures. The problem with them lies not in the position of the limbs, but in the temptation to remain in one stance, statuelike, while concentrating on what is coming out of your mouth.

So, what *do* you do with your hands? First, do nothing distracting such as nervously shredding notecards, drumming on the table, or making other kinds of unproductive hand movements:

| *The Lady Macbeth:* | Hands wrung compulsively and continuously to wash out the "stain" of having to speak |
| *Happy pockets:* | Keys, change, and other pocket articles set to jingling by restless hands, the sound competing with the speaker's voice |

Second, do nothing contrived—no rehearsed gestures. What matters most is that your arms, wrists, and fingers are relaxed so that your hands can move if you find a need for that movement arising naturally.

35f. Eye contact

In any speech, even a manuscript speech, you should have eye contact 85 percent of the time, looking down only to read technical material or to refer briefly to your notes. Most important, be sure to maintain eye contact throughout your introduction and conclusion and during the most telling points and pivotal arguments.

Be familiar enough with your material that you can look at as many members of your audience as possible, as often as possible. Maintaining eye contact allows you to read your listeners' faces to get feedback on how your message is being received. Advice to fake eye contact by looking between heads or just over the heads of the people in the back row misses the whole point.

Actually look into the eyes of the individual audience members and hold that contact for at least three seconds. Do not skim across rows of faces. Move your eye contact randomly throughout the room. Do not fall into a head-bobbing pattern: left, center, right, center, left . . .

> **KEY POINT** **Smile** The *one* expression that has the same mean-
> ing in every culture is the smile. Most public speakers underuse or
> misuse this powerful tool. A constant, fixed, jaw-aching grin is as bad
> as a deadpan expression. A smile at a sad or serious moment is inap-
> propriate. However, remind yourself to smile genuinely whenever it
> can reinforce your message. It is one of the easiest ways to establish
> rapport, show your goodwill, and put you and your audience at ease.

CHAPTER 36

Using Presentation Aids

Whether discrete or continuous, hand-held or projected, seen or
heard, your presentation aids should be a seamless part of your
speech, not an interruption. Choosing appropriate aids that supplement and augment your points will go a long way toward easing this
blending (see **27**). Beyond the structural appropriateness of the aid or
aids you select, there are a few simple things you can do to smooth
your aids' introduction.

36a. Practice with your aids

Your aids should be prepared early enough that you can practice
with them several times. (See **33b.3**.) This will alert you to any
changes that might be necessary. Become comfortable with them
so that you do not fumble around during the presentation.

36b. Have your aids ready to go

For audio aids, have the tape or CD cued to the spot so you have
only to press a button. If you are projecting off a computer, have
the program launched and the file(s) open. Don't subject your audience to a navigation exhibition through your folder structure.

36c. Face the audience

Be so familiar with your material that you can look at your listeners while explaining a visual aid. Often, a speaker will turn away
from the audience and talk directly at the visual aid. This deprives
the speaker of feedback and strains the listeners' hearing.

36d. Keep talking

Avoid long pauses when demonstrating a process. If there is some
complexity, or if many steps are needed to produce your desired

result, you might take a hint from television cooking shows and prepare a series of aids to demonstrate the various phases. Doing so will eliminate those periods when both you and the audience are waiting for something to happen. For example, a speaker could say, "Then you apply glue to the two blocks, press them together like this, and let the bond dry. Here are some that have already dried. Now, I'll show you the next step. . . ." When you cannot avoid a time lag introduced by some process, have a planned digression—some bit of history related to the process, perhaps—to fill the gap.

36e. Do not become secondary to your slides

It is a common scene in conference and convention settings: One or two large screens dominate a room holding dozens or hundreds of people; dwarfed by the screens, a speaker is partially hidden behind a bank of computer monitors, hunched over in the dim light, clicking away at the mouse while talking into the body mike, and often commenting on some glitch with the system. Obvious problems here are lack of connection with the audience because of the darkened room and the focus on the machine, confinement of the speaker to the space in front of the computer, and the "aid" becoming an impediment.

If you are in a situation in which this sort of projection will be used, take steps to counteract the potential difficulties. Enlist a colleague or friend to operate the computer so that you are free to move around and make eye contact with the audience. If you cannot avoid operating the equipment, or if you must compensate for dim lighting, use vocal variety to counterbalance immobility and lack of visibility. (See **34b**.) If possible, use the slides for key illustrations and points, but leave the screen blank the rest of the time.

36f. Do not let your aids become distractions

Keep your visual aids out of sight, turned off, covered, or turned away from your audience until you are ready to use them. Remove or recover them immediately after they have served their purpose. If you are using an overhead projector or similar device, turn it off whenever you can to eliminate the cooling fan noise. For a continuous visual aid like a PowerPoint presentation of charts and graphs that support particular points, introduce a blank slide between each content slide. When you have finished addressing the point related to one of the content slides, move to the blank slide until it is time to reveal the next content slide as you get to the point it illustrates. If you use a flip chart, use every other sheet when you are preparing it—this gives you the same effect as the blank slide, and you should use it in the same way.

Refrain from passing objects around the room; it will cause a ripple of inattention. This rule is flexible, especially when you are dealing with an unusual object and a small audience, but still it is probably best to share the item *after* the speech—say, during the discussion period. By the same token, handouts should be distributed after a speech. You want the audience to listen now and read later. (Of course, there are some contexts, primarily business, where this is not necessarily the norm. See **7**.)

Finally, presentation aids are most distracting when you are clumsy with them. Be sure that your charts are in the right order, your models are set up, and your equipment is in perfect working order.

KEY POINT **Avoiding Presentation Aid Fiascoes** Practice carefully, arrive in plenty of time for setup, and bring interface cables, pins, tape, extension cords, extra projector bulbs, CD-ROM backups, and the like to ensure that what you envision comes to pass.

If you are using electronic aids, find the outlets in the room and actually test both your aids and the outlets for proper functioning. If you are being provided with equipment, insist that it come with spare bulbs, batteries, and so on. If you are using a computer, make sure it is compatible with the projection system.

CHAPTER 37

Answering Questions

The **question-and-answer period** is a great opportunity to further the goals of your speech. While you spoke, you attempted to address the needs of your audience, and now you can see how close you came. From your listeners' questions, you can learn what points are unclear or what arguments and objections they have. Communicate an eagerness to interact with your listeners and to hear their ideas on your topic.

Do not lose your delivery skills just because the speech is over. Maintain eye contact, and avoid fidgeting or mumbling.

37a. Come prepared

As you prepare your speech, anticipate the questions that will arise naturally from each of your points. You can also have the friends who listen to your practice sessions ask you questions afterward. Although you can never predict the exact questions that will come up, certain ones are more probable than others. Rehearse aloud possible answers to the most complicated and difficult ones. This is how public figures prepare for news conferences.

Ideally, your research has been so extensive that you have much more material than you were able to use, and you have reviewed this extra material so you are familiar enough with the content to use it in response to questions.

37b. Invite questions and be direct in your answers

Do not worry if there are not any questions immediately, or if at first there are long pauses between questions. It usually takes your listeners a moment to collect their thoughts. In some cases, you can start the ball rolling yourself by asking a question of the audience.

Call on questioners in the order they sought recognition, and maintain eye contact while a question is being asked. If you are not sure you understand the question, paraphrase it and ask the questioner if it is accurate. When both of you are satisfied, restate or paraphrase it for the entire audience and direct the answer to them.

Be sure you *answer* the question. To avoid oversimplification, you want to elaborate, expand, or qualify your answer, but if your discussion becomes too diffuse, you will appear to be avoiding the issue. Consequently, always include a one-sentence, direct answer in your response to a question. For emphasis, place this sentence first or last, as in these examples:

First: *Yes, I do oppose building nuclear power plants,* at least until several safety questions are answered satisfactorily. My reasons include . . .

Last: . . . so, because of all these serious problems I see, my answer to your question would be *Yes, I do oppose building new nuclear power plants at this time.*

37c. Manage self-indulgent questioners

The purpose of a question-and-answer period is to clarify issues for the entire audience. When individual audience members attempt to use this time for detailed consultation on a specialized problem or to get on their favorite soapbox, you have an obligation as speaker to bring the interaction back on its true course. Be prepared to keep control of the situation by dealing in a firm and tactful manner with several types of distracting questioners.

■ *The person who wants to give a speech.* This person may agree or disagree with you, or may have a favorite ax to grind that is only tangentially related to your topic. It becomes obvious that, rather than asking a real question, the person is taking advantage of an assembled audience to hold forth. It is rarely effective to ask, "What is your question?" The person will just say,

"Don't you agree that . . ." or "What do you think of the position that . . ." and take off for another five minutes. You have to jump in at the end of a sentence, manufacture a question somewhat related to the person's ramblings, answer it, and recognize another questioner on the opposite side of the room.

- *The person who wants to have an extended dialogue.* This person might begin with a genuine question but, after you respond, may refuse to relinquish the floor by countering with follow-up questions, commenting on your answer, or opening new lines of discussion. The best way to deal with this sort of person is to end the exchange firmly but with a compliment: "Thank you, you've given me quite a number of interesting insights here."

- *The person who wants to pick a fight.* Intellectual confrontation and probing, penetrating questions are to be expected, and even welcomed, from audience members who disagree with you. But sometimes questioners become inappropriately argumentative and mount hostile, personal attacks against a speaker. Rather than seeking an answer to a question they are trying to destroy your credibility. Do not let them succeed by becoming angry or by defending yourself against generalized name-calling. Pick out the part of such a person's diatribe that contains the kernel of a question, paraphrase it, and answer it calmly and reasonably.

Q: What about all this poisonous junk that you greed-crazed despoilers dump into our rivers to kill our children and whole species of animals?

A: The questioner has brought up the valid and difficult subject of toxic waste disposal. What is our company doing about it? Well . . .

In short, respond to these disruptive people diplomatically. Do not take cheap shots or direct humor at them to shut them off.

Likewise, when you are taken aback by incomprehensible questions or questions that demonstrate gross ignorance or misinformation, you should react positively. Avoid language that embarrasses the questioner or points out errors:

Not: You've totally confused fission and fusion!

But: Many of those problems relate to nuclear *fission*. The *fusion* reaction is quite different. It works like this. . . .

Try to find ways to dignify bad questions and turn them into good ones. Your listeners' empathy is with the questioner, who may be nervous or confused. Your efforts to put others at ease will earn you an audience's goodwill.

Sample Speeches and Outlines

This appendix contains two sample persuasive speeches and the out-lines used in creating them, as well as a sample outline for an informa-tive speech—the "comic book outline" referred to in various chapters of this handbook. Annotated versions of these materials are available via *The Speaker's Compact Handbook* online resources.

A. Sample persuasive speech transcript (1)

In a persuasive speaking course, students were required to develop a 10-minute persuasive message that was adapted to the specific audience in the class. The speaker had given previous speeches on environmental topics to this class. Based on that experience and through an audience survey she concluded that her listeners were generally favorably disposed to these issues but were not ex-tremely well informed.

Rainforests Are in Need of Defense

by Karen McNeil

"Save the Rainforest!" But for what and from whom? The rainfor-est issue has had great media coverage, and we are all too familiar with this slogan. I'm not sure, though, that we're actually aware of what is at stake. I know I wasn't, even being really concerned about the environmental issues that face this planet, until I came across the orangutan. I'm an anthropology minor, and this semes-ter I'm taking a class that details the habitats of primates. This is where I got to know more about orangutans, the threats they face, and what it means to the rest of us.

Do you know where orangutans live? In the wild, these great apes live on two Indonesian islands: Borneo and Sumatra. Their habitat is exclusively tropical rainforest. They are frugivorous, which means that they rely on fruit as their source of nutrition. Because of this, they need a wide range of habitat to provide them with fruit year-round. Orangutans used to free-range in Southeast Asia, but development has pushed them out of these areas. The primary threat to these animals is habitat destruction—destruction of the tropical rainforests. I was alarmed to see that almost all of the primates live exclusively in tropical rainforests. Suddenly I had a new perspective on what we stand to lose as we continue to de-stroy these tropical zones.

These, then, are the questions that I want to address today: What are we saving when we save the rainforests? Who are we saving them from? What can we do that can actually make a difference?

First, I'll briefly outline the threats to the ecology of the rainforest and then detail some of the investment policies of the World Bank, which is the institution that contributes to major destruction of the tropical rainforests. And then finally I have some suggestions for what you can do to ensure the well-being of our planet.

To understand the seriousness of the current threat to the rainforests, we need to recognize what they represent ecologically, culturally, and economically. These elaborate ecosystems are a kaleidoscope of biological diversity. The vegetation in these towering forests is divided into dozens of layers, each of which provides a distinct habitat for different plants and animals, literally thousands of species. Within the tropical belt that circles the equator there exist more plant and animal species than in the rest of the world combined! The rainforests are also home to millions of indigenous people. Thousands of tribal groups exist in rainforests throughout the world. Most of these peoples live as hunters and gatherers or they conduct small agricultural projects that fit the cycle of the land. Their centuries-old cultural practices have grown up in harmony with their environment. Another value of the rainforests is the important role they play in our weather patterns, both locally and globally. In fact, they are often referred to as the lungs of our planet. Economically, these regions are a bountiful source of rubber, hardwood, food products, and essential medicines for heart disease and cancer.

Although lush, these ecosystems are really quite fragile. Similar to the old-growth forests that run from the northern part of our state up through the Pacific Northwest, these interdependent biological systems took centuries to develop. Without the constant renewal of the protective overgrowth and dense canopies the inhabitants of the lower levels—plants, animals, birds—die from exposure to the sun. The laterite soil on which the forests are built turns to clay and erodes quickly when cleared, as many farmers and ranchers are beginning to discover. Topsoil is swept away by floods. Sediment flows into the rivers and affects fishing. Most of the damage is irreversible. You can see why deforestation for farming, ranching, and logging has such a devastating effect.

Yet it goes on, and worsens, even as we speak. To give you some sense of the scope and urgency of the situation, let me cite some statistics from *The Rainforest Book* by Scott Lewis. Half of the earth's rainforests have already been destroyed. Thirty-five million acres a year are eliminated. That's an area the size of New York State gone forever. The rates of deforestation have doubled in the last decade and they are continuing to rise. In the name of progress, the industrialized Western world destroys these irreplaceable plants and animals. It alters the environment of the region and the climate of the world. It wipes out indigenous cultures of rainforest peoples without even realizing the rich traditions that they have to offer us. These tribal people are not in a position to resist change that others define as progress. Imagine what it would be like if you had to defend your own home against lawyers of a multinational logging firm. Would you have any chance of winning? If it would be an uphill fight for someone like you, think what it would be like for someone from a community that has no grounding in Western-style law and that has no connection to the Western economic system.

Profits are the major factor that lead to rainforest destruction. My next point highlights the destructive investment practices that lead to environmental ruin. One investment institution that can be credited with funding a majority of the environmental devastation is the World Bank. After World War II the world community assembled the World Bank to help war-torn countries rebuild. After they completed that work, they turned to the Third World. The Rainforest Action Network of San Francisco argues that the World Bank has turned the Third World into a resource colony for the Western industrialized nations. The World Bank has become a power that dictates what's developed and created by countries, and also even at times how governments treat their own people. The World Bank is an organization funded by money that is borrowed on international markets and also money contributed by 148 member nations. The United States is the most influential of these members. We have 20 percent of the overall vote. The president of the World Bank, Robert Zoellick, is a United States citizen. U.S. members of the World Bank are given direction by the United States Department of Treasury and the Congress. The money the United States supplies to the World Bank comes from the taxpayers. The World Bank prefers to finance huge megaprojects: hydroelectric dams, massive relocations and resettlements, agricultural and industrial projects that involve building roads into areas that have previously been inaccessible. Bruce Rich of Environmental Defense states that over half of the loans given by the World Bank and its three regional counterparts in recent years have gone to support projects in sectors that can seriously affect tropical forests. Survival International, an organization that advocates the rights of tribal people and serves as a watchdog of the World Bank, makes these recommendations for the bank's reform. First, they want public access to all information regarding the bank's projects. They want the World Bank's staff to include people that are trained in ecology as well as in socioeconomic analysis. Systematic involvement of organizations representing the environment and indigenous people should be a part of all projects. The bank should increase its proportion of ecologically beneficial programs. These Survival International recommendations reflect their analysis that the World Bank has been developing projects solely on economic criteria without regarding or understanding the environmental effects of their actions. If you're shocked that these practices continue, and with our country's support, I'm glad. I want you to see how important it is that we understand these issues. I have some recommendations that I want you to consider adopting in your own lives.

My suggestions begin with learning more about this complex problem and then taking action both individually and collectively. Education is the key to bringing about change. Read some of the books that discuss the rainforest. Here is one concise (and inexpensive) one: *The Rainforest Book* by Scott Lewis, published in 1990. Share your knowledge about environmental subjects with children and support them as they try to make sense of these issues. Take some classes that are offered here at San Jose State that promote a global perspective on environmental issues. For instance, I know that many of you are communication studies majors or minors. You might be especially interested in a course that Dr. Dennis Jaehne will be offering next fall called Communication and the Environment. I took it the first time it was offered and it was excellent! Whenever you possibly can, travel to other countries and see for yourself what's going on. I've traveled four times around the world, and I wouldn't trade those experiences for anything. It's one thing to understand intellectually that our industrially advanced lifestyle and Western values are not universal. But it becomes meaningful in a different way when you have the chance to experience firsthand the incredible diversity of this planet. You realize how privileged we are in terms of material goods and political freedom. Yet you also see that there are places in this world of unbelievable physical beauty and cultures of such depth and richness that they must be preserved and cherished. Travel, especially off the beaten path of the usual tourist spots, really dramatizes the choices before those of us who live in rich and powerful societies. We can either expand our consumerism more and more by exploiting other parts of the world or we can start evaluating the impact of our economic policies on the rest of the world. Through education, as you continue to learn about how we are all complicit in the problems of the rainforest, you will want to take some direct action. There are several ways to do this.

First, you can boycott products that are known to cause destruction of the rainforest. A typical four-ounce fastfood hamburger that's been made from "rainforest beef" took 55 square feet of rainforest to produce. Is one hamburger worth that destruction? We can insist on clearer labeling of meat so that we know where it comes from. Disposable chopsticks are oftentimes made from tropical timber, or in some cases whole stands of rainforest are cleared to plant trees that produce a color of wood more popular for chopsticks. In 1979 Japan used enough disposable chopsticks to build 11,000 timber-frame family dwellings. You can imagine what those statistics would be today. You may not use many chopsticks, but you can be aware of the exotic wood products that are being stripped from these regions. I've included a list of these woods on a handout that I'll give you in a few minutes.

Next, you can support organizations that are involved with saving the rainforest. I've listed several of them on the same handout. It is only through collective action in organized groups like these that we have any chance of influencing the policies of government and of the World Bank. The decision makers will continue to listen to business interests unless we show them how many of us there are that value long-term social and environmental goals over short-term material gains.

Finally, I encourage you all to stop by the Art Quad before three o'clock today and buy a scoop of Rainforest Crunch ice cream. Representatives of Ben & Jerry's Ice Cream are going to be here today, and they are going to donate the proceeds of the ice cream sales to SAFER, Students Affiliated for Environmental Respect, the campus environmental group. Rainforest Crunch is made from Brazil nuts, thus making it advantageous for the trees in at least one rainforest to be left standing. You'll find the address of the Rainforest Action Network printed on every carton of Rainforest Crunch they sell. This is just one example of how business organizations can take steps to be socially responsible while still making a profit and offering a quality product.

Since I began this presentation, 1,000 acres of rainforest have been destroyed or degraded severely. These fragile ecosystems need to be protected; once they're destroyed they're gone forever. My studies about the primates intensified my interest in the rainforest because I realized how fragile they are and that these precious creatures have become very close to extinction. It isn't the Brazilian or Malaysian or Indonesian farmers who pose the real threat to these areas. It is the governments of the developed countries in cooperation with multinational development banks that initiate large projects and create real havoc in these areas. As Americans we contribute to the problem in a number of ways. As we drive the world market through our obsessive consumption, we entangle developing nations in outrageous debts. As American taxpayers we're helping to fund the World Bank's destructive policies through the taxes we pay. There are other organizations worldwide that we could support, groups that are committed to grassroots development. These smaller projects often are far more beneficial to the local people in other countries. The only way that we can hope to get a realistic picture of this problem is through education and involvement. We can no longer afford to think merely on a local or national level. We must learn to think on a global level and feel that the well-being of humanity and this planet is a responsibility we all share. Although the problem is a huge one, we as individuals should not feel powerless. By taking even a small step, you can begin to make a difference. Please, don't wait. Take a step now.

B. Sample persuasive speech outline (1)

Here is a sample speech outline for the preceding speech. This is just one illustration of the sort of speech outline that helps a speaker get organized. Some outlines are more spare and compact, and others are more like argumentative briefs containing full citations of all evidence.

Notice that the main points listed here are never stated in precisely those words in the speech transcription. The outline is a logical plan, a place to set down your main points in propositional form, to fit the subpoints beneath the main points, and fit your support beneath the subpoints. Uncluttered with transitions and extra words, and properly indented, the outline allows the reader to see the basic speech development at a glance.

Along with the outline of the body of the speech, we include the thesis sentence and identify the text that delineates the parts of the introduction (attention-getter, psychological orientation, logical orientation) and conclusion (logical closure, psychological closure, clincher).

Thesis The continuing and accelerating destruction of the tropical rainforests, due largely to the policies of industrialized nations, poses a serious threat to the global environment and community—a threat that must be met by immediate action from concerned individuals.

Introduction

Attention-Getter "Save the Rainforest!" But for what and from whom? . . . what is at stake.

Psychological Orientation I know I wasn't, even being really concerned about the environmental issues . . . we continue to destroy these tropical zones.

Logical Orientation These, then, are the questions that I want to address today . . . well-being of our planet.

Body

    I. Tropical rainforests, important to the well-being of the planet, are being subjected to rampant destruction, with irreversible effects.

       A. Rainforests are an important component of the planet.

          1. Ecologically complex systems

            a. Towering forests divided into layers

            b. More plant and animal species than rest of world

          2. Thousands of tribal groups live there.

            a. Hunters and gatherers/small agriculture

            b. Irreplaceable ancient cultures

          3. Rainforests affect weather patterns.

      4. Economically important
        a. Rubber, hardwood, food products
        b. Medicines for heart disease and cancer
  B. Rainforests are in serious danger.
      1. They are fragile.
        a. Need dense canopies to protect inhabitants of lower layers
        b. When exposed, laterite soil turns to clay, erodes
        c. Topsoil swept away, affects rivers
        d. Damage is irreversible
      2. Rainforests are being destroyed.
        a. By farming, logging, ranching
        b. Half of world's rainforests already gone
        c. 35 million acres a year, size of New York
        d. Rate of destruction is doubling
        e. Tribal people powerless to resist
II. Short-sighted economic policies of the industrially advanced countries, carried out through multilateral development agencies like the World Bank, are responsible for the destruction.
  A. The World Bank's policies tend to serve the industrialized nations.
      1. History
        a. Formed to rebuild after WWII
        b. Later took on Third World development
      2. U.S. plays major role in the World Bank's policies
        a. Of the 148 member nations, U.S. funds 20 percent
        b. President, Robert Zoellick, is U.S. citizen
        c. Directed by U.S. Department of Treasury and Congress
  B. World Bank policies are destructive to the rainforests.
      1. Tends to fund huge projects such as hydroelectric dams
      2. Half of its loans have gone to projects that endanger rainforests
  C. Reforms of World Bank have been suggested.
      1. Public access to records
      2. Staff should include ecologists
      3. Should collaborate with environmental organizations and representatives of indigenous peoples
      4. Should consider more than economic criteria in selecting projects
III. Concerned individuals can help save the rainforests through education and collective action.
  A. Education is a key to saving the rainforests.
      1. Read books
      2. Educate children

        3. Take courses

        4. Travel

    B. Boycott products that cause destruction to rainforests.

        1. Need to label meat so we can tell if it is "rainforest beef"

        2. Wood from tropical lumber

           a. Chopsticks from light wood could have built 11,000 houses

           b. List of exotic woods to avoid will be on handout

    C. Support organizations to save the rainforests.

        1. Several national and international groups listed on handout

        2. Campus organization SAFER

           a. Ice cream social today until three at Art Quad

           b. Ben & Jerry's Rainforest Crunch saves nut trees

Conclusion

Logical Closure Since I began this presentation, . . . education and involvement.

Psychological Closure We can no longer afford to think merely . . . not feel powerless.

Clincher By taking even a small step, you can begin to make a difference. Please, don't wait. Take a step now.

C.   Sample persuasive speech transcript (2)

The speaker gave this speech at a speech tournament. He was required to give a memorized speech no longer than 10 minutes in length, and to provide a preparation outline that included a section of works cited. As you read this speech, note the organizational pattern the speaker used to enhance his persuasive message. Also consider the ethics of his persuasive methods.

No More Sugar!
by Hans Erian

Arnell Scott was 15 years old and weighed over 300 pounds. One day his mother noticed that he was losing weight rapidly and was constantly thirsty, so she took him to the hospital. There the doctors diagnosed this 15-year-old with Type 2 Diabetes. According to *Newsday,* July 20, 1999, Type 2 Diabetes—which is usually associated with adults—is now increasing among an alarming rate in children, leaving them open to life-threatening complications like blindness, kidney disease, heart disease, and stroke at ages as young as thirty. Dr. Barbara Linder of the National Institute of Diabetes and Digestion and Kidney Diseases attributes this rise in Type 2 Diabetes to a rise in obesity, and obesity is on the rise because of sugar.

According to the *New York Times* of February 16, 2001, of the top 10 most bought foods at supermarkets, most are sugar-rich junk foods. A Georgetown University study shows that 25 percent of the calories adults consume are from sugar, but for kids it's closer to 50 percent. That means that the average person in this room consumes about 125 to 150 pounds of sugar per year. *Consumer Reports on Health* of August 2001 says that when blood sugar levels rise, so does the risk of disease and even death. Americans are consuming too much sugar; it's destroying our health, but most don't even realize it. Today we'll look at the misconceptions average Americans have regarding their intake of sugar. Next, we'll look at what these misconceptions lead to. And, finally, we'll explore some ways you can overcome your lethal sweet tooth.

So why are Americans consuming all of this sugar? The two main reasons are ignorance and an increased consumption of soda pop. We often consume sugar without even realizing it. This is partly due to the food-labeling process. The FDA and the Sugar Association have been fighting a linguistic tug-of-war since about 1970 over the definition of sugar. Let's look at the basics: Fructose is good sugar that you find in fruits and vegetables, and sugar is what you find in most of the items you eat. These types of sugar go by many different names, including sucrose, dextrose, corn syrup, and high-fructose corn syrup. The last one, high-fructose corn syrup, may cause some confusion at first because it has the word *fructose* in it, but don't be fooled! This is just another type of refined sugar.

Now, let's take a look at a few common items that you can find at any local Safeway to see the confusion in action. Here we have a cranberry tangerine mix—a juice that we expect to be healthy for us—but notice that the second ingredient is high-fructose corn syrup. Now let's take a look at Wheaties, supposedly one of the healthiest breakfast cereals on the market—even their slogan promotes health. Let's look at the ingredients: Number one is whole wheat, and number two is sugar. And we also have corn syrup (another bad sugar) and brown-sugar syrup (another bad sugar). All of this sugar can't be in the breakfast of champions! These are the kinds of "health foods" that we put into our bodies daily, and we assume that they are healthy for us, but they're not.

The other reason Americans consume so much sugar is because of the increased consumption of soda pop. Let's take a look at Coca-Cola. Notice that its second ingredient is high-fructose corn syrup and/or sucrose. (Here the manufacturer used the chemical name for sugar, sucrose.) The average can of Coke has about 10 teaspoons of sugar. According to the *San Jose Mercury News* of January 17, 1999, since the mid-80s, U.S. soda pop consumption has increased by 43 percent to more to 85 gallons per American per year. That's 555 cans annually for every American. How much soda do you drink?

Now that we've seen that Americans are consuming too much sugar because of ignorance and an increased consumption of soda pop, let's look at how all this sugar has had a negative impact on our health. The *New York Times* of September 9, 2001, says that there is convincing new evidence about the relationship between weight gain in children and soda pop consumption. The *New York Times* goes on to say that obesity is directly linked to soda pop consumption, regardless of the amount of food you eat or the lack of exercise. Part of the explanation for this may be that the body has trouble adapting to such intense concentrations of sugar taken in liquid form. Obesity has been linked to high blood pressure, high cholesterol, and heart disease. Obesity is also linked to cancer. In fact, obesity is now considered the number-two killer in the United States because of its link to cancer, according to the *New York Times* of October 9, 2001. The *Hindu* of April 26, 2001, says that obese people are 70 percent more likely to get pancreatic cancer, which has a 95 percent mortality rate. The U.S. Department of Health affirms the claim that obesity causes several types of cancer, including postmenopausal breast cancer and colon cancer.

Along with causing cancer, obesity is also a key cause of diabetes. According to the Hartford Chronic of September 9, 2001, since 1991 adult obesity has increased by 60 percent and the percentage of overweight kids has doubled in the last decade. Helping to put significant numbers of children and adolescents among the ranks of Type 2 diabetics, Type 2 Diabetes usually comes on after the age of 45. Dr. Gerald Bernstein predicts that left unchecked, the onset of more diabetes could have a huge impact, with more than 500 million diabetics worldwide in 25 years. We're looking at a tidal wave of suffering and an avalanche of healthcare bills if people don't change their ways.

Now we've seen that Americans are consuming too much sugar and that it's destroying their health, one bite or sip at a time. We obviously need to decrease our sugar intake. So now we'll look at what we could do at a national level. Next, we'll look at what we can do as individuals. On a national level, we need to do two things: increase awareness and decrease soda pop consumption. Kelly Brownwell, director of Yale University's Eating and Weight Disorders, has suggested that we regulate food advertisements directed at children to provide equal time for pro-nutrition and physical-activity messages. She also suggests that we change the price of foods to make healthier foods less expensive. Nationwide, schools should mimic what nearly a dozen states are already considering, and that is to turn off school vending machines during class time, stripping them of sweets, or to impose new taxes on soda pop machines. The *New York Times* of February 16, 2001, says that taking these actions will discourage kids fiom buying sweets. We can even take this proposal one step further and not only impose taxes on school vending machines but also on soft drinks in general. These are a few ways we can create incentives for people to eat healthily and decrease their sugar intake.

Now, we would all like someone else to make us healthy, but what is really needed is a personal commitment to health. You know the answer to the question "How do I get rid of my sugar addiction?" Simple. Start off slow and follow Dr. Ralph Gowen's advice: moderation. The author of *Optimal Wellness* has suggested that dessert a few times a week or a can of pop once or twice a week isn't going to hurt anyone's health. In fact, the World Health Organization has suggested that between 0 to 10 percent of your daily calories come from sugar, and this will still be considered within a safe range. Try to stick to good foods, though, like fruits, vegetables, and fruit juices that don't have any added sugar. Become a label reader and be aware of what you're eating.

Today we've looked at the misconceptions about sugar, looked at where these misconceptions lead, and have found some solutions to our sugar addiction. Americans have become unhealthy because they're eating too much sugar. Americans need to decrease their sugar intake before more of them end up like 15-year-old Arnell Scott, having to take daily insulin injections just to stay alive.

D. Sample persuasive speech outline (2)

Here is the sample speech outline for the preceding speech. Note the source citations at the end of the outline. Can you identify the attention-getter, the psychological orientation, and the logical orientation for this speech?

Thesis The health problems that many Americans have as a result of misconceptions about the effect of too much sugar in their diets can be alleviated by taking action at the national level and on a personal level.

Introduction

    I. Arnell Scott was 15 years old and weighed over 300 pounds.

        A. He was losing weight rapidly and was constantly thirsty, so his mother took him to the hospital.

        B. There the doctors diagnosed him with Type 2 Diabetes.

    II. According to *Newsday,* July 20, 1999, Type 2 Diabetes is increasing alarmingly in children.

        A. Type 2 Diabetes is usually associated with adults.

        B. This type of diabetes can cause life-threatening complications like blindness, kidney disease, heart disease, and stroke at ages as young as thirty.

        C. Dr. Barbara Linder of the National Institute of Diabetes and Digestion and Kidney Diseases attributes this rise to a rise in obesity caused by the overconsumption of sugar.

III. According to the *New York Times* of February 16, 2001, the top 10 most bought foods at supermarkets are sugar-rich junk foods.

   A. A Georgetown University study shows that 25 percent of the calories adults consume are from sugar, but for kids it's closer to 50 percent.

   B. The average person in this room consumes about 125 to 150 pounds of sugar per year.

   C. *Consumer Reports on Health* of August 2001, says that when blood sugar levels rise, so does the risk of disease and death.

IV. Americans are consuming an unhealthy amount of sugar, but most don't realize it.

   A. Today we'll look at the misconceptions Americans have about their sugar intake.

   B. We'll also look at the health problems these misconceptions lead to.

   C. Finally, we'll explore how you can overcome your lethal sweet tooth.

Body

I. The two main reasons Americans consume so much sugar are ignorance and an increased consumption of soda pop.

   A. We often consume sugar without even realizing it.

      1. The food-labeling process is confusing in regard to sugar, whose definition has been debated by the FDA and the Sugar Association since 1970.

         a. Fructose is good sugar found in fruits and vegetables.

         b. Bad sugar is found in most other foods and is called many different names, including sucrose, dextrose, corn syrup, and high-fructose corn syrup.

         c. The last one, high-fructose corn syrup, causes some confusion because it includes the word *fructose*, but it is a type of refined sugar.

      2. Common items found at any local Safeway—and commonly thought to be healthy for us—illustrate the confusion.

         a. The second ingredient in cranberry tangerine mix is high-fructose corn syrup.

         b. The first ingredient in the breakfast cereal Wheaties is whole wheat, but the second ingredient is sugar, followed by the two bad sugars, corn syrup and brown-sugar syrup.

      c. We eat these "health foods" daily, assuming they are healthy for us.

  B. Americans consume too much sugar as a result of drinking too much soda pop.

    1. Let's take a look at the amount of sugar in Coca-Cola.

      a. Its second ingredient is high-fructose corn syrup and/or sucrose.

      b. The average can of Coke has about 10 teaspoons of sugar.

    2. According to the *San Jose Mercury News* of January 17, 1999, since the mid-80s, U.S. soda pop consumption has increased by 43 percent to more to 85 gallons per American per year.

      a. That's 555 cans annually for every American.

      b. How much soda do you drink?

II. Sugar has had a negative impact on our health because it causes obesity, which can lead to a number of health problems, including diabetes.

  A. The *New York Times* of September 9, 2001, cites new evidence that links obesity in children directly to soda pop consumption.

    1. The body has trouble adapting to such intense concentrations of sugar in liquid form.

    2. This overconsumption of sugar leads to obesity, which has been linked to a number of serious health problems.

      a. Obesity can cause high blood pressure, high cholesterol, and heart disease.

      b. Additionally, obesity is now considered the number-two killer in the United States because of its link to cancer, according to the *New York Times* of October 9, 2001.

        i. The *Hindu* of April 26, 2001, says that obese people are 70 percent more likely to get pancreatic cancer, which has a 95 percent mortality rate.

        ii. The U.S. Department of Health affirms the claim that obesity causes several types of cancer, including post-menopausal breast cancer and colon cancer.

  B. Along with causing cancer, obesity is also a key cause of diabetes.

    1. According to the *Hartford Courant* of September 9, 2001, since 1991 adult obesity has increased by 60 percent and the percentage of overweight kids has doubled in the last decade.

       a. This increase in obesity has led to Type 2 Diabetes in significant numbers of children and adolescents.

       b. Type 2 Diabetes usually comes on after the age of 45.

    2. Dr. Gerald Bernstein predicts that left unchecked, the onset of more diabetes could have a huge impact.

       a. More than 500 million people worldwide could develop diabetes in 25 years.

       b. We're looking at a tidal wave of suffering and an avalanche of healthcare bills if people don't change their ways.

III. To improve our health, we need to decrease our sugar intake, both at a national and a personal level.

  A. On a national level, we need to increase awareness about the hazards of sugar and decrease soda pop consumption.

    1. Kelly Brownwell, director of Yale University's Eating and Weight Disorders, suggests we increase awareness and provide incentives to eat more healthily by regulating food advertisements and amending the cost of food.

       a. Regulate food advertisements directed at children so they provide equal time for pro-nutrition and physical-activity messages.

       b. Change the price of food to make healthier foods less expensive.

    2. We can decrease soda pop consumption by making it more difficult to purchase soft drinks, especially in schools.

       a. Nationwide, schools should turn off school vending machines during class time, strip them of sweets, or impose new taxes on soda pop machines.

       b. We can also impose new taxes on soft drinks in general.

  B. To get rid of our addiction to sugar, we must make a personal commitment to health.

    1. Start off slow and eat sugar in moderation.

       a. Dr. Ralph Golan, author of *Optimal Wellness*, suggests that dessert a few times a week or a can of pop once or twice a week isn't going to hurt anyone's health.

       b. The World Health Organization suggests that between 0 to 10 percent of your daily calories can come from sugar and you'll still be safe.

      c. Try to stick to good foods like fruits, vegetables, and fruit juices that don't have any added sugar.

    2. Become a label reader and be aware of what you're eating.

Conclusion

I. Today we've explored the hazards of sugar and how we can avoid these hazards.

    A. We've looked at common misconceptions about sugar.

    B. We've looked at the health problems that can result from these misconceptions.

    C. We've explored some solutions to our sugar addiction.

II. Americans have become unhealthy because they're eating too much sugar.

    A. Americans need to decrease their sugar intake.

    B. If they don't, more of them will end up like 15-year-old Arnell Scott, having to take daily insulin injections just to stay alive.

Works Cited

Brody, Jane E. "Don't Lose Sight of Real, Everyday Risks." *New York Times*. 9 October 2001.

Condon, Garret. "Diabetes Epidemic Menaces the U.S.: Costs, Suffering Expected to Soar." *Hartford Courant*. 9 September 2001.

Diet, Nutrition, and the Prevention of Chronic Diseases. Posted 26 April 2002. World Health Organization. Accessed 29 June 2002. http://www.who.int/hpr/nutrition/26Aprildraftrev1.pdf

Geiger, Debbe. "Diabetes' Changing Face: Number of Type 2 Cases among Children Is Increasing." *Newsday*. 20 July 1999.

Golan, Ralph. *Optimal Wellness*. New York: Ballantine Books, 1995.

National Desk. *The New York Times*. "Extra Soft Drink Is Cited as a Major Factor in Obesity." 16 February 2001.

"Not Diabetic? Glucose Still Counts." *Consumer Reports on Health*. August 2001.

Overweight and Obesity: Health Consequences. U.S. Department of Health. Accessed 30 June 2002. http://www.cdc.gov/nccdphp/dnpa/obesity/consequences.htm.

Sevrens, Julie. "The *Mercury News* Food Group Volunteers Put Their Diets to the Test." San *Jose Mercury News*. 17 January 1999.

Winter, Greg. "States Try to Limit Sales of Junk Food in School Buildings." *New York Times*. 9 September 2001.

E. Sample informative speech outline

Thesis Statement With their scope, history, and influence, comic books are an interesting component of American popular culture.

I. Comic books are not merely "comic," but rather explore a range of subject matter.
   A. Funny animal comics and kid comics are parables and parodies of the human condition.
      1. Elmer Fudd and Bugs: Tradition versus the pioneering spirit.
      2. Barks's ducks: Epic adventure and human foibles.
      3. Harvey's rich kids: Capitalism with a human face.
   B. True-love and teen comics present a hackneyed, boring, and sometimes disturbing picture of male/female relationships.
      1. True-love girl meets, loses, gets, marries boy (and vows never to be so stupid as to put her needs above his again).
      2. Teen comic girl fights other girls for the favors of a jerk male like Archie, who her father thinks is a twerp.
      3. True-love and teen comics foster the "us versus them" view of the male/female world.
   C. Western and adventure comics concentrate on the triumph of good over evil.
      1. Western cattle barons learn that six-gun-slinging saviors arise naturally from oppressed common folk.
      2. Adventure stories pit virtuous types against the blind malice of uncaring nature.
   D. Horror and mystery comics investigate ethics and morality while titillating and scaring readers.
      1. Eternal punishment for an unethical choice is a recurring theme of horror comics.
      2. The tempting hedonism of wrongdoers is graphically displayed in mystery comics—until the ironic twist of fate on the last page.
   E. Superhero comics manifest the unspoken and sometimes frightening fantasies and aspirations of the American people.
      1. Superman is the supremely powerful spokesman and policeman for the American definition of the "right way."
      2. The jackbooted hero, Blackhawk, was created in World War II to fight totalitarian fire with fire.
      3. Mar-Vell personifies the desire for total knowledge and the wisdom needed to use it.
      4. Spider-Man is the embodiment of the perennial underdog triumphant.

II. Comic books started as anthologies of another medium but soon grew into a separate art form developing along a path of its own.

   A. Early comic books were mostly reprints of Sunday newspaper comic strip sections.

      1. "Foxy Granpa" was reprinted in a number of comic books just after the turn of the century.

      2. The following decades saw strips like "Mutt & Jeff," "Little Orphan Annie," and "Moon Mullins" reprinted.

      3. Reprint books in the thirties included such titles as "Tarzan" in Tip Top Comics and "Terry and the Pirates" in Popular Comics.

   B. By 1938, the majority of comic books contained original work, and, with the appearance of Superman, the golden age of comics began.

      1. Detective Comics was the first single-theme, all-original comic.

      2. Superman, the first costumed superhero, was featured in Action no. 1.

      3. More than 150 titles were in print by the end of 1941.

   C. During the decade after the war, comic books for the most part went into a slump.

      1. With the Axis powers defeated and the Cold War not yet focused, the perceived need for superheroes lessened, and the sales of their books slacked off.

      2. Many horror, mystery, superhero, adventure, true-love, and teen comics fell before the wave of censorship following the publication of *Seduction of the Innocent.*

      3. Funny animal comics and kid comics retrenched behind the strongest series.

   D. By the late fifties, comic books had started to recover, overcoming their tarnished image.

      1. In creating the Comics Code Authority, publishers hoped to reassure worried parents and legislators.

      2. The silver age of comics began with the reintroduction of long-idle golden age characters.

   E. In the early sixties the trend toward emphasizing characterization, motivation, and involvement with issues initiated a new and still-developing era in superhero comics, the effects of which were eventually felt in the other comic genres.

      1. The Fantastic Four, Spider-Man, and the Hulk were the first fallible and self-questioning superheroes.

      2. Comic books became accepted by a wider, more literate audience.

3. Concern with ethical and even political questions became more evident, even in kid comics and funny animal comics.

III. Comic books have an effect beyond their entertainment value.
   A. Comic books are a unique and vigorous art form.
      1. Comic books have developed exciting and innovative methods for transcending the static nature of the panel format (series of distinct pictures across and down the page) to produce a sense of motion and drama.
      2. The art of comics is not confined to the work within a single panel, but also touches the arrangement of panels on a page.
      [as a result]
   B. Comic books can be seen to influence other media.
      1. Many filmmakers' use of split screens and quick cuts demonstrates a stylistic adaptation of the comic panel format.
      2. Camp and pop art drew heavily on comic book themes and styles.
      [and as a result]
   C. Comic books are in demand with collectors.
      1. Some issues of rare comics can bring prices in the thousands of dollars.
      2. Every year there are many large conventions around the United States where comics can be bought, sold, and traded.

Citation Guidelines

Two standard formats for citing references in reference lists or other collateral materials are "APA style" as set out in the *Publication Manual of the American Psychological Association,* and "MLA style" as set out in the *MLA Handbook for Writers of Research Papers.* See **16d.** The following is a sampling of reference citations for both print and nonprint sources done in both styles.

Selected Reference List Entries in APA and MLA Styles

Print Sources

Publication Manual of the APA	*MLA Handbook*
Book, single author	
Lastname, A. A. (date). *Title of work*. City: Publisher.	Lastname, Firstname. Title of Work. City: Publisher, date.
Pagels, E. (1995). *The origin of Satan*. New York: Random House.	Pagels, Elaine. The Origin of Satan. New York: Random House, 1995.
Book, two authors	
Lastname, A. A., & Lastname, B. B. (date). *Title of work*. City: Publisher.	Lastname, Firstname, and Firstname Lastname. Title of Work. City: Publisher, date.
Crossan, J. D., & Reed, J. L. (2001). *Excavating Jesus: Beneath the stones, behind the texts*. San Francisco: HarperSanFrancisco.	Crossan, John Dominic, and Jonathan L. Reed. Excavating Jesus: Beneath the Stones, Behind the Texts. San Francisco: Harper, 2001.
Book, edited	
Lastname, A. A. (Ed.). (Date). *Title of work*. City: Publisher.	Lastname, Firstname, ed. Title of Work. City: Publisher, date.
Smiley, J., & Kenison, K. (Eds.). (1995). *The best American short stories 1995*. Boston: Houghton.	Smiley, Jane, ed., and Katrina Kenison, series ed. The Best American Short Stories 1995. Boston: Houghton, 1995.
Book, no author or editor (anonymous)	
Title. (Edition.). (date). City: Publisher.	Title. Edition [if any]. City: Publisher, date.
The New York City Public Library Desk Reference. (3rd ed.). (1998). New York: Macmillan.	The New York City Public Library Desk Reference. 3rd ed. New York: Macmillan, 1998.
Periodical, journal	
Lastname, A. A. (date). Title of article. Periodical, volume, pages.	Lastname, Firstname. "Title of Article." Periodical volume (date): pages.
Hughes, M. (2002). Moving from information transfer to knowledge creation: A new value proposition for technical communicators. *Technical Communication, 49*, 257–285.	Hughes, Michael. "Moving from Information Transfer to Knowledge Creation: A New Value Proposition for Technical Communicators." Technical Communication 49 (2002): 257–285.

Publication Manual of the APA	*MLA Handbook*

Periodical, magazine

Lastname, A. A. (date). Title of article. *Periodical,* volume, pages.

Schoenfeld, S. (1997, May/June). An experience in culture. *Timeline,* 33, 3–4.

Lastname, Firstname. "Title of Article." Periodical date: pages.

Schoenfeld, Samantha. "An Experience in Culture." Timeline May–June 1997: 3–4.

Newspaper

Lastname, A. A. (date). Title of article. *Newspaper* [add city in brackets if necessary], pages.

Guido, M. (2003, September 11). Lawmakers seek to plug loophole: Chipmakers got refunds but paid no tax to state. *San Jose Mercury News,* pp. C1–2.

Lastname, Firstname. "Title of Article." Newspaper date [edition, if named]: pages.

Guido, Michelle. "Lawmakers Seek to Plug Loophole: Chipmakers Got Refunds but Paid No Tax to State." San Jose Mercury News 11 Sep. 2003, Peninsula/SF ed., C1–2.

Nonprint Sources

Television series (single episode)

Writername, A. A. & Directorname, A. A. (date). Title of episode. In Producername, A. A. *Series title*. City: Station/Network.

Ward, G. C. (Writer) & Burns, K. (Director). (2001). Gumbo [Television series episode]. In K. Burns & L. Novick (Producers). *Jazz.* Washington, DC: WETA.

"Episode." Series. Narrator/Producer. Director. Network, Station, City. Date.

"Gumbo." Jazz. Narr. Keith David. Dir. Ken Burns. PBS, WETA, Washington DC. 8 Jan. 2001.

Internet document (nonperiodical, no author)

Organization publishing website. (date). Document title in *Section*. Retrieved date from address

League of American Bicyclists. (n.d.). How to commute by bicycle. *Better bicycling fact sheets*. Retrieved September 10, 2003 from http://www.bikeleague.org/educenter/factsheets/commuteemployee.htm

"Document Title." Site. Date. Organization publishing site. Date of retrieval <address>

"How to Commute by Bicycle." League of American Bicyclists. 2003. League of American Bicyclists. 10 Sep. 2003 <http://www.bikeleague.org/educenter/factsheets/commuteemployee.htm>

Internet periodical (newsletter)

Lastname, A. (date). Title of article. *Publication*. Retrieved date from address

Hansen, S. (2003, June 4). For poorer or for poorer: For young couples trying to start a new life together, the dismal economy means more fighting, postponed weddings—and less sex. *Salon*. Retrieved September 10, 2003 from http://www.salon.com/mwt/feature/2003/06/04/couples/index.html

Lastname, Firstname. "Title of Article." Publication Date. Date of retrieval <address>

Hansen, Suzy. "For Poorer Or For Poorer: For Young Couples Trying To Start a New Life Together, The Dismal Economy Means More Fighting, Postponed Weddings—And Less Sex." Salon 4 June 2003. 10 Sep. 2003 <http://www.salon.com/mwt/feature/2003/06/04/couples/index.html>

Publication Manual of the APA	*MLA Handbook*

Message posted to online forum

[Only if forum threads are archived, otherwise considered personal communication not included in reference list.]

Lastname, A. A./Screenname (date). Subject line/Thread. Message posted to address.	Lastname, Firstname. "Thread/Subject Line." Online posting. date. Forum Name. date of retrieval <address>
Randya (2003, Aug. 28). Taking the lane, and not quiet about it [Msg 18]. Message posted to http://www.bikeforums.net/showthread.php?threadid=35868	Randya. "Taking the Lane, and Not Quiet About It." Online posting. 28 Aug 2003. BikeForums.net. 10 Sep. 2003 <http://www.bikeforums.net/showthread.php?threadid=35868>
E-mail (Personal communication not included in reference list.)	Lastname, Firstname. "Subject Line/Description." E-mail to Firstname Lastname. date.
	Thor, Leifur. "Info on the Design Science Initiative Project." E-mail to Doug Stuart. 2 May 2003.
Interview conducted by the speaker (Personal communication not included in reference list.)	Lastname, Firstname. Personal/Telephone/E-mail interview. Date.
	Thor, Leifur. Telephone interview. 5 May 2003.

APPENDIX C

Common Pronunciation and Usage Errors

For a speaker, pronunciation and usage errors are impediments to intelligibility and credibility. Well-reasoned points and lively descriptions can lose their impact if a mispronounced or misused word lands with a clunk to interrupt the concentration and attention of your listeners. In this appendix we list just a few of the common errors that can crop up; references at the end describe many more usage and word choice snares to which you should be alert. You can find pronunciation references in **34c2**.

Problems in Pronunciation

Word	Proper	Improper
get	get	git
just	just	jist
across	a cross	a crost
nuclear	nu clee ar	nu cyou lar
perspiration	pers pir a tion	press pir a tion
strict	strict	strick
escape	es cape	ex cape
compulsory	com pul sory	com pul so rary
recognize	rec og nize	reck a nize
library	li brar y	li berry
mischievous	mis che vous	mis chee vious
theater	THEE a ter	thee A ter
picture	pic tchure	pit chure
surprise	sur prise	sup prise
comparable	COM per able	com PARE able
larynx	lar inks	lar nix
relevant	rel a vant	rev a lant
drowned	drowned	drown ded
et cetera	et cet era	ek cet era
February	feb roo ary	feb you ary
temperature	temp per achure	temp achure
athlete	ath leet	a thuh leet
err	ur	air

Word Choice Errors

Wrong Use	*Comments*
adverse/averse	
"I would be adverse to adopting this plan."	Because the speaker is talking about an aversion to something, the proper adjective is "averse." When describing feelings, use averse; when describing things, use adverse, e.g., "Without restructuring, we shall end up working in adverse conditions."
alternative/alternate	
"Or, we could adopt an alternate plan."	"Alternate" means to switch back and forth between two things. In this case, the speaker should have said "alternative," meaning a second choice.
affect/effect	
"The affect of the plan could be very beneficial."	Usually "affect" is a verb. Properly, this sentence should use "effect" in its definition of "result."
bi/semi	
"Under this plan, paychecks will be distributed bimonthly on the 1st and 15th."	One should use bi for "every two" and semi for "twice a," so in this case it should be "distributed semimonthly on the 1st and 15th."
disinterested/uninterested	
"Some of you may be disinterested in the workings of this plan."	"Disinterested" means having no stake in the outcome, or neutral, as in "a disinterested third party will judge the results." If you mean "lack of interest," use "uninterested."
nonplussed/nonchalant	
"The opponents of this plan seem remarkably nonplussed in their calm acceptance of the status quo."	When one is nonplussed, one is bewildered or perplexed, not "nonchalant" or "calm."
tortuous/torturous	
"The torturous logic of the opponents of this plan is hard to fathom."	Because the speaker means "twisted or complex"—not "painful"—in this context, "tortuous" would have been the better choice.
imply/infer	
"I'm not inferring this plan will solve everything."	Imply means to suggest something that has not been stated explicitly and infer means to draw a conclusion from something not

stated explicitly. So, correct use would be either "I'm not implying this plan will solve everything," or something like, "You may have inferred that I think this plan will solve everything; that is not the case."

less/fewer

"There are less opponents to this plan than supporters."

If something can be counted in discrete units, it should be modified by "fewer" rather than "less." So, "there are fewer opponents" is correct. Note that changing to "there is less opposition than support" makes the usage correct, too.

ironic/coincidental

"It's ironic that, after working on this plan, Alexis and I discovered we both changed our original positions."

Irony is more than mere coincidence. There has to be some incongruity rising from a result that was different from the one expected. So, unless the speaker and Alexis had both vowed repeatedly that they were going to be steadfast in their original positions, a better sentence would have been, "Coincidentally, Alexis and I discovered we both changed our original positions after working on this plan."

comprise/compose

"Let's look at the three actions that comprise this plan."

A whole comprises its parts, so this sentence is backward with "comprise" in it. *Compose* or *constitute* would be correct. For "comprise" to be correct, the sentence might look like, "The plan comprises three actions; let's look at them now." Also, using "is comprised of" is not correct.

flaunt/flout

"One thing about this plan is that it makes it less easy for users to flaunt our guidelines."

"Flaunt" means to show off; "flout" means to treat with disregard or scorn. They are not interchangeable.

i.e./e.g.

"Some parts of this plan, i.e., restructuring, won't take place immediately."

This is wrong at two levels. First, i.e. is an abbreviation of the Latin *id est*, meaning "that is." It does *not* mean "for example"— that role is taken by e.g., from Latin *exempli gratia*. Second, a speaker should not use these abbreviations orally, but should use plain English "that is" and "for example" instead.

Some Grammar and Usage Problems

Wrong Use	*Comments*
Dangling/Misplaced Modifier	
"Having failed twice before, I wouldn't support any more attempts by the Baker committee to come up with a plan."	As constructed, this sentence makes the speaker the one who has failed twice. To be grammatically correct, and certainly less confusing, the sentence could be, "Having failed twice before, the Baker committee won't get my support for any more attempts to come up with a plan," or "I wouldn't support any more attempts by the Baker committee to come up with a plan because they have failed twice before."
Subject-Verb Agreement	
"The source of these failures are to be found in the incomplete research done."	"Of these failures" is a phrase that modifies the singular subject of the sentence, "source," and the fact that the noun in the phrase is plural has no impact on the verb. Because the subject is singular, the verb should be singular as well: "The source of these failures is to be found in . . ."
Misuse of Reflexive Pronoun	
"The people who looked over the plan were David, Carla, and myself."	"Myself" is the reflexive form of the pronoun, and the reflexive ordinarily is used only where the object of a sentence is the same as the subject ("I overworked myself on this project"), an object of a preposition that refers to the subject ("I worked on this project by myself"), or to emphasize the subject ("Although others helped with the research, I wrote the plan myself.") The sentence in this case should use the objective case for the pronoun: "The people who looked over the plan were David, Carla, and me." Be alert to the misuse of other reflexive pronouns like himself, herself, yourself, themselves.
Misuse of Pronouns in the Subjective Case	
"The composition of the Baker committee came as a surprise to Alexis and I."	"I" is reserved, as a pronoun in the subjective case, for use as the subject of a sentence, such as, "Alexis and I were surprised by the composition of the Baker committee." For a sentence in which the speaker is the object

of the verb, the objective case is appropriate: "The composition of the Baker committee came as a surprise to Alexis and me." A preposition (to, by, from, etc.) is usually a dead giveaway to use the objective case of a pronoun.

Here are two good resources for information on correct usage and word choice:

The American Heritage Book of English Usage. Boston: Houghton Mifflin, 1996.

Website: www.bartleby.com/64/

Brians, Paul. *Common Errors in English Usage.* Wilsonville, OR: William, James & Co., 2003.

Website: www.wsu.edu/~brians/errors/errors.html

GLOSSARY

A

acronym A term created from the first letter of each word in a phrase. **(21b)**

ad hominem fallacy An error in reasoning that consists of attacking a person identified with a position instead of refuting the position itself. **(21f.1)**

agenda A planned order of events for a meeting or group function. It provides structure and helps minimize conflict over what will be discussed, in what sequence, and, perhaps, for how long. **(7f.1)**

alliteration A stylistic device that consists of the repetition of a consonant sound. For example, "big, brutal bullies" is stronger and more memorable than "large, mean bullies." **(29d.2)**

antithesis A stylistic device that consists of two contrasting ideas set up in opposition. **(34a.3)**

appeal Any part of a speech designed to evoke a response from the audience. A direct appeal is often found in the conclusion of a speech when the speaker asks the audience to take a particular action. **(31b.2)**

articulation The ability to produce the sounds of speech correctly so that words are understandable. **(31a.3)**

assonance A stylistic device that consists of the repetition of a vowel sound. "People are dreaming of pie in the sky, by and by" repeats the long i sound, which makes it memorable. **(29d.2)**

attention-getter The opening one or two sentences of a speech introduction designed to immediately engage the listenersí interest. **(31a.2)**

B

bar graph A format for displaying data that compares related items by representing their amounts with columns or bars of different lengths or heights. **(27a.3)**

C

causal reasoning The justification for an argument claiming that one thing is the direct result of another. A causal claim should not be confused with mere coincidence or correlation. **(21d; 24c)**

cause–effect pattern A way of organizing speech points that begins with the origin of the situation and moves to the consequences. **(19a.3)**

central idea The core idea of a speech and the touchstone for its development; less formal than a thesis sentence (a subject–predicate assertion). **(11d.1)**

chronological pattern A way of organizing speech points that follows a time order; it might be historical or it might follow the steps in a process. **(19a.1)**

circular reasoning An error in reasoning that occurs when a speaker assumes the truth of the conclusion and uses it as the starting point for developing an argument, instead of building a case for the conclusion. **(21f.9)**

claim A proposition that a speaker advances as a conclusion. The claim might be the thesis of the speech, a main point, or a subpoint. Typically, a claim is a controversial statement that does not earn automatic acceptance but needs to be proven by the development of an argument. **(21a)**

clincher The carefully thought-out closing sentence of a speech conclusion that is memorable and gives a sense of finality. A good speech can be spoiled if it just "trails off" without a clincher. **(31b.3)**

cognitive restructuring A treatment for communication apprehension that involves discovering the underlying statements driving one's fear, analyzing their logic, and replacing them with more realistic statements.

ating the statements can eventually restructure the way a
bout speaking. **(4d.2)**
A nonlinear technique for organizing ideas in order to
in points of a speech. A circle diagram or notecards are
similar ideas. **(17b.2)**

context Features such as time, space, and degree of formality that shape
the core message of a speech. Specific contexts, such as the workplace
or the political arena, have norms that shape public speaking in them.
(5)

coordinate points Points of equal importance in an outline, for example,
points I, II, and III, or points A, B, and C. **(18d)**

core values Beliefs about right and wrong that are central to the identity
of the person who holds them. These values are very difficult to change.
(25c.2)

credibility A speaker's believability over and above the logical message
and the emotional impact. Credibility comes from the ability to project
qualities such as competence, trustworthiness, concern, and dynamism.
Other things being equal, speakers perceived as having these qualities
will be more persuasive. **(26)**

D

deduction A form of reasoning that demonstrates how the relationship among established premises lead to a necessary conclusion. The
deductive relationship is often expressed in an if/then or either/or
syllogism. **(21c, 24b)**

E

evocative Designed to call forth an emotion or shared feeling. An evocative speech is sometimes called a speech to entertain, but evocative
speaking is broader and can arouse feelings of sympathy or grief as well
as feelings of happiness or amusement. **(9)**

extemporaneous The most common mode of delivery. An extemporaneous speech is a structured speech delivered in a conversational manner
from general notes. The speaker is thoroughly familiar with the order
of points and subpoints and with key phrases, but the speech is not
written out or memorized. **(28a)**

F

factual example Specific, directly verifiable or commonly accepted instance used to illustrate or to prove a general point. **(16a.1)**

fallacies Errors in reasoning that make a particular argument or position
invalid. **(21f)**

fallacy of the absurd extreme (*reductio ad absurdum*) An error in reasoning that makes a potentially sound argument appear groundless by
extending it to a point where it can be easily ridiculed. **(21f.8)**

false dichotomy An error of reasoning that results from the assumption
that there are only two alternatives in a situation when in fact there are
many. **(21f.4)**

full-sentence outline A plan for a speech that states each main point and
at least the first level of subpoints in complete subject–predicate sentences. This attention to detail helps ensure that every part of the
speech is logically related. **(20b)**

H

hasty generalization An error in inductive reasoning that results from
making a premature inductive leap and basing a generalization on
insufficient data. **(21f.5)**

hypothetical example A plausible story created by the speaker to illustrate a point. In contrast to factual examples, hypothetical examples can be used only to clarify a point but not to prove it. **(16a.2)**

I

impromptu A mode of delivery that requires the speaker to speak "off the cuff" without formal preparation. An impromptu speech can, however, have elements of other types of speeches, such as a theme, planned first and last sentences, appeals to the audience, and lots of examples. **(28b)**

inductive reasoning A pattern of reasoning in which a series of specific observations lead to a probably general conclusion. **(21b.1)**

internal preview A forecast in the course of a speech of one or more points that will be covered. This is a device to unify a speech and to emphasize key points. **(32b.2)**

internal summary A restatement in the course of a speech of one or more points that have been covered. Like the internal preview, this is a device to unify a speech and to emphasize key points. **(32.b.2)**

introduction The opening section of a speech that serves to get attention and orient audience members before the first main point is developed. **(31a)**

J

jargon Terms that relate to a particular activity and are familiar to the people who practice it. **(29c.2)**

K

keyword or key-phrase outline A tool used in speech preparation. It consists of words and phrases to be used and is more developed than brainstorming tools, such as concept mapping, but less detailed than a topic outline or a full-sentence outline. **(28a)**

L

line graph A format for displaying data represented as points connected by lines; it indicates changes over time or distance. **(27a.3)**

logical orientation A section of the introduction to a speech that provides the intellectual framework, often including the thesis sentence and previewing the main points. **(31a.4)**

M

main points The ideas that are central to the development of the thesis of a speech. **(18b)**

major premise The basic statement about a relationship between two terms that underlies a deductive argument. **(21c)**

manuscript speaking A mode of delivery in which the speech is written out word for word (preferably in the oral style). The speech is practiced until it is familiar enough to sound conversational when it is delivered. **(28c)**

Maslow's hierarchy of needs A ranking of human needs from basic survival needs through needs for security, belonging, and esteem and culminating in the need for self-actualization. **(25b)**

memorized speech A mode of delivery in which the speech is written out (preferably in the oral style) and then practiced until it can be delivered word for word. **(28d)**

metaphor A stylistic device that equates two different things—for example, "My job is a nightmare." **(29d.2)**

minor premise The part of a deductive argument that introduces some data. **(21c)**

motivated sequence An organizer for persuasion that is based on the mental stages through which listeners progress during a speech. **(23c.1)**

g A speech that has the purpose of changing the ides of the audience members. **(23a)**

ons Presentation aids that visually depict an object; tographs, sketches, and videos. **(27a.3)**

symbols Presentation aids that represent abstract concepts; examples are graphs, charts, diagrams, and maps. **(27a.3)**

pie chart A format for displaying data as segments of a circle; it shows the relative size of parts of a whole. **(27a.3)**

pitch How high or low a speaker's voice is. Speakers should try to use a pitch that is natural, and they should occasionally vary their pitch to reinforce meaning. **(34b)**

post hoc fallacy An error in reasoning that results from assuming that an event that follows another event is caused by the first event. This error confuses sequence with cause. **(21f.6)**

presentation aid An object that adds another communication dimension to a speaker's content and delivery. **(27,36)**

presentation software Computer software used to create presentation aids. **(27a.2)**

preview An organization tool that gives listeners a road map of the topics to come. **(31a.4)**

primacy The persuasive effect of placing a point first or early in a speech in order to give it greater impact or make it memorable. **(23c.2)**

primary audience outcome The most important result that a speaker wants to achieve, phrased in terms of what the audience will do after the speech. **(11c)**

probability The condition that exists when a conclusion is likely to be true but cannot be established with absolute certainty. When speakers try to persuade listeners, they often compare costs and benefits so that the "odds" favor their position. **(21b.2)**

problem–solution pattern A way of arranging the main points of a speech that begins with a description of something that needs changing and moves to a proposal for the remedy. **(19a.4)**

project proposal A workplace presentation in which a plan and its rationale are described; examples are research proposals and sales presentations. **(7c)**

project status report A workplace presentation that describes the progress on a project. This interim report is used to reassure colleagues or customers about what is being done, to alert them to any problems, and to seek feedback. **(7d)**

proposition of fact A claim that something is or is not true. **(11d.3)**

proposition of policy A claim that a certain course of action should or should not be adopted. **(11d.3)**

proposition of value A claim that something is good or bad. **(11d.3)**

PSR statement A problem–solution–result (PSR) statement is a brief but memorable personal success story that states a problem, describes a solution, and lists the results; it should be delivered in 90 seconds or less. **(7a.4)**

public speaking A communication setting in which one person has primary control and direction of the resources of communication. It may happen in a formal or informal setting, but it involves preparation, and the focus is on the speaker for all or most of the time. **(1b)**

Q

question-and-answer period A time allotted after the conclusion of the main speech when audience members can ask for clarification or elaboration on the topic. **(37)**

quotation The words of another person. Quotations are used because the language is more powerful than the speaker could create or because the person being quoted has some special credibility. Direct quotations use the exact words of another, and indirect quotations paraphrase another person's words; both should be attributed to the source. **(16c.2)**

R

rate The speed at which one speaks. Ideally, the rate must be fast enough to hold attention, slow enough to be understood, and varied as necessary to enhance meaning. **(34a.2)**

reasoning by analogy A form of reasoning in which conclusions can be drawn about unfamiliar events or things based on what is known about familiar events or things. **(21c, 24d.2)**

recency The persuasive effect that comes from placing a point last or late in a speech to give it greater impact or make it memorable. **(23c.2)**

S

semantic fallacy An error in reasoning that occurs when a word is used in different senses in different parts of the argument. **(21f.3)**

signpost An organizational technique that keeps listeners informed about how a speech is unfolding. Signposts can tell what has been covered, what is still to come, and when changes in direction are about to occur. **(22b)**

simile A stylistic device that compares two different things, such as "Managing a group of scientists is like herding cats." **(29d.2)**

slang Nonstandard words and expressions. **(29c.2)**

slippery slope fallacy An error in reasoning that claims the first step in some direction will inevitably lead to a disastrous outcome. **(21f.2)**

spatial pattern An organizational pattern according to some relationship of components in space; examples are geographical regions or galleries in a museum. **(19a.2)**

speech notes Working notes designed for quick reference and easy readability during a speech. They contain key words and phrases, organizational cues, and information that must be cited exactly. **(33b)**

statistical evidence Data that has been systematically collected and coded in numerical form. **(16b)**

straw figure fallacy An error in reasoning that stems from stating an argument in weaker form than its advocates use and then proceeding to demolish that weak argument. **(21f.7)**

style The effective use of language. Style consists of being clear and concise and using various linguistic devices to enhance the impact of language. **(29)**

subordinate points The lesser points that support or elaborate on the main points of a speech. **(18d)**

supporting materials The parts of a speech that expand on or prove the claims made in main points or subpoints. These examples, definitions, statistics, and testimonies are the building blocks of a speech. **(16)**

T

team presentation A speech prepared and delivered collaboratively by a small group of presenters, each of whom typically has special expertise or perspective. **(7b.1)**

testimony A form of supporting material that reports the experience or opinions of another person, who is typically an expert or has direct experience with the topic. **(16c)**

text A message captured in words. All the nonverbal, psychological, and cultural factors that surround this core message and help shape its meaning are called the *context*. **(5)**

topic outline An outline that identifies the points to be covered and the relationships among them but does not spell out all the logical connections that are present in a full-sentence outline. **(17b.1)**

topical pattern A way of organizing the main points of a speech that grows naturally out of a topic that does not lend itself to sequential or spatial organization. **(19b.5)**

training presentations Usually a series of workshops or seminars related to the workplace; the goal is to teach a specific set of work-related skills or body of knowledge. **(7e)**

V

values Beliefs about what is good and bad (or wise or foolish, just or unjust, pretty or ugly, etc.). **(25c)**

vocal variety Changes in the tone and pitch of the voice to provide interest and emphasis; the opposite of a monotone. **(34b)**

vocalized pauses Filler phrases such as "um," "er," "y'know," and "like" that break the fluency of speaking and can be distracting to listeners. **(34d.3)**

volume The loudness or softness with which one speaks. **(34a.1)**

W

whiteboard A board with an erasable shiny surface that can be used during a speech for quick drawings or words. **(27b.1)**

INDEX

Index

CHECKLISTS

KEY POINTS